Russia's Interventions in Ethnic Conflicts

James J. Coyle

Russia's Interventions in Ethnic Conflicts

The Case of Armenia and Azerbaijan

palgrave
macmillan

James J. Coyle
Newport Beach, CA, USA

ISBN 978-3-030-59572-2   ISBN 978-3-030-59573-9 (eBook)
https://doi.org/10.1007/978-3-030-59573-9

This Palgrave Macmillan imprint is published by the registered company Springer Nature Switzerland AG
The registered company address is: Gewerbestrasse 11, 6330 Cham, Switzerland

Preface

In 2018, I published a book entitled *Russia's Border Wars and Frozen Conflicts*.[1] The thesis of the book was that Russia has used a ju-jitsu foreign policy to project power and influence far beyond its geopolitical weight. With the exception of its nuclear arsenal and landmass, Russia is a mid-level power. Politically, its system is run by a group of oligarchs led by the former KGB Colonel Vladimir Putin—not a system that most people in the world would want to emulate. The country's conventional military armaments and tactics are/were far outclassed by those of the North Atlantic Treaty Organization, as evidenced by the ease in which Western forces triumphed over countries that follow Russian military doctrine and fight with Russian armaments. The population of 145 million is less than half that of the United States, and the GDP of its natural resource extractive economy is only on par with Italy.

Despite these drawbacks, Russian diplomatic prestige is as high as it ever has been because of three factors: its potential peer competitors are in political or economic disarray; it has used its energy policy to make Europe, including Turkey, dependent on its good graces; and, it has skillfully manipulated ethnic unrest on its borders to grant itself an overlarge role in maintaining the region's peace.

[1] Coyle, James J. *Russia's Border Wars and Frozen Conflicts* (New York: Palgrave Macmillan, 2018).

It is this third topic to which most of *Border Wars* dedicated itself. Looking at conflicts in Azerbaijan, Georgia, Moldova, and Ukraine, I discerned a pattern of Russian support for ethnic minorities, the arming of these minorities' militant groups, encouraging them directly or indirectly to revolt against the internationally-recognized central government, offering to mediate a peace conference, and ensuring that the conference never creates a workable peace plan. Russia then becomes indispensable: the conflict enters a "frozen" state (although various levels of combat still continue) in which Russia controls the level of violence. This is most obvious with the War in Ukraine between the government in Kyiv and Russian-backed separatists in the East.

After *Border Wars* was published, many individuals asked for additional information on the four conflicts. As the original book was already over 270 pages in length, I decided not to expand the text further but to write four books: one on each of the frozen conflicts. I decided to tackle the four alphabetically, and so this volume (Armenia and Azerbaijan) is the first in a hoped-for series. The book consists of six chapters: one on the roots of the conflict, and subsequent chapters describing it through military, political, economic, and diplomatic lenses. There is a final chapter with analytic conclusions. Modern conflicts, particularly frozen conflicts, do not rely on a single element of power, but rather rely on multiple instruments. These conflicts may be limited in scope, but they are full spectrum conflicts for the societies affected.

I hope you, the reader, will enjoy reading an in-depth discussion of a conflict in an area little known to American or European audiences.

Newport Beach, USA James J. Coyle, Ph.D.

Contents

Base 802741AI (C00132) 8-02

Armenia (*Source* US Government Printing Office)

Azerbaijan (*Source* US Government Printing Office)

CHAPTER 1

Roots of the Conflict

Geography

Inside the Republic of Azerbaijan is a wooded area of approximately 1700 square miles (4400 square kilometers) of jagged mountains and deep valleys. It is known as Nagorno-Karabakh, an interesting title as it mixes both the Russian and Turkish languages. "Nagorno" is Russian for "mountainous," and "Karabakh" is Turkish for "Black Garden." The name captures the nature of the area perfectly. The rich soil of this high garden allows trees to grow so strongly that the forests appear black against the sun.

Nagorno-Karabakh is not contiguous with any other country, surrounded by seven Azerbaijani provinces. The closest international border is the Azerbaijan-Armenia border, approximately 6 miles away across a strip of land known as the Lachin corridor. When the Soviet Union collapsed, there were approximately 200,000 residents there. These were divided between ethnic Armenians (140,000) and ethnic Azerbaijanis (60,000).[1] There was also a small smattering of other ethnicities: Russians, Kurds, and Greeks. By contrast, the population of the seven surrounding provinces was almost 100% ethnic Azerbaijani. Within five years (1988–1993), the area became 100% ethnic Armenian as it was

[1] Croissant, Michael P. *The Armenia-Azerbaijan Conflict* (Westport: Praeger Publishers, 1998), 10.

J. J. Coyle, *Russia's Interventions in Ethnic Conflicts*,
https://doi.org/10.1007/978-3-030-59573-9_1

captured by Armenian forces. Today Nagorno-Karabakh holds approximately 145,000 inhabitants,[2] and the seven surrounding provinces are a depopulated security perimeter. How this happened, and what steps are being taken because of this situation, is the subject of this study.

Azerbaijan itself is one of the three countries that make up the South Caucasus, along with Armenia and Georgia. Azerbaijan is slightly smaller than the state of Maine and is bounded by Russia to the north, Iran to the south, Armenia and Georgia to the west, and the Caspian Sea to the east. A tiny border of about 15 miles connects Turkey with Nakhichevan, an exclave of Azerbaijan separated from the main territory by Armenia.

Demographics

The population of Azerbaijan is mainly Azerbaijani Turkish, but some ethnic minorities—including Armenians—still live in the area under Azerbaijani control. A country of 10 million people, the 2009 census revealed the population to be 91% Azerbaijani, 2% Lezgin, 1.3% Armenian, 1.3% Russian, and numerous other nationalities.[3]

While Azerbaijani ancestry is mixed, the spoken language points to membership in the Oguz Turkish tribal confederation. This people originated in the Ural-Altay region and migrated west in the ninth thru twelfth centuries. The area had originally been occupied by the Khazar kingdom. In 965, a military treaty was concluded by the Oghuz and the Russian prince Svyatoslav that led to the destruction of the Khazar state, which had been a rival of ancient Rus.[4] Other groups that may have added to the Azerbaijan ethnic mix are Albanian Caucasians and Iranians. These groups would have an even longer historical residency in Azerbaijan, assimilating into the newly-arrived Turkish population eight to nine centuries ago. By the fourteenth century, the majority of the population of Nagorno

[2] Artsakh Republic National Statistical Service. "The Results of 2015 Population Census of the Republic of NKR," Web. Retrieved 30 April 2019. http://www.stat-nkr.am/en/-2015/-2015.

[3] State Statistical Committee of the Republic of Azerbaijan. "Population of Azerbaijan." (Baku, 2018), 21.

[4] Agajanov, S.G. "The State of the Oghuz, the Kimek, and the Kipchak," Web. Retrieved 30 April 2019, 73. https://en.unesco.org/silkroad/sites/silkroad/files/knowledge-bank-article/vol_IVa%20silk%20road_the%20states%20of%20the%20oghuz%2C%20the%20kimek%20and%20the%20kipchak.pdf.

Karabakh was Azerbaijani ruled by a small Armenian elite. This situation continued until the eighteenth century, when the elite destroyed itself through infighting. In Karabakh, an ethnic Azerbaijani leader Panah Ali Khan founded an independent Khanate that would survive until Russia conquered the area in 1805.[5]

The second ethnic group in Nagorno Karabakh is the Armenians, also with long historical ties to the Caucasus region. In Nagorno-Karabakh, however, Armenians are relatively recent arrivals. They trace their origins in the area to the 1828 Treaty of Turkmenchay. This treaty ended the Russian-Persian War of 1826–1828. One part of the treaty guaranteed the Russian protection of ethnic Armenians who left the Persian empire. Many of these people came to the Nagorno-Karabakh area. Many of the Armenians in Yerevan also date their arrival from this period: 8249 Armenian families (approximately 50,000 people) moved from Iran into the governates of Yerevan, Karabakh, and Shamakhi.[6] The influx of Armenians was supplemented by the 1829 Treaty of Adrianople which allowed Armenian migration from the Ottoman Empire. This influx into the Caucasus continued through the next century, primarily from Ottoman lands.

The inclusion of resettlement in the treaty of Turkmenchay may have been the result of secret negotiations between Armenian Archbishop Nerses and Russian Infantry General Paskevich on the one side, and Czar Nicholas I on the other. According to a nineteenth-century Russian historian, the original text of the treaty had no provision for the resettlement of Armenians. After several secret messages from Armenian representatives to the Czar, however, the Russians agreed to including the provision. The Armenian intent was to create the basis for an independent Armenian kingdom.[7] As Commander of the Caucasus Corps, General Paskevich was in charge of the resettlement. He wanted the Armenians settled in the current Republic of Armenia but, when informed that the area could not

[5] Cornell, Svante E. "The Nagorno-Karabakh Conflict," Report no. 46. Department of East European Studies, Uppsala University (1999), 4–5.

[6] Bolukbasi, Suha. *Azerbaijan: A Political Hist*ory (New York: IB Taurus, 2011), 23.

[7] Shafiyev, Farid. *The Russian-Soviet Resettlement Policies and Their Implications for Ethno-Territorial Conflicts in the South Caucasus.* Doctoral Dissertation (Ottawa: Carleton University, 2015), 78.

accommodate additional settlers, Paskevich approved them being sent to Karabakh.[8]

Before the treaty, there were few Armenians. In a census performed by the Czar's representatives in 1805, only 8% of the population of Karabakh and the surrounding regions were Armenian.[9] After the treaty, however, things changed. According to Paskevich, "On March 9, 1828, the last Russian army left Tabriz ... According to the Turkmenchay Treaty, Armenians moved from different villages to Karabakh."[10]

Another Russian author of the period wrote, "We started the imperial policy in Transcaucasia by the placement of other peoples, not of the Russian population here. In the 1828–1830s, we move 40,000 Armenians from Iran and 84,000 Armenians from Turkey and deported them to the provinces of Yelizavetpol and Irevan ... where the Armenian population were in minority. The mountainous part of the Yelizavetpol province (the mountainous part of Karabakh) and the shores of Lake Goycha are inhabited by Armenian displaced persons...The number of displaced and unofficially displaced were more than 200,000 people...As a result of this relocation, more than 1 million of the 1.3 million Armenians living in the Transcaucasia in the early 20th century were not 'indigenous people of the region', but were transferred by us."[11]

According to quotations posted publicly by the government of Azerbaijan in the town of Terter, the Armenian historian B. Ishkhanyan reported on the Armenian arrival into the area. "As for the Armenians living in the territory of Nagorno-Karabakh, some of them were ancient aboriginal Albanian tribes, who maintained Christianity. The other part of the population consists of refugees fleeing Iran and Turkey and finding asylum in Azerbaijani lands. Armenians have come to different parts of the Caucasus region only in the last centuries."[12] Another Russian historian, writing in 1930, stated, "Karabakh has never belonged to

[8] Shafiyev, op cit. 85.

[9] Kruger, Heiko. *The Nagorno-Karabakh: A Legal Analysis* (New York: Springer Press, 2010), 8.

[10] Glinka, S. *Transfer of Azerbaijani Armenians to the Russian Borders* (Moscow, 1831), 99–100.

[11] Shavrov, N. *New Threat to Transcaucasia for Russia* (St. Petersburg, 1911), 59–61.

[12] Ishkhanyan, B. *Peoples of the Caucasus* (Petrograd, 1916), 18.

Armenian cultural centers."[13] To mark their arrival in the area, in 1978 the Armenian community in the town of Maragha (on the outskirts of Nagorno-Karabakh) built a monument commemorating the 150th anniversary of their arrival in the area.

The treaty of Turkmanchay did not deal only with the area of modern Azerbaijan, but also with Iranian Azerbaijan. While the Russians seized control of the area north of the Aras (Araxes) river, an annex to the treaty said that if the Shah of Iran did not pay an indemnity of twenty million silver rubles within six months Russia would also claim Iranian Azerbaijan. The Iranian court could not pay the funds, and the British provided the funds to stop Russian expansion.[14]

In 1834, the Czar issued an imperial decree establishing the Armenian oblast, even though only 20% of the population in the area was Armenian. In Karabakh during the same time period, there were 19,000 Armenians and 35,000 Muslims according to Russian census figures. By 1871, there were 878,000 "Tatars" and 292,000 Armenians in the Elizavetpol guberniia; there were 465,000 "Tatars" and 52,000 Armenians in the Baku guberniia. By 1888, however, Muslims had become the minority in Erivan guberniia, 211,000–286,000 Armenians.[15] From these figures, it would appear that by 1888 Armenians were in the majority within the borders of the modern Republic of Armenia, and their numbers continued to grow in other parts of the Caucasus. The growth of the figures establishes, however, that this majority is a relatively modern phenomenon.

With the growth in population came a growth in intercommunal violence. The first such eruption was in Baku, starting on 6 February 1905. In the fighting that followed, called the Tatar-Armenian War, 128 Armenian and 158 Muslim villages were destroyed or pillaged. The major center of the fighting was in Nagorno-Karabakh. More Muslims were killed than Armenian, and so the Western press declared an Armenian victory. Among the Muslim community, however, the attacks by the Armenian guerrilla forces, the Dashnaks, united them. Azeri groups who previously fought separately began to unite their efforts, and the

[13] Petrushevksi, I. *The Pre-Christian Beliefs of Nagorno-Karabakh Peasants* (Baku, 1930), 8.

[14] Swietochowski, Tadeusz. *Russia and Azerbaijan: A Borderland in Transition* (New York: Columbia University Press, 199), 6–7.

[15] Swietochowski, ibid., 11, 12, 16.

Azeri intelligentsia also became involved. A clandestine group in Ganja named *Difai* (Defense) was created, and they sponsored Muslim fighting squads, including a 400-man unit in Shusha. Difai was not aimed at Armenians, however, but at Russia whom they blamed for the intercommunal fighting.[16]

Short-Lived Independence of Armenia and Azerbaijan Followed by Soviet Domination

During and after World War I, Germans, British, White Russians, Mensheviks, and Bolsheviks all took their turn as the dominant power in the region. Between 31 March and 2 April 1918, Dashnaks in Baku, many of them refugees from Anatolia, took advantage of the political turmoil and staged an unprovoked massacre of the city's Muslims—resulting in at least 3000 fatalities.[17] The New York Times reported the number of dead as high as 12,000.[18] The Bolsheviks took advantage of the unrest to seize power and create the Baku commune.

The Democratic Republic of Armenia (DRA) and the Democratic Republic of Azerbaijan were seven days old when they signed their first treaty, the Treaty of Batumi (4 June 1918). The formal name of the treaty, which was never ratified, was "The Treaty of Peace and Friendship between the Republic of Armenia and the Ottoman Empire."[19] Modern Armenian historians claim this treaty was imposed upon the new Armenian Republic by the Ottoman Empire. Given the relative youth of the state and the fact the Ottoman Third Army was only seven kilometers from Yerevan, this is probably true. Regardless, the treaty was signed by the Chairman of the Armenian National Council and the DRA's Minister of Foreign Affairs. The treaty recognized the independence of the DRA.

[16] Swietochowski, ibid., 39–41.

[17] Swietochowski, ibid., 66–67.

[18] "Land of Eternal Fires," New York Times, 19 October 1919.

[19] Sahakyan, Vahe. *Between Host Countries and Homeland: Institutions, Politics and Identities in the post-Genocide Armenian Diaspora*. Dissertation (University of Michigan, 2015), 56.

Article two outlined the DRA's territory as the 12,000 square kilometers of Erivan and Echmiadzin districts. Karabakh and its surrounding territory were not included in the new Republic.

The Baku Commune was overthrown by non-Communist parties, and the new government invited the British army to protect them from assault by the Ottomans. The British remained about 40 days, after which the Ottomans seized the city. On 15 September 1918 following the retreat of the British, Baku was occupied by the Turkish-led Caucasus Islamic army. In the next three days, the troops engaged in massive looting and massacred many of the local mostly non-Muslim population. Nobody knows exactly how many people died in Baku (according to various sources some 9000 Armenians died).[20]

The British returned two months later, in November 1918. The commander of the British North Persian Force, General W. M. Thomson, in mid-January 1919 put Nagorno-Karabakh under Azerbaijani administration. They confirmed a Muslim (i.e., Azerbaijani) governor in Shusha, Khosrow Sultanov. For his part, Sultanov succeeded in getting the Armenian Assembly in Nagorno-Karabakh to accept Azerbaijani rule.[21] With the exception of Dashnaks (Armenian Revolutionaries) who engaged in guerilla warfare in the mountains, the inhabitants acceded to the arrangement in February 1920.[22] The Nagorno-Karabakh Peoples Congress signed an agreement making Karabakh an autonomous region within Azerbaijan. The Paris Peace Conference then concurred that the area should stay within Azerbaijan. When the Dashnaks tried to seize the area, they were repulsed by forces of the Azerbaijani regional governor. Thus, by 1920 Karabakh's status as a part of Azerbaijan was confirmed by Armenia in an international treaty signed by the Chairman of the Armenian National Council, by locals through the actions of the Nagorno-Karabakh Peoples Congress, and by the international community in the Paris Peace Conference.

The Red Army seized Baku in April 1920, ending the first iteration of an independent Azerbaijan. Armenia fell some months later. As the Soviets

[20] Akhmedov, Afgan. *British Foreign Policy in Azerbaijan 1918–1920.* Dissertation (University of Lancaster, 2018), 78.

[21] Swietochowski, ibid., 76.

[22] Cornell, ibid., 7.

seized control of the DRA, the government of Soviet Azerbaijan sent an olive branch to the new Armenian government in the form of a telegram stating boundaries had no meaning between Soviet peoples. Once the Red Army had full control over Armenia, however, the Bolshevik leader of Azerbaijan Nariman Narimanov repudiated the telegram. In response to this turn of events, Joseph Stalin wrote, "It is essential to take sides firmly with one of the two parties, in the present case, of course, Azerbaijan."[23]

In 1921, the Caucasian Bureau of the Communist Party stated that Karabakh belonged to Armenia. Outraged, party delegate Narimanov warned the decision would lead to anti-Communist activity in Azerbaijan. The threat had its desired effect. At first, the Bureau reaffirmed Karabakh went to Armenia. The day after a meeting attended by Stalin, however, without a formal vote the Bureau reversed itself (possibly at Stalin's request). The Bureau declared that Karabakh remained a part of Azerbaijan and would receive the status of autonomous region.[24]

As for Nakhichevan, an area that has a 14-mile border with Turkey but is otherwise surrounded on three sides by Armenia and the fourth side by Iran, its status as a part of Azerbaijan was decided in the March 1921 Azerbaijani Friendship Treaty with Moscow. It received a guarantee from the government of Turkey in the October 1921 treaty of Kars. When the Soviet Union was officially announced in 1922, Nakhichevan became an Autonomous Socialist Republic under the Azerbaijan Soviet Socialist Republic.[25]

While the situation appeared to be resolved from the viewpoint of national law (within the USSR) and international law, Armenian nationalists remained dissatisfied. In 1926–1927, Armenian immigrants to Karabakh circulated petitions demanding that Armenian authorities reopen the question of the region's status. In 1936, the first secretary of the Armenian Communist Party raised the question shortly before being executed.

In the period 1948–1953, Soviet authorities attempted to clear Armenia of Azerbaijanis. There were two reasons given: the need for workers to grow cotton in the Azerbaijani lowlands, and the need to make room for Armenians arriving from the diaspora. Both reasons were not

[23] Croissant, ibid., 18–19.

[24] Croissant, ibid., 19.

[25] Swietochowski, ibid., 105–106.

true: the lowlands were not prepared by the Ministry of Agriculture to grow cotton (the canals had not been built), and the attempt to remove Azerbaijanis continued until 1953 despite the fact the Armenian repatriation effort was canceled in 1948. It appears that Moscow bowed to pressure from Armenian elites.

On 6 June 1945, the First Secretary of the Armenian Communist Party, Grigory Arutunov, approached Stalin to discuss the incorporation of Nagorno-Karabakh and Nakhichevan into the Armenian SSR. Stalin rebuffed Artunov, noting it was no easier to change borders within the Soviet Union than outside of the USSR.

Later that year, in the fall, Azerbaijan Communist Party First Secretary Mir Jafar Baghirov met with two influential members of the Soviet Politburo: Anastas Mikoyan, an Armenian, and Lavrenti Beria, a Georgian. They told him that the size of the Azerbaijan SSR would soon double after the USSR absorbed Iranian Azerbaijan. They then proposed jokingly that Baghirov could transfer Nagorno-Karabakh to Armenia and other northern regions of Azerbaijan to Georgia. When Baghirov replied it was too early to be discussing such ideas, Arutunov sent a letter to Stalin in November requesting the transfer of Nagorno-Karabakh. Stalin turned the matter over to the secretary-general of the Communist Party, who asked Baghirov his opinion. Baghirov's response was a sarcastic proposal that parts of Armenia and Georgia be transferred to Azerbaijan, using many of the ethnic arguments that Arutunov used in his letter to Stalin.

Baghirov's opposition had little effect. In the end, according to the Ministry of Agriculture of Azerbaijan, in 1948–1953, 11,914 households or 53,000 people were resettled from Armenia. The number of returnees by the end of 1954 was about 1500 households, or approximately 7500 people—only 14% of all settlers from Armenia.[26]

There were additional petitions and demonstrations in Armenia demanding unification throughout the 1960s, in 1977, and in 1983.[27]

[26] Shafiyev, Farid. "The Forced Resettlements of Azerbaijanis from Armenia, 1948–1953," *Journal of Muslim Minority Affairs*, 13 June 2019, pp. 178, 185–186. https://www.tandfonline.com/doi/full/10.1080/13602004.2019.1620002.

[27] Kaufman, Stuart J. *Modern Hatreds: The Symbolic Politics of Ethnic Wars* (New York: Cornell University Press, 2001), 51.

End of the Soviet Era[28]

As Mikhail Gorbachev implemented his policies of glasnost and perestroika, he did not realize he was laying the groundwork for the collapse of the Soviet empire. In the republics, the new freedoms provided the political space for ethnic unrest to surface. Karabakh was no exception.

It began in 1986 with Igor Muradian, an ethnic Armenian Karabakhi working as an economist at Gosplan. He established contact with Dashnak underground cells and began procuring from abroad small arms for Karabakh separatists. Muradian later stated at that time all the Karabakh organizations—including the Komsomol (Communist youth organization similar to the Boy Scouts)—were under arms.

The chief economic advisor to Mikhail Gorbachev, Abel G. Aganbegyan, traveled to Paris in 1987 and met with a group of French Armenians. Over dinner, he made some remarks about Nagorno-Karabakh's possible unification with the Armenian SSR. Aganbegyan claimed he only mentioned the question was under study by a commission, but the French newspaper L'Humanite quoted him as saying Karabakh and Armenia deserved to be united. Foreign observers believed this was one of the causes of the rise in separatist activity in Karabakh.[29] Separatists believed that if their cause was embraced publicly by someone so close to Gorbachev, that the Kremlin must support their objectives.

Azerbaijanis living in the Armenian countryside faced increased levels of violence. In November 1987, two freight trains carrying Azerbaijanis from the southern Armenian town of Kafan arrived in Baku. By the end of January 1988, 2000 more refugees from Kafan arrived, many bearing wounds from beatings or fights. Armenian gangs were raiding villages, beating and shooting Azeris, burning homes and forcing villagers to flee. By the end of 1988, there were dozens of deserted villages and 200,000 Muslim ethnic Azeris and Kurds had fled.[30]

[28] Unless otherwise indicated, most of this section is derived from de Waal, Thomas. *Black Garden: Armenia and Azerbaijan Through Peace and War*. 10th Anniversary Edition (New York: New York University, 2013), 11–44.

[29] Smith, Hedrick. "On the Road with Gorbachev's Guru," *The New York Times*, 10 April 1988. Web. Retrieved 7 May 2019. https://www.nytimes.com/1988/04/10/magazine/on-the-road-with-gorbachev-s-guru.html.

[30] Bolukbasi, ibid., 86.

Armenians submitted ten volumes of signatures, over 75,000, to Moscow demanding unification of Karabakh to Armenia. Armenian delegations were sent to Moscow to make the case. This led to the Armenians in Karabakh holding an unsanctioned political rally on the night of 12 February 1988 calling for the unification of the Autonomous Region of Nagorno-Karabakh (ARNO) with the Armenian SSR. It was the first of its kind within the Soviet Union, an unsanctioned political gathering threatening the Communist party's central control of the Empire. Soon, in the Armenian SSR capital of Yerevan, crowds of up to a half million were gathering to demand unification.

The Armenians in Karabakh were not concerned with any reaction from Moscow. Muradian said he felt Stepanakert (known as Khankendi in Azerbaijan) was "in his hands" before the rally began. He said police, law enforcement organs, and local party officials had all told him that he could rely on them. "They gave us information about what the KGB was up to, who was coming from Baku, who was coming from Moscow. It was full information, there were no secrets."

Asked about the 30% of the Karabakh population that was ethnically Azerbaijani, Muradian was dismissive. "We weren't interested in the fate of those people," he told British journalist Thomas de Waal. "Those people were the instruments of power, instruments of violence over us for many decades, many centuries. We weren't interested in their fate and we're not interested now." This depersonalization of the "other" is an aspect in all conflicts, but it is jarring to read how callused Muradian was in describing his neighbors.

The demonstration in Karabakh was followed a week later by a resolution of the Karabakh Soviet requesting the Supreme Soviet of the USSR approve the transfer of Nagorno-Karabakh from the Azerbaijan SSR to the Armenian SSR. To maintain the status quo and keep the peace, Gorbachev sent a Ministry of Interior motorized battalion from Georgia to Karabakh. At the same time, he counseled Azerbaijani party officials not to use force against the demonstrators.

Immediately after the Karabakh Soviet passed its resolution, Gorbachev convened a meeting of the Politburo in Moscow. He noted there were nineteen potential territorial conflicts throughout the Soviet Union. He would not establish a precedent by making concessions. The Central Committee passed a resolution condemning the Karabakhi Armenians as "extremists." The members of the Karabakh Soviet who voted for the resolution were eventually arrested and transferred to Moscow,[31] supposedly for interfering with the delivery of earthquake relief aid following the Spitak earthquake of December 1988.[32]

Gorbachev tried to defuse the situation by receiving two leading Armenian intellectuals who were separatist leaders, journalist Zori Balayan and poet Silva Kaputikyan. He assured his guests of material assistance for Nagorno-Karabakh, but the area would remain an autonomous region of Azerbaijan. He reiterated his opposition to changes in territorial boundaries within the Soviet Union. He branded events in Karabakh a "knife in the back" of his attempts to reform Soviet society. He would never endorse the transfer of Karabakh to Armenia because it would "dislodge the rock from the mountain and thereby let loose an avalanche." Balayan returned to Yerevan convinced for some reason that Gorbachev supported the separatist position.[33]

Armenians in Nagorno-Karabakh created the Karabakh Committee in February 1988. Their goal was the unification of the oblast with the Armenian SSR. In support of their efforts, demonstrations and school boycotts broke out throughout Nagorno-Karabakh. The demonstrations soon spread to Yerevan, in the Armenian SSR.

The first military sparks of the 1992–1994 war were ignited on 22 February 1988. A group of angry pro-Azerbaijan demonstrators marched from Aghdam (90% ethnic Azerbaijani population) to Stepanakert—where pro-Armenian demonstrations were taking place. They were met near the town of Askeran by policemen and Armenian villagers armed with hunting rifles. Two of the Azerbaijani demonstrators were killed, Ali Hajiyev and Bakhtiyar Guliyev. The Aghdam population was furious but restrained themselves from retaliating.

[31] "Gorbachev's Mounting Nationalities Crisis," The Heritage Foundation, 9 March 1989. Web. Retrieved 3 May 2019. https://www.heritage.org/europe/report/gorbachevs-mounting-nationalities-crisis

[32] Cornell, ibid., 21.

[33] Taubman, William. *Gorbachev: His Life and Times* (W.W. Norton, 2017). Web. Retrieved 8 May 2019. https://books.google.com/books?id=FpFYDgAAQBAJ&pg=PT320&lpg=PT320&dq=gorbachev+karabakh+june+1988&source=bl&ots=e9RlKSN6zu&sig=ACfU3U1lpZScaUBbC8OQJbAh6nuprBj4ng&hl=en&sa=X&ved=2ahUKEwiZrdLjuoziAhUXvJ4KHX2IAU04MhDoATAAegQICBAB#v=onepage&q=gorbachev%20karabakh%20june%201988&f=false.

Sumgait

As ethnic violence escalated, many Armenians living in the Azerbaijan capital of Baku abandoned the city for Sumgait, an industrial town about 22 miles away. This was also the home of Azerbaijani refugees who had fled violence in the Armenian SSR, making it a volatile place. Five days after the deaths in Askeran, the USSR Deputy Prosecutor General Alexander Katusev announced on Central TV that the individuals killed at Askeran were Azerbaijani. This sparked a three-day anti-Armenian pogrom in Sumgait by some local elements in late February-early March 1988. Six Azerbaijanis and 26 Armenians died in the rioting.

Katusev blamed gangs of youths hunting Armenians. "In Sumgait," he told the Azerbaijani Communist Party newspaper Bakinsky Rabochy, "there were massive disorders, accompanied by pogroms, arson and other outrages ... the most terrible crimes."[34]

As bad as the violence was, not all Azerbaijanis in Sumgait participated. There were many stories of Azerbaijanis who tried to help their Armenian neighbors. Members of the Komsomol brought Armenians to the safety of the Palace of Culture in the central square. Soviet media depicted one woman, Mrs. Ismailova, as a hero for her role in protecting several families in her apartment. A doctor's wife, Natevan Tagieva, hid Armenians from her apartment block on the top floor of the building. Vigilante groups guarded Armenian patients in the hospital.[35]

The identity of who initiated the attacks remains a mystery. The majority opinion, as prosecutor Katusev explained, was that this was a spontaneous uprising of Azerbaijani youths outraged over the treatment of their co-ethnics at Askeran. Many of the rioters were Azerbaijani natives of Karabakh who had been driven from their homes by the fighting there.

There are at least three other theories, however, that need to be considered. According to Arzu Abdullayeva, the chairwoman of the Azerbaijani National Committee of the International Helsinki Federation of Human Rights, the demonstrations were instigated by the KGB. Her reasoning was that there was a Soviet military unit stationed a half hour

[34] "Soviet Tells of 'Pogroms' by Rioters in Azerbaijan," *The Washington Post*, March 15, 1988. Web. Retrieved 3 May 2019. https://www.washingtonpost.com/archive/politics/1988/03/16/soviet-tells-of-pogroms-by-rioters-in-azerbaijan/56dc16e1-9aeb-40cd-9ffd-0f176a55a223/?noredirect=on&utm_term=.502a9239b33d.

[35] de Waal, ibid., 37.

out of the city, but it did nothing for the first 24 hours to stop the violence. Abdullayeva said she asked a Soviet soldier for help in stopping the killing, but the soldier replied he was barred from intervening.[36] When the rioting began, there were cameras pre-set on the rooftops to record the violence.[37] How was it possible that cameras would have been there before the outbreak of spontaneous demonstrations, unless it was all planned by the security forces? Abdullayeva's theory is intriguing but, on the other hand, no Western academic has written that they have ever seen footage from the rumored cameras, so it is possible the entire story is apocryphal.

Another possibility is that the pogrom was a *Reichstag* fire event. According to this reasoning, Armenia wanted an excuse to remove ethnic Azerbaijanis from its territory, and popular outrage over a riot such as Sumgait would provide the needed spark. According to court depositions in the case of an Armenian from Sumgait (one of two Armenians convicted of involvement in the riots; 82 Azerbaijani) Armenian victims of the violence identified Armenian Edward Grigorian as one of the organizers of the riots. Grigorian had lists of flats inhabited by Armenians and, along with three other Armenians, personally took part in violence against his co-ethnics.[38]

The third possibility is that the Azerbaijan Communist Party orchestrated the violence. Following this logic, the real target of the violence was not the Armenian community, but decision-makers in Moscow. The communists wanted to demonstrate that unless the Kremlin acted fast, popular uprising in Azerbaijan could harm stability in the Caucasus. If this was indeed a communist plot, it worked—at least initially. Moscow intervened and demanded that the Azerbaijan, Armenia, and Nagorno-Karabakh Oblast communist parties stop the recriminations. All three followed the orders from the center, but it didn't last.[39]

[36] Naegele, Jolyon. "Azerbaijan: Armenians and Azerbaijanis Remember Suffering," RFE/RL, 9 March 1998. Web. Retrieved 3 May 2019. https://www.rferl.org/a/1088062.html.

[37] Goltz, Thomas. *Azerbaijan Diary* (New York: M.E. Sharp, 1999), 83.

[38] Azimov, Araz. "Armenia-Azerbaijan Nagorno-Karabakh Conflict: Historical Background, Legal Aspects and Negotiation Process," in Petersen and Ismailzade, eds., *Azerbaijan in Global Politics: Crafting Foreign Policy* (Baku: Azerbaijan Diplomatic Academy, 2009), 264.

[39] Bolukbasi, ibid., 10.

Soviet government authorities were slow to react. The deputy chief of the KGB arrived that evening. He was appalled at the destruction he witnessed. He decided a military intervention was necessary. A regiment of Soviet Interior Ministry troops arrived several hours later, backed up by cadets from the military academy in Baku. The rioters attacked these symbols of the Soviet state, who were under orders not to use lethal force. The following day, Gorbachev ordered a military curfew. It did not stop the rioting, however. Throughout February 29, the attacks and killings continued. It was not until the evening of the 29th that a company of marines and a parachute regiment restored order.

Soviet military commander Grigory Kharchenko, who had come to Sumgait with the KGB deputy chief, was taken a hostage by some of the 5000 Armenians taking shelter in the Palace of Culture. The hostage takers demanded a plane for Kharchenko's release. They wanted the plane to fly them to safety elsewhere in the Soviet Union. Kharchenko noted that none of the Sumgait Armenians wanted to go to Armenia. "No one in Armenia needs us," said one of the Armenian refugees from Karabakh. "They don't think of us as real Armenians, we are not real Armenian." Given the efforts of the intelligentsia in the Armenian SSR to convince the Supreme Soviet that Karabakh was Armenian territory, it is interesting that members of Azerbaijan's Armenian community were not considered Armenian at all.

To the residents of the Armenian SSR, Sumgait brought back memories of 1915 in Anatolia. Armenian writer Vardges Petrosyan approached Soviet leader Gorbachev with his concerns but was met with a complete lack of understanding. "How can you talk about Genocide?" Gorbachev asked. "You know what kind of word it is and the weight it carries. You are flinging around accusations you will regret for the rest of your life."[40]

Armenians in Yerevan swore revenge before a rally of an estimated 300,000. Ashot Manucharyan, a member of Armenia's nationalist Karabakh Committee, openly called for Armenians to create "self-defense units." "If our government will not carry out its duties," said Manucharyan, "we must organize to defend ourselves ...We must trust no one but ourselves."

In reviewing what occurred in Sumgait, it is important to keep it in perspective. "There was no overall Azerbaijani plan to rid Azerbaijan of

[40] Kaufman, ibid., 75.

Armenians, certainly not to murder them systematically," reported the Armenian American historian Ronald Gregor Suny in a co-authored study of ethnic conflicts. "Even today some Armenians manage to live in Baku without overt threat or ethnic slurs."[41]

The importance of Sumgait is twofold: it triggered a mass population exchange between the two Soviet Socialist Republics, and later a larger Armenian massacre of Azerbaijanis at Khojaly on its anniversary. In the aftermath of Sumgait, the 14,000 Armenians in the city fled, and thousands more joined the exodus from throughout Azerbaijan. As the violence continued, more Armenians would flee Azerbaijan and more Azerbaijanis would flee Armenia and Armenian-controlled areas in Nagorno-Karabakh.

The Communist Party chief and the mayor of Sumgait were dismissed in March because of their inability to handle the riots, but it was not enough to stop the violence. Attacks against Azerbaijanis took place in the Armenian towns of Spitak, Gugark, and others. According to Azerbaijani sources, 216 Azerbaijanis were killed, including 57 women, 18 children, and five infants.[42] Villagers in the Spitak region were set upon by armed gangs after Armenian government officials demanded they leave. As the Azerbaijanis left in buses, they were fired upon. The Armenian atrocities were probably coordinated by Armenian Communist Party officials and their allies supporting Karabakh independence.[43]

The events of Sumgait were not swept under the rug. The Soviet press organs had daily updates on how many had been arrested, convicted, or were under investigation. Within six months, nine people had been convicted, 33 were on trial, and another 52 were under investigation. Reports came in of similar atrocities, only this time it was Armenian violence against Azerbaijanis. "You see there are a lot of Sumgaits," said

[41] Laitin, David D. and Ronald Grigor Suny. "Armenia and Azerbaijan: Thinking a Way Out of Karabakh," Middle East Policy Council VII/1, 1999. Web. Retrieved 8 May 2019. https://www.mepc.org/journal/armenia-and-azerbaijan-thinking-way-out-karabakh.

[42] Balayev, Bahruz. *The Right to Self-Determination in the South Caucasus: Nagorno Karabakh in Context* (New York: Lexington Press, 2013), 22.

[43] Yunusov, Arif, "Pogromy v Armenii v 1988–1989 Godakh," *Ekspress-Khronika* 9 (186), 26 February 1991, as quoted by de Waal, ibid., 64.

Sumgait's new leader of the Communist party. "Every Azerbaijani area of Armenia is a little Sumgait."[44]

Gorbachev charged the Central Committee of the Communist Party to resolve the Karabakh problem. Andrei Gromyko, leader of the Supreme Soviet, said that unification of Nagorno-Karabakh with Armenia through the efforts of "extremist organizations" was intolerable.[45] Instead, the Kremlin passed resolutions to improve the social and economic development of the oblast. It was not enough.

Six months after Sumgait, the cities of Stepanakert and Shusha erupted in Armenian violence against Azerbaijanis. Scores of homes and apartments were burned, and their inhabitants set upon. Robert Kocharyan, future president of Armenia, approved of the violence as an appropriate reprisal. The Soviet Internal Affairs Ministry Commander, Col. Yuriy V. Shatalan, announced he would provide additional troops to supplement the 4500 assigned to Karabakh.[46]

Azerbaijanis were now systematically forced out of Armenia, especially from the Ararat and Zangezur regions. Similarly, rioting in Baku and throughout Azerbaijan put Armenians on the road. In November and December, an estimated 250,000 Armenians left Azerbaijan and 240,000 Azerbaijanis left Armenia. By the end of 1991, there were no Azerbaijanis left under Armenian control, and only a handful of Armenians remained in Azerbaijan.[47]

The result of these massive population flows, and the traumatic circumstances under which they occurred, was the homogenization of two societies that would make future compromise extremely difficult. "Almost the entire Armenian population of Baku (close to 220,000) was forced to flee, as were Armenians in other parts of Azerbaijan, except in parts of Karabakh where they resisted. Simultaneously, the entire Azerbaijani population of Armenia (160,000) was intimidated to leave or forcibly

[44] Keller, Bill. "Riots Legacy of Distrust Quietly Stalks a Soviet City," *The New York Times*, 31 August 1988. Web. Retrieved 23 May 2019. *AcademicOneFile*. http://link.galegroup.com/apps/doc/A175926235/AONE?u=chap_main&sid=AONE&xid=3f0a7786.

[45] Bolukbasi, ibid., 94.

[46] Keller, Bill. "A Deadly Feud Tears at Enclave on Gorbachev's Southern Flank," *The New York Times*, 5 September 1989. Web. Retrieved 23 May 2019. , http://link.galegroup.com/apps/doc/A175760687/AONE?u=chap_main&sid=AONE&xid=20ac8387.

[47] Cornell, ibid., 19–20.

expelled. This mutual ethnic cleansing was the culmination of a decades-long process of homogenization in the two republics. As a result of these forced population transfers, a massive refugee problem emerged in both countries." These figures do not include an estimated 750,000 additional Azerbaijanis who were later expelled from Karabakh and the seven surrounding provinces during the 1992–1994 war.[48]

In Moscow, the Supreme Soviet did not remain silent. Still motivated by Gorbachev's concerns about the potential for ethnic conflict throughout the Soviet Union, they followed up the Central Committee's resolution and rejected the Nagorno-Karabakh Soviet's petition to join Armenia. There was no appeal to their decision. To keep the situation calm, Moscow sent troops to Yerevan, but the troops did little to change the situation. Disregarding Moscow's rejection of Nagorno-Karabakh's petition, the Armenian SSR's Soviet announced the annexation of Nagorno-Karabakh in June 1988. The motion was shepherded through the legislative body by the new, Moscow-approved leadership, possibly to defuse the possibility of street violence. Television coverage of the debate over the motion was canceled when demonstrators demanded changes to the language, indicating the authorities were supporting the resolution as written.[49]

The USSR Supreme Soviet again exercised its veto power, two days later. Gorbachev addressed the Politburo. "The one thing that we can never agree to is to support one people to the detriment of another," he said. "We must never be blackmailed into this. We will not permit, we must in no case allow the truth to be sought through blood!"

The resolution did more than anger Gorbachev; it essentially ended Moscow's efforts to find a compromise. "At some point," wrote the former secretary-general, "it seemed that a possible solution was to give Karabakh, like Nakhichevan, the status of autonomous republic, while keeping it as part of Azerbaijan. There was a time when this proposal was on the point of being implemented. However, it was just at this moment that the Supreme Soviet in Yerevan passed a resolution to incorporate Nagorno-Karabakh as part of Armenia and so everything fell apart. It

[48] Panossian, Razmik. "The Irony of Nagorno-Karabakh: Formal Institutions versus Informal Politics," *Regional and Federal Studies* 11/3, 8 September 2010, 145–146.

[49] Keller, Bill. "Armenian Legislature Backs Call for Annexing Disputed Territory," *The New York Times*, 16 June 1988. Web. Retrieved 8 May 2019. https://www.nytimes.com/1988/06/16/world/armenian-legislature-bakcs-calls-for-annexing-disputed-territory.html.

fell apart because of internal antagonism, because the battle for power, for replacement of the ruling elite, was already in full swing there. If fell apart because the Armenian national movement, which was formed on the basis of the Karabakh committee, was in a hurry to seize power."[50]

The Rise of Nationalism

In response to the rise in Armenian nationalism, Abulfaz Elchibey and others founded the Azerbaijan National Front (ANF) on 16 July 1988. It was a hodge-podge of anti-Soviet nationalists. Elchibey wanted to create an Azerbaijani nationalism based on pride in their own community. For most members of the ANF, however, Azerbaijani nationalism meant being opposed to Armenian nationalism.[51]

The ANF platform called for sovereignty within the USSR, while demanding a seat in the United Nations. It said the name of the people of Azerbaijan was "Azerbaijani Turks," and demanded that Baku retain control over Nagorno-Karabakh. They began holding large demonstrations in Baku to call attention to the situation in the oblast. The demonstrations grew in number until 12 August 1989, when 200,000 took to the streets. The demonstrations were followed by a series of strikes, which the ANF ended in late September in return for the government issuing a declaration of sovereignty. The declaration stated the government of the Azerbaijan SSR reserved the right to withdraw freely from the USSR and could enter into direct relations with foreign states. As for Nagorno-Karabakh, it was an inalienable part of the republic.[52]

In September 1989, the USSR commander of all interior security forces, Col. Gen. Yuri V. Shatalin, visited the region and announced plans to deploy more troops on the perimeter of Karabakh. He then traveled with the military commandant of Nagorno-Karabakh, Maj. Gen. Vladislav F. Safonov, and a third general to the Azerbaijani-majority city of Shusha, to meet with local officials in the Shusha cultural center. A crowd of thousands of Azerbaijanis, many of them refugees from Armenia, gathered outside. About 100 of the protesters stormed the cultural center,

[50] Gorbachev, Mikhail. *Memoirs* (New York and London: Doubleday, 1996), 333–340.

[51] Remler, Philip. *Chained to the Caucasus: Peacemaking in Karabakh 1987–2012* (New York: International Peace Institute, 2016), 23.

[52] Shaffer, Brenda. *Borders and Brethren: Iran and the Challenge of Azerbaijani Identity* (Cambridge: MIT Press, 2002), 132–135.

encircled the military officers and refused to let them leave until they agreed to transfer two Azerbaijanis arrested the previous day for shooting at a nearby Armenian settlement. The two prisoners were moved from Stepanakert, which is almost entirely Armenian, to a prison in Shusha. The crowd had not carried weapons and the generals had an armed escort, but the military officers decided trying to force their way out would worsen the conflict. The incident demonstrated the tenuous nature of Moscow's hold on the region. It was almost inconceivable that a crowd could hold three Soviet generals for several hours and not have suffered severe retribution.[53]

In the political arena, Nagorno-Karabakh separatists took another vote. This time they did not vote to unify with Armenia, but only to secede from Azerbaijan. Again, the Supreme Soviet in Moscow rejected the measure. The Kremlin tried its hand at peacekeeping by sending Viktor Volsky as the "Representative of the Politburo" to Karabakh. He tried to separate the two communities and then bring the leaders together in reconciliation ceremonies. Things went well until 18 September 1988 when a Soviet/Armenian convoy was trying to resupply Stepanakert and an Azerbaijani militia attacked them. In revenge, Armenians attacked several Azerbaijani villages.[54]

Mother Nature intervened in the middle of the nationalist fervor. On 7 December 1988, a massive earthquake struck Spitak Armenia, killing approximately 50,000 people. Thousands more were left homeless. Aid poured in from international relief agencies. The Soviet government lost an airplane with 78 aboard delivering emergency supplies, including relief workers rushing to the scene from Baku. Through it all, Armenian separatists kept up their drumbeat. Armenian protestors were suspicious of the central government's motives in the tragedy, asking why Moscow had not predicted the quake in advance and whether Russia was going to take children orphaned by the tragedy. Troops had to fire on the crowds with bricks and pipes in Yerevan who were attacking soldiers engaged in salvage efforts. Others believed the Kremlin was using the excuse of the natural disaster to reimpose order and eliminate the nationalist movement. "To

[53] Keller, Bill. "Soviet Drama: 3 Generals Held by Crowd," *The New York Times*, 8 September 1989. Web. Retrieved 23 May 1989. *Academic OneFile*. http://link.galegroup.com/apps/doc/A175759206/AONE?u=chap_main&sid=AONE&xid=3505a6be.

[54] Remler, ibid., 32.

behave like this at such a time," fumed Gorbachev. "What sort of morals do these people have?"[55]

Moscow was fed up: in January 1989 Gorbachev placed the NKAO under the authority of a six-person committee headed by Volsky reporting directly to the Kremlin. It was the sort of compromise for which Gorbachev was famous: pleasing no one. To the Armenians, it represented a loss of authority from the local Armenian officials within the autonomous region; to the Azerbaijanis, it meant that Moscow was taking over control of their legal territory. Parliaments of both soviet socialist republics demanded that the central government withdraw from the enclave.[56] Armenian residents of the oblast began organizing themselves into a parallel, underground government. Soviet authorities arrested members of the Karabakh Committee and held them for six months before finally releasing them without a trial. Moscow's direct control would continue almost eleven months. Control of the NKAO was returned to the authorities in Baku in November 1989.

In protest, Armenians in Karabakh called a general strike. This resulted in Soviet troops and tanks being deployed in Stepanakert.[57] The enclave held out almost until the end of Moscow's control. In September 1989, however, the Karabakh Armenian leadership called an end to the strike which was hurting Karabakh's economy.[58]

Repulsed by Moscow when acting separately, the Soviets of Armenia and Nagorno-Karabakh tried to achieve success by operating jointly. On 1 December 1989, the two bodies passed the "Joint Resolution of Armenia SSR and Nagorny Karabakh Oblast on Reunification." The resolution referenced the principle of self-determination and the desire for "unification of the two segments of the Armenian people pulled apart by force."

[55] Keller, Bill. "Amid the Rubble, Armenians Express Rage to Gorbachev," *The New York Times*, 12 December 1988. Web. Retrieved 23 May 2019. *Academic OneFile*. http://link.galegroup.com/apps/doc/A176016925/AONE?u=chap_main&sid=AONE&xid=b6374148.

[56] Clines, Francis X. "Violence Flares Again in Azerbaijan Republic," *The New York Times*, 17 September 1989. Web. Retrieved 23 May 2019. *AcademicOneFile*. http://link.galegroup.com/apps/doc/A175757618/AONE?u=chap_main&sid=AONE&xid=0469d7c9.

[57] Human Rights Watch, ibid., 2.

[58] Keller, Bill. "A Deadly Feud Tears at Enclave on Gorbachev's Southern Flank," *The New York Times*, 5 September 1989. Web. Retrieved 23 May 2019. http://link.galegroup.com/apps/doc/A175760687/AONE?u=chap_main&sid=AONE&xid=20ac8387.

The Armenian SSR recognized the NKAO "National Council" as the sole legal authority in force in the oblast, and then stated the NKAO wanted to be a part of Armenia. They added that they (in Yerevan) assumed the obligation to represent the national interests of Armenians in the NKAO.[59] This was a revolutionary step. By stating that the NKAO representatives were the sole legitimate authority in the oblast, the resolution effectively declared secession of the NKAO from the Soviet Union. It was only by taking such a step that the authorities could ignore the USSR 's constitutional requirements that border changes would require approval of the Supreme Soviet. Article 78 of the Soviet Constitution specifically stated "Territory may be altered only by mutual agreement of the concerned republics, and subject to the ratification of the USSR."[60] It is an interesting legal feat that one resolution could both tear the NKAO out of the Soviet Union and, at the same time, integrate it back into the Soviet Union as part of the Armenian SSR.

Neither the Azerbaijan SSR nor the Supreme Soviet of the USSR were amused at this usurpation of their authority. The Praesidium of the Azerbaijan SSR declared the resolution illegal, null, and void. They stated that the resolution was an "impermissible interference in the sovereign Azerbaijan SSR's territorial integrity," and added that the resolution was not helpful to efforts to stabilize the situation and restore normal relations.[61] Of course, what the Praesidium missed was that the very goal of the resolution was to block the restoration of normal relations. The resolution was a statement from the periphery that it was accepting responsibility for its own actions, and there was no longer a role for the center in governance. In that respect, the resolution was a harbinger of what was to come with the dissolution of the Soviet empire.

[59] "Joint Resolution of Armenia SSR and Nagorny Karabakh Oblast on Reunification," 1 December 1989. Web. Retrieved 8 May 1989. https://www.legal-tools.org/doc/67c50c/pdf/.

[60] "Constitution of the Union of Soviet Socialist Republics, Adopted at the Seventy (Special) Session of the Supreme Soviet of the USSR," Ninth Convocation, 7 October 1977. Web. Retrieved 8 May 2019. http://www.departments.bucknell.edu/russian/const/77cons03.html.

[61] "Decision of the Supreme Soviet of the Azerbaijan SSR in Connection with the Decision of the Supreme Soviet of the Armenian SSR on Uniting the Armenian SSR and the NKAO," 6 December 1989. Web. Retrieved 8 May 2019. https://www.legal-tools.org/doc/883cb8/pdf/.

As the 1990 New Year came to Azerbaijan, ethnic fighting continued. There was an upsurge in sabotage throughout Nagorno-Karabakh. Authorities had to airdrop food and medical supplies into the region.[62] In Shaumyan and Khanlar, military helicopters without identification marks fired shots at Azerbaijani forces.[63] The clashes culminated in riots in Baku after two members of the Azerbaijani Popular Front told an Armenian family to leave. The Armenians resisted, with at least one person attacking the Azerbaijanis with an ax. One of the APF members died, and the other was hospitalized with severe injuries.

In the fighting that followed, at least 25 people were killed including several soldiers from the internal security forces. TASS, the Soviet news agency, described the fighting as a pogrom in which gangs of hooligans were committing atrocities. The fighting lasted three days as it spread to other districts. Moscow flew in a division of riot troops to restore order. As in Sumgait, not all Azerbaijanis participated in the fighting. A Moscow radio correspondent reported that members of the militia were able to save many people, and many Azerbaijanis again sheltered their Armenian neighbors from the mob.

The Kremlin sent to Baku a special Communist Party delegation, headed by Yevgeny Primakov, to resolve the crisis. Primakov was one of the top officials of the Soviet Union, and would eventually serve as head of the KGB, Minister of Foreign Affairs, and Prime Minister. A second group, headed by Politburo member Nikolai Slyunkov, went to Yerevan.[64] Another delegation was sent to Nagorno-Karabakh, but were turned back at the airport.[65]

[62] Clines, Francis X. "Upheaval in the East: Soviet Union; Sharp Rise in Sabotage Reported in Ethnic Conflict in Azerbaijan," *The New York Times*, 9 January 1990. Web. Retrieved 23 May 2019. *AcademicOneFile*. http://link.galegroup.com/apps/doc/A175414177/AONE?u=chap_main&sid=AONE&xid=e3a27915.

[63] Balukbasi, ibid., 128.

[64] Parks, Michael. "Soviet Riots Kill 25 Armenians: Azerbaijan: Russians in the Capital of Baku Tell of Atrocities Against Minority Group. Moscow Flies in a Division of Troops," *Los Angeles Times*, 15 January 1990. Web. Retrieved 8 May 2019. https://www.latimes.com/archives/la-xpm-1990-01-15-mn-191-story.html.

[65] de Waal, ibid., 108.

Black January

The Communist officials sent to review the situation had few good ideas. Finally, the Kremlin decided to take decisive action—too little and too late. By this point, the Popular Front had become a significant political factor in Baku that was interfering with the Communist party's ability to govern. Seeking to halt the rise in Azerbaijani nationalism and to make an example for other Soviet republics, the Kremlin decided to invade Baku and other parts of Azerbaijan. KGB General Filipp Bobkov commanded Operation Strike in which Soviet Ministry of the Interior (MVD) troops were sent to Baku, Nagorno-Karabakh, and the Armenian-Azerbaijan border. Bobkov worked under the direction of the Minister of Defense Dimitri Yazov who had come to Baku with Minister of the Interior Vadim Bakatin to join Politburo members Primakov and Girenko. Over the night of 19–20 January 1990, up to 26,000 Soviet troops invaded and occupied a capital city of one of their own socialist republics. Somewhere between 131 (the official estimate) and 300 (an unofficial estimate) Azerbaijani civilians were killed in the invasion.

The event became known in Azerbaijan as Black January, and it is commemorated every year on 20 January. One resident described the events he experienced. "Soviet army soldiers shot people at point-blank range with special brutality, carried out deliberate assaults of tanks and armored personnel carriers on cars, and bombarded hospitals, prevented the medical personnel from helping the wounded. The personnel of the troops wounded the wounded with bayonet knives. ... A terrible sight represented Baku at dawn on January 20: bloodstained streets and squares of the city, the remains of mutilated corpses, crushed cars, riddled bullet-riddled houses, and asphalt. This night, the whole population of Azerbaijan, especially Baku, experienced a real tragic shock. I was then 15 years old...Like many other people in my city, for the first time in my life I heard shots from tanks and machine guns."

Another former resident of Baku, photographer Boris Dobin, said, "It cannot be forgotten. The events of January 1990 are an open wound for me, which will never cease to cause pain... I remember the development of these days in details...I was working as a photographer in two places: in the city musical art history museum and the traffic police department. On January 20, early in the morning the head of the department called me and said that we had to make a raid on the streets to picture the damage committed to the city infrastructure. Tanks drove across Baku and crashed everything in their path; they ran over parked cars on purpose…It was terrible to walk down the streets. Bodies were everywhere. It was clear that the army fired at unarmed people who could not and did not try to resist. Even though it was morning already and General Lebed had withdrawn his troops from Baku, shots could be heard in the city."[66]

In Moscow, Prime Minister Gorbachev blamed Communist Party and state authorities in both Azerbaijan and Armenia as having caused the problems that required the military to intervene. He said the officials had caved into pressures of nationalist groups.[67] He put more blame on Azerbaijan, much to the consternation of Azerbaijanis who began to perceive a bias on the part of the Kremlin.

The Soviets followed the invasion with a declaration of martial law. Defense Minister Yazov defended his actions imposing military control on the 20th, but not stopping the riots two weeks earlier. He claimed there were not enough troops available at the beginning of the month. Yazov's failure to act in the one instance, and willingness to act in the other, demonstrated that restoration of public order was not the purpose of Bloody Sunday. Rather, it was to destroy the nationalist freedom movement in Azerbaijan, as personified by the Azerbaijan Popular Front (APF). He admitted at a press conference the military occupation was designed to prevent the Front from seizing power from the Communist Party. His goal was to smash the "structure of power" created by the nationalists whom he branded "extremists". Prime Minister Gorbachev said there were growing calls for a seizure of power by force. Soviet deputy foreign minister Alexander Bessmertnykh justified the Soviet invasion as preventing a virtual coup by the APF. "A headquarters was established whose purpose was in essence to remove the legal authorities from power, and to take power themselves," he said.[68]

Yazov seemed genuinely concerned about the military situation. He said that Azerbaijan SSR Interior Ministry officials were helping the

[66] Gut, Arye. "Bloody 'Black January' Became the Starting Point for Independence of Azerbaijan," *The Jerusalem Post*, 19 January 2018. Web. Retrieved 10 May 2019. https://www.jpost.com/Blogs/News-from-Arye-Gut/Black-January-became-the-starting-point-for-independence-of-Azerbaijan-537065.

[67] Swietochowski, ibid., 206.

[68] Keller, Bill. "Troops Storm City: Militants Stage Protest, Vowing to Defy Army with Civil Unrest," *The New York Times*, 21 January 1990, 1.

Front, by providing activists with information on Soviet troop movements and weaponry, including the latest model Kalashnikov submachine gun. Approximately, 40,000 Azerbaijani militants possessed automatic weapons, machine guns, and various kinds of rifles, he said. It was not just the military situation; however, the Front appeared to have the support of the workers. Immediately after the invasion, the Popular Front called for a general strike. Four days later, Yazov reported that only 22 of about 350 factories in Baku were working normally.[69]

When it was over, an independent military investigation concluded that the Red Army had waged war on one of its own cities. It called for criminal proceedings against Minister Yazov, whom they concluded had personally commanded the operation. This was important, since the use of the army internally appeared to violate the Soviet Constitution. Articles 50 and 51 promise freedom of speech and assembly (and Yazov admitted the military intervention was designed to stop both). Article 72 gave the union republics the right to freely secede from the USSR (and therefore would protect the rise of nationalist movements). Article 73 discusses safeguarding the frontiers and territory of the USSR, (implying the role of the military was external). Article 81 said that the sovereign rights of union republics would be safeguarded by the USSR, (not trampled militarily by the USSR). Article 137 said the highest authority of state authority in a Union Republic was the Supreme Council of that republic, and Article 145 said local authority was in the local council of people's deputies (not Moscow). Article 164 said that responsibility for supervising observance of laws was with the Procurator General (not the military).[70] Of course, these articles were never meant to be interpreted in a strictly legalistic way, but in the Gorbachev era of glasnost people were paying more attention to the letter of the law.

Nagorno-Karabakh was also placed under martial law and occupied. By the summer of 1990, Soviet military checkpoints had been set up on all roads leading to Stepanakert and travel within Nagorno-Karabakh generally was reported to be under Soviet military control.[71] Armenian leaders accused the Soviet military of siding with Azerbaijan's Interior Ministry

[69] Dobbs, Michael. "Soviets Say Troops Used to Avert Coup in Baku: Nationalists Said to Plan Seizure of Power," *The Washington Post*, 27 January 1990, A13.

[70] Soviet Constitution of 1977, ibid.

[71] Human Rights Watch, ibid., 3.

special troops to maintain Azerbaijani control of the oblast. In response, ethnic Armenians purchased weapons and shipped them into Karabakh. They also raided USSR weapons depots within the Armenian SSR. In one incident, Soviet interior ministry troops killed 20 Armenian separatists attempting to raid depots at the Yerevan train station and at a military base south of the city.

The government of the Armenian SSR declared a day of mourning for the separatists who died trying to pilfer weapons from the USSR itself. Soviet press said similar raids were occurring throughout the republic. Armenians had seized 1200 automatic rifles from police stations over the previous months. The head of Soviet internal security troops, General Yuri Shatalin, fretted over the large arsenal that the separatists had acquired. "Our troops do not want this bloodshed," he said, "but the terrorists are forcing them into it." Shatalin met with leaders of the armed Armenian groups and demanded they lay down their arms. The Armenians rejected the request from the central government's representative. USSR Interior Minister Bakatin complained that Armenia was not doing enough to stop the lawlessness.[72]

In Yerevan, a group of Soviet troops escorting a train was surrounded by an angry crowd. According to an Armenian journalist, the crowd was peaceful and demanded the troops leave Armenia. According to Soviet press, the crowd attacked the soldiers. Regardless of how it began, the troops opened fire and killed six civilians. The Armenian National Front claimed that the troops had opened fire because of Soviet unhappiness over upcoming local elections that would include voters in Nagorno-Karabakh.[73] Gen. Yuri Shatalin said that the "bloodshed in Yerevan" was brought about by "open connivance of the republic leadership and law enforcement agencies with illegal armed groups." He accused local leaders of ignoring signs that separatists in the capital were acquiring stolen vehicles and weapons. Shatalin said he had met with "leaders of illegal armed

[72] Dobbs, Michael. "Armenia in Mourning After Clashes Kill 22; Soviets Blame Nationalists' Quest for Arms," *The Washington Post*, 29 May 1990, A18.

[73] "Evolution in Europe: Soviet Troops Kill 6 in Armenian Capital," *The New York Times*, 28 May 1990. Web. Retrieved 23 May 2019. *AcademicOneFile*. http://link.galegroup.com/apps/doc/A175495619/AONE?u=chap_main&sid=AONE&xid=76ede82c.

formations," but that they had rejected his request that they voluntarily surrender their arms.[74]

An Armenian paramilitary group, the Armenian National Army (ANA) began patrolling the borders of Nagorno-Karabakh. They caused numerous deaths in skirmishes with Azerbaijani civilians and Soviet authorities. As an example, TASS reported that when five busloads of Soviet Interior Ministry troops were escorting a convoy of 16 trucks and a bus carrying Azerbaijanis, they came under attack by heavily armed Armenian militants.[75] The ANA did not survive until independence, as the Armenian SSR disbanded the organization. Despite its fleeting existence, however, it had one long-term effect: the head of the ANA Levon Ter-Petrosyan was elected chairman of the Armenian Supreme Soviet.[76] He would later become the first president of Armenia.

Gorbachev ordered all paramilitary groups disbanded within 15 days. The Armenian Supreme Soviet responded with a resolution on 31 July 1990 suspending Gorbachev's ban on illegal armed groups, declaring that the Soviet Constitution did not give Gorbachev the power to issue such a decree.[77] Soviet troops continued to find themselves in firefights. In the Kazakh border region of Azerbaijan, Soviet troops expelled hundreds of Armenian fighters who had been harassing Azerbaijani villages. The fighters were armed with heavy weaponry, including rocket and grenade launchers.[78]

Azerbaijani militias now found themselves in constant skirmishes with armed formations inside Karabakh. To halt the fighting, in April 1991 the Kremlin sent into action elements of the 23rd Motorized Rifle Division of the Fourth Army. They joined with Azerbaijan SSR security forces and

[74] Fein, Esther B. "Evolution in Europe: Armenian Fighting Levels Off; Toll is 23," *The New York Times*, 29 May 1990. Web. Retrieved 23 May 2019. *AcademicOneFile*. http://link.galegroup.com/apps/doc/A175495895/AONE?u=chap_main&sid=AONE&xid=fab73d5f.

[75] "Evolution in Europe: Soviets Say 3 Died in Armenian Ambush of a Convoy," *The New York Times*, 13 July 1990. Web. Retrieved 23 May 2019. *AcademicOneFile*. http://link.galegroup.com/apps/doc/A175528692/AONE?u=chap_main&sid=AONE&xid=fff810c3.

[76] Croissant, ibid., 38.

[77] Bolukbasi, ibid., 151.

[78] "Soviets Oust Armenia Fighters in Azerbaijan," *The New York Times*, 23 August 1990. Reuters. Web. Retrieved 23 May 2019. http://link.galegroup.com/apps/doc/A175545635/AONE?u=chap_main&sid=AONE&xid=2cfe9e0c.

launched Operation Ring, an effort to locate and seize the illegal weapons cache. Operation Ring occurred both within and without of the borders of Karabakh. In the villages of Getashin and Martunashen, the security forces rousted the Armenian inhabitants and gave their homes to Azerbaijani refugees who had previously fled from Armenia. Eventually, security forces would empty twenty-four villages in Karabakh, accusing the residents of assisting separatists. Armenian irregular forces put up a spirited defense against troops supported by tanks and heavy artillery. Much of the weaponry came from the government of the Armenian SSR. Minister of Interior Ashot Manucharian admitted in 2000 that he had supplied the fighters with weapons he had brought from Soviet bases in Georgia.[79]

Gorbachev ordered the militias disarmed, but his demands were ignored. In August 1991, a Soviet armored personnel carrier was blocked by ethnic Armenian inhabitants of a town called Aterk. Twelve Soviet troops were captured. Later, an additional 21 soldiers were seized. The Armenians originally demanded the release of an Armenian who had been arrested for carrying a machine gun and ammunition; later they demanded the release of 15 Armenians detained in the previous months.[80] They threatened that if the Armenian prisoners were not released, that the soldiers would be transferred to the Armenian SSR. The Soviet Ministry of Interior rejected the idea of a prisoner exchange and threatened the leaders of the Armenian SSR with unnamed consequences if the soldiers were not released.[81]

In Moscow, the new president of the Russian SSR Boris Yeltsin was a fierce critic of Operation Ring. He perceived actions of the center against separatist forces in Azerbaijan as a bad precedent. Yeltsin was moving to give Russia as much independence as possible from the USSR, and he did not want to create any justification for the Kremlin to halt his activities. By opposing Operation Ring, Yeltsin laid the foundation for the future alliance between Russia and Armenia.

[79] Bolukbasi, ibid., 166.

[80] "Armenian Militants Reported to Capture 33 Soviet Soldiers," *The New York Times*, 15 August 1991. Web. Retrieved 23 May 2019. *AcademicOneFile*. http://link.galegroup.com/apps/doc/A175306117/AONE?u=chap_main&sid=AONE&xid=8d215d5c.

[81] "8 More Soviet Troops Seized by Armenians," *The New York Times*, 16 August 1991. Web. Retrieved 23 May 2019. *AcademicOneFile*. http://link.galegroup.com/apps/doc/A175304791/AONE?u=chap_main&sid=AONE&xid=569c761c.

The results of Operation Ring were the continued transfers of populations and a hardening of mutual feelings of animosity.[82] When Armenian military recruiters mentioned these military actions, volunteers would flock to defend their Armenian co-ethnics in Karabakh. There was a third effect that, if pursued, may have brought some calm into the area. Impressed at the willingness of the central government to use such overwhelming force, the Armenians decided it was time for peace feelers. This was the first time that either side considered compromise from their maximalist positions. The Armenian parliament approved a proposal from the leaders of Nagorno-Karabakh, for "all sides to reconsider all anti-constitutional decisions regarding Mountainous Karabakh." The leaders wrote to Azerbaijan's leader, Ayaz Mutalibov, proposing talks based on the Soviet and Azerbaijani Constitutions with a long list of preconditions. There was only one meeting after which one of the Armenian negotiators was assassinated. Armenian moderates feared this was a signal from the hardliners that they could not accept a negotiated settlement.[83]

Declarations of Independence

The final collapse of the Soviet Union began on 17 August 1991, when Soviet hardliners answered the call of KGB chairman Vladimir A. Kryuchkov to meet in a bath house. The prime minister, defense minister, and a handful of others agreed that Soviet leader Gorbachev's treaty proposal for a looser federation of soviet republics would mean the end of the USSR. To save the state, he would have to be removed. A group flew to Crimea to ask Gorbachev to resign while the other coup plotters stayed in Moscow. On 19 August, they announced the state was under the authority of an emergency committee, led by Soviet Vice President Gennadi Yanayev.[84] For three days, the world remained spellbound; the coup plotters were in the Russian White House, home of the country's parliament. The newly elected leader of the Russian SSR, Boris Yeltsin, emerged on top of a tank as the most powerful figure in Russian politics. The army remained neutral, fearful of starting a civil war. On 21

[82] Croissant, ibid., 42.

[83] Kaufman, ibid., 77–78.

[84] Sebestyen, Victor. "The K.G.B.'s Bathhouse Plot," *The New York Times*, 21 August 2011. Section SR, Pg. 4.

August, the emergency committee ordered the KGB's Alpha Group to storm the demonstrators that were keeping them imprisoned inside the White House. The KGB refused to comply and the coup failed. The coup plotters' efforts to save the Soviet Union had hastened its demise. Within days, Yeltsin banned the Communist Party inside the future Russian Federation. Within four months, the Soviet Union would be a memory. On 25 December, Mikhail Gorbachev celebrated the West's Christmas Day by resigning from office. The red flag was lowered for the last time from the Kremlin's towers.

In the aftermath, Soviet forces discontinued their formal operations in Karabakh. Both Armenians and Azerbaijanis took advantage of the ensuing chaos to arm themselves with Soviet weaponry. Some were purchased from the departing troops, while more was seized as the Red Army left them behind. The withdrawal of the troops hurt Baku more than Yerevan, as Baku had remained loyal to the Kremlin and relied on Soviet military support. By contrast, the Armenians had been organizing their own militias and paramilitary groups for some time. Without a Soviet military presence, Azerbaijan was relatively defenseless against Armenian aggression.

Emboldened by the weakness in the Kremlin, on 29 August 1991 Azerbaijan's parliament passed a declaration of independence that was overwhelmingly ratified (99% approval) on 29 December by a popular referendum. On 2 September 1991, the Nagorno-Karabakh National Committee followed suit and declared its own independence. Since the Soviet Union was not to collapse for several more months, the declaration was as illegal as all the other attempts to secede from the Azerbaijan SSR. Under Article 72 of the Soviet Constitution of 1977, only Union Republics had the right to secede from the USSR. Nagorno-Karabakh, however, was an oblast (a subunit of a republic). It therefore was bound by Article 78's insistence that changes in the borders of union republics required the approval of all republics involved. Two weeks later, on 21 September, the Republic of Armenia exercised its constitutional right to leave the USSR.

Nagorno-Karabakh's attempt to gain its independence preceded the Republic of Armenia's by almost three weeks. While support for Karabakh independence had been a major rallying cry for Armenian nationalists in Yerevan as they sought to obtain power, from this moment on the leaders in Karabakh would pursue its own interests—even if it did not align completely with Yerevan's. This was not a frequent condition, however, as post-independent Armenia was controlled by Karabakh leaders for almost its entire existence. As one Karabakh leader answered if he was happy with the support he was getting from Yerevan, "Yes, and if we are ever less than satisfied, we can change the government of Armenia."[85]

Russian President Boris Yeltsin tried to burnish his international credentials by teaming up with Kazakh strongman Nursultan Nazarbayev to sponsor peace talks. They offered a peace plan that rejected claims of Karabakh independence but proposed strong autonomy within Azerbaijan. Newly elected Azerbaijani President Ayaz Mutalibov pronounced himself completely satisfied with the position of the two visiting leaders. Armenian President Ter-Petrosyan said he was willing to negotiate, but he did not say he agreed to the proposals.[86]

Yeltsin and Nazarbayev brought the two presidents together for talks in a town called Zheleznovodsk. Also present was Robert Kocharyan from Nagorno-Karabakh. Ter-Petrosyan told the assembled leaders that Armenia did not want any of Azerbaijan's territory. The leaders of Russia, Kazakhstan, Azerbaijan, and Armenia signed a declaration stating any unconstitutional laws would be repealed, legitimate bodies of power would be recognized, all non-Soviet troops would be withdrawn from the combat zone (not further defined), and Armenia and Azerbaijan would begin bilateral negotiations.[87]

The Russian-Kazakh mediation effort came to a fiery conclusion on 20 November 1991, when an Armenian rocket shot down an Azerbaijani MI-8 military helicopter carrying members of the peacekeeping mission. This included 13 high-ranking members of the Azerbaijani government, including the Secretary of State, the Public Prosecutor General, and the Minister of Internal Affairs. In addition, there were a number of Russian and Kazakh officials. All 22 people on board were killed. In retaliation for the crash, Azerbaijan imposed a full rail blockade on Armenia and cut communication links with Stepanakert, the Armenian-controlled capital of Nagorno-Karabakh. The two newly-formed Republics—stood on the brink of war over Nagorno-Karabakh.

[85] Remler, ibid., 26.

[86] Keller, Bill. "Yeltsin, in Azerbaijan, Proposes Pact on Enclave," *The New York Times*, 22 September 1991. Web. Retrieved 23 May 2019. http://link.galegroup.com/apps/doc/A175322917/AONE?u=chap_main&sid=AONE&xid=bedbc8f0.

[87] Remler, ibid., 37–38.

CHAPTER 2

The Military Face of a Frozen Conflict

Introduction

Academic literature discusses the Nagorno-Karabakh War as one of many frozen conflicts on the periphery of the former Soviet Union. The term "Frozen Conflict" is a misnomer. It is really a longstanding simmering conflict with low-level fatalities, punctuated by periods of hot war. Armed skirmishes began as early as 1988, but actual fighting between organized military units did not break out until 1992.

Russia traditionally and historically supported Armenians in the region. In the immediate aftermath of the collapse of the Soviet Union, however, her soldiers took part in military operations on both sides of the conflict. This was not a conscious decision on the part of the Kremlin, but the result of the physical location and makeup of the "Russian" troops. The 366th Motorized Rifle Regiment contained large numbers of Armenian officers and enlisted personnel. Karabakh Armenians hired tanks from the regiment on numerous occasions. By contrast, the 23rd Motorized Rifle Division was bivouacked in Ganja, Azerbaijan, and its number included many Azerbaijanis. There were also independent operators, petty thieves within the units who sold equipment to the highest bidder. In one case, an officer tried to sell his tank to an American for $3000, thinking that

J. J. Coyle, *Russia's Interventions in Ethnic Conflicts*,
https://doi.org/10.1007/978-3-030-59573-9_2

the man was a weapons trader.[1] One commentator referred to the period as the privatization of the Soviet army.[2]

Armenia was the Russian favorite. Soviet weaponry that was being left behind for the new Republics was not shared equally, but most went to Armenia. The Russian Ministry of Defense in 1992 promoted the commander of the Seventh Army in Armenia, citing his leadership in the Karabakh campaign.[3]

The secessionists in Karabakh acquired much of its equipment from the four regiments of the Soviet Interior Ministry who had been stationed there. "It was a very solid foundation," said Robert Kocharyan. "All of the equipment stayed, we did not allow it to be removed." Sometimes, the weapons transfers were by force. According to official records of the Soviet Interior Ministry, on 22 December 1991 armed Armenians broke into a barracks in Stepanakert, forced the troops there to abandon their post, and then seized their weapons, ammunition and vehicles. De Waal noted, however, that this official version may well have been a cover story for a business deal.[4]

The government of Armenia did not hide its continuing involvement in Karabakh despite protestations of neutrality. "The government is dropping the pretense of being just an interested observer," wrote a reporter. "In downtown Yerevan, a pile of rocket-propelled grenades sits in the office of the special government committee that handles relations with Karabakh. A staffer keeps an AK-47 behind his desk and fiddles absent-mindedly with his side arm as he makes phone calls. Armed guerillas with luxuriant Fidel-style beards and wearing rumpled fatigues walk diffidently in the boardroom size office."[5]

The fighting moved from intercommunal skirmishes to war. Faced with Nagorno-Karabakh's unilateral declaration of independence, the Azerbaijan government decided to end the insurrection by force. On 31 January 1992, it launched a military operation against the rebel capital

[1] Bolukbasi, Suha, ibid., 189.

[2] de Waal, ibid., 180.

[3] King, Charles. "The Benefits of Ethnic War: Understanding Eurasia's Unrecognized States," *World Politics* 53, July 2001, 539.

[4] de Waal, ibid., 179.

[5] Quinn-Judge, Paul. "Stepanakert Postcard: Revenge Tragedy," *The New Republic* 206/14, 6 April 1992, 11.

of Stepanakert. The attack was beaten off by Armenian defenders, and Azerbaijan fell back onto the tactic of firing rockets and artillery on the capital from the heights surrounding the town.[6]

Khojaly Massacre

In February 1992, Armenian forces began a major assault on Khojaly, a town north of Stepanakert. Khojaly, an Azerbaijani populated town, was being used by the Azerbaijanis as an artillery base, and it housed the only airport in Nagorno-Karabakh that could use large, fixed-wing aircraft. As such, it was a target of tremendous military worth. In many ways, Khojaly was an Azerbaijani island in the middle of an Armenian sea. Paramilitary forces had cut the road in October 1991, so the only way the population could be resupplied was by air. By February, there were about 3000 civilians left in town, protected by 160 lightly armed men. The rest had been taken out by helicopter.

The Russian 366th Motorized Rile Unit became involved in the fighting on 23 February. After supposedly spending months in the region maintaining their neutrality, Air Marshall Yevgeny I. Shaposhnikov gave the unit approval to exercise the right of self-defense if attacked. Shaposhnikov was the top military commander for the Commonwealth of Independent States. He gave the order after the Russians' base came under Azerbaijani artillery shelling.[7]

On the night of 25 February 1992, elements of the 366th, working in unison with Armenian forces, surrounded the town. They left a "humanitarian corridor" open so the civilians could escape as they engaged the town's few defenders. Armenian forces had given an ultimatum to the head of the Khojaly militia, Alif Hajiyev, to abandon the town or face an attack. Hajiyev warned the civilians, and most of the militia and townspeople fled down the corridor. A small number stayed behind.

The Armenians did not give the civilians safe passage. In fact, the "humanitarian corridor" was a field of fire. The Russians and Armenians opened fire on the fleeing civilians trying to reach the relative safety of Aghdam. They killed 613 Azerbaijanis, including up to 300

[6] Croissant, ibid., 78.

[7] Dahlburg, ibid.

women, children, and elderly. Over a thousand people were taken prisoner. Many were subjected to torture. When Western reporters were flown in several days after the killing spree, they found a mountainside riddled with corpses. Many showed evidence of being shot at close range; others were mutilated. According to Human Rights Watch, Khojaly was "the largest massacre to date in the conflict." Executive Director Holly Cartner wrote, "We place direct responsibility for the civilian deaths with Karabakh Armenian forces... The circumstances surrounding the attack ... on those fleeing Khojaly indicate that [Karabakh] Armenian forces and the troops of the 366th CIS regiment ... deliberately disregarded this customary law restraint on attacks (on civilians.) Nagorno-Karabakh officials and fighters clearly expected the inhabitants of Khojaly to flee since they claim to have informed the town that a corridor would be left open to allow for their safe passage ... Under these circumstances, the killing of fleeing combatants could not justify the foreseeably large number of civilian casualties."[8]

The timing of the Khojaly attack, two days after the Russians received the self-defense authorization, the fact that Khojaly had military value because of its airport' and eyewitness testimony of survivors point to the Russians' involvement. Deserters from the 366th would eventually admit the unit had been involved in the fighting.[9] Almost immediately, Shaposhnikov ordered the 366th Motorized Rifle Regiment to withdraw from Karabakh. They relocated to Georgia.[10] Once the unit was safely outside the international borders of Azerbaijan, it was disbanded on 10 March. Many members of the unit and much of the military equipment stayed behind. The regiment's Major Seyran Ohanyan and over 100 other

[8] Cartner, Holly. "Response to Armenian Government Letter on the Town of Khojaly, Nagorno Karabakh," Human Rights Watch, 23 March 1997. Web. Retrieved 26 May 2019. https://www.hrw.org/news/1997/03/23/response-armenian-government-letter-town-khojaly-nagorno-karabakh.

[9] Schmemann, Serge. "Armenians Block Exit by Former Soviet Army," *The New York Times*, 4 March 1992. Web. Retrieved 23 June 2019. *AcademicOneFile*. http://link.galegroup.com/apps/doc/A174814864/AONE?u=chap_main&sid=AONE&xid=0dc14ab7.

[10] Dahlburg, John-Thor. "Armenia-Azerbaijan War Troops Old Soviet Regiment: Caucasus: The Soldiers Want No Part of the Ethnic Conflict, and Moscow Has Finally Ordered Them Out," *Los Angeles Times*, 29 February 1992. Web. Retrieved 27 May 2019. https://www.latimes.com/archives/la-xpm-1992-02-29-mn-2372-story.html.

Armenian officers defected to Nagorno-Karabakh separatists.[11] Ohanian was later rewarded by being named military commander of Karabakh's forces. The other officers included all three battalion commanders, who took with them at least 60 T-72 tanks.[12]

The weapons were greatly prized by the Armenians, to the point that they had barricaded the entrance to the 366th Regiment's base with dump trucks to prevent the T-72 s from departing with the unit. The big fear was that the tanks would fall into the hands of Azerbaijan. "We cannot permit Azerbaijan to get their hands on that equipment," said future Armenian president Serzh Sargsyan. "It could be decisive."[13] Not only were the weapons important, but Armenia also wanted the 366th to stay. They initially blocked the roads so that the unit could not depart. Russia had to finally airlift the unit out of Karabakh by helicopter.

Russia at first denied that its troops were involved in the massacre. They insisted that their troops had remained neutral in the conflict. Just as the Kremlin originally claimed that the "little green men" who fought in Crimea were volunteers (later admitted by President Vladimir Putin to be Russian military forces), the Russian Ambassador to Turkey reluctantly admitted that it was possible that some of the individuals involved may have been Russian acting in an unofficial capacity. "We reject rumors that our military units may have taken part in these incidents. However, we have to consider the armed men who have deserted their units. They are paid large sums of money. There are Slavic troops on both sides, either as volunteers or mercenaries," he said.[14]

The Armenians also denied that their forces had participated in a massacre, although they did not deny the attack itself. "It is a great victory for Armenians," said a parliamentary spokesman in Yerevan.[15] Their original story was that when their forces arrived, Khojaly was virtually empty. They were able to seize the town facing no resistance. An Armenian police officer however, hinted strongly that the massacre was revenge for the

[11] Gore, Patrick. *'Tis Some Poor Fellow's Skull: Post-Soviet Warfare in the Southern Caucasus* (Lincoln, NE: iUniverse, 2008), 20.

[12] Kaufman, ibid., 73.

[13] Dahlburg, ibid.

[14] Croissant, ibid., 99.

[15] "Armenians Gain in New Battles with Azerbaijanis," *The New York Times*, 27 February 1992. Web. Retrieved 23 May 2019. *AcademicOneFile*. http://link.galegroup.com/apps/doc/A174790176/AONE?u=chap_main&sid=AONE&xid=05744d36.

anti-Armenian pogrom in Sumgait four years earlier. He noted that 25 February was the fourth anniversary of Sumgait, and that many of the Armenians in the Khojaly action were natives of Sumgait.[16]

There would be many examples of intentional killing of civilians on both sides during the conflict, none of which would reach the scale of Khojaly. Future Armenian president Sargsyan admitted the Khojaly massacre was an intentional attack on the civilian population to prove the willingness of Armenian forces to wage total war. "I think the main point is this," he told British journalist Tom de Waal. "Before Khojalu the Azerbaijanis thought that they were joking with us, they thought that the Armenians were people who could not raise their hand against the civilian population. We needed to put a stop to all that. And that's what happened. And we should also take into account that among those boys were people who had fled from Baku and Sumgait … If civilians stay there, even though they had a perfectly good chance to get out of there, it means they are also taking part in the fighting."[17]

By May 1992, the Armenians had completed their conquest of Nagorno-Karabakh. They captured Shusha, the historic capital of Nagorno-Karabakh and the cradle of Azerbaijani music and culture, because no real defense of the city was made. It was Azerbaijan's last outpost in the former oblast. Almost 40,000 Azerbaijani inhabitants were expelled. With the fall of Shusha the Armenian forces moved out of Nagorno-Karabakh proper. They began attacking Azerbaijani-majority districts that surrounded the highlands. They seized the town and district of Lachin later in May, again expelling the entire Azerbaijani population. This was a crucial victory for the Armenians, in that it established a land bridge between Nagorno-Karabakh and the Republic of Armenia, eliminating the need for resupplies from Armenia to cross six miles of Azerbaijani territory. There was now a physical link between the two Armenian-controlled entities.

In June 1992, the tide of battle turned in Azerbaijan's favor. Launching a lightening attack with Russian mercenaries driving Russian tanks, Baku seized back the northern half of Nagorno-Karabakh. In a panic, the Armenians turned to their ultimate defender, the Kremlin. The Russian army intervened directly in the fighting, flying military attack helicopters. And

[16] Quinn-Judge, ibid., 12.

[17] de Waal, ibid., 356, n.28.

so, in this battle, Russians were fighting on both the offensive and defensive sides. Later that summer when Russia provided the Armenians with an antiaircraft system, they manned the system with Russian operators.[18]

Russia also intervened to maintain a military balance between the Republics of Armenia and Azerbaijan. Under the terms of the 1992 Tashkent agreement governing the distribution of Soviet (non-nuclear) military equipment among the new republics, both Armenia and Azerbaijan were allocated equal amounts of weaponry: 220 battle tanks, 220 armed combat vehicles, 285 artillery pieces, 100 warplanes, and four armed attack helicopters each. In reality, if the weapon had been on a republic's territory before independence, it stayed there. Because there was more military equipment around Baku (a major port and oil producer) than in the farming communities of Armenia, it meant that Azerbaijan was inheriting about three times as much equipment as Armenia. An Armenian estimate of Armenian ammunition supplies was 500 railroad cars, while Azerbaijan would have 10,000 carloads.[19]

This alarmed Armenian president Levon Ter-Petrosyan. He contacted his friend in Moscow, Boris Yeltsin, and asked what could be done. Despite Moscow's professed commitment not to arm either side in the conflict, Yeltsin arranged an illegal billion-dollar (650 million pounds) military aid package.[20]

According to the chairman of the Russian Duma's defense committee, General Lev Rokhlin, between 1992 and 1996 Russian Defense Minister Pavel Grachev and his successor General Igor Rodionov violated a UN arms embargo by sending weapons to Armenia. The defense ministers shipped 84 T-72 battle tanks, 50 BMP armored troop carriers, 72 howitzers, 24 Scud missiles with eight launchers, and millions of rounds of ammunition to Yerevan. During the time of the war (1992–1994), Russian transport aircraft ferried 1300 tons of ammunition into

[18] Bolukbasi, ibid., 95.

[19] Bolukbasi, ibid., 193–194.

[20] Ter-Petrossian interview in de Waal, ibid., 212.

Armenia.[21] The transfers during this period came from a Russian military base in North Ossetia.[22]

Other evidence of Russian support to the Armenians came in September 1992 when Azerbaijani forces captured six Russian special forces (Spetznaz) soldiers. They were members of the Russian Seventh Army, assigned to Yerevan. At the time of their capture, they were listed as being on active duty and were only declared AWOL after they received death sentences (one received a prison sentence) for being mercenaries. As AWOL service members, the Russian state asked Azerbaijan for mercy and deportation for trial in Russia. Azerbaijani prosecutor Roshvan Aliev categorically denied they were mercenaries, however, and insisted they were working for the Russian state. "We have no evidence and no means of obtaining any specific Russian orders dispatching the men to go kill our people on the front," he told American journalist Thomas Goltz. "But as a citizen of what was once the Soviet Union, I can assure you that no Russian soldier could take the sort of extended absences from duty that these men took without some sort of collusion much higher up."

At their trial, the men stated they had been recruited from their units in the Seventh Army by Colonel Jena, previously an officer in the 366th Motorized Rifle Regiment whose tanks had assisted in the Khojaly massacre. Jena offered them cash bonuses, and a six-month reduction in their mandatory military service, if they joined his new unit to fight in Karabakh. The men would be listed on their original units' rosters, so they would not be considered deserters. On 13 June 1992, they were dispatched to the northern front to shore up the Armenian defensive line, at that time reeling under an Azerbaijani assault. They said they killed an estimated 40 Azerbaijani soldiers, and destroyed some armor before returning to their barracks in Yerevan in July 1992. They were capture on a reconnaissance mission on 3 September. Azerbaijan had asserted many times that the Russian military was supporting the Armenians in the war;

[21] "Inquiry into Covert Arms Supplies to Armenia," *The Irish Times*, 9 April 1997. Web. Retrieved 27 May 2019. https://www.irishtimes.com/news/inquiry-into-covert-arms-supplies-to-armenia-1.60400.

[22] Mirzoyan, A. *Armenia, the Regional Powers and the West: Between History and Geopolitics* (New York: Palgrave Macmillan, 2010), 33.

the capture of these Spetznaz troops was the first concrete proof of the assertion.[23]

In October 1992, Armenian president Ter-Petrosyan appointed Vazgen Manukian to be defense minister. In interviews with de Waal, Manukian admitted that the Republic of Armenia's army was active in the Karabakh fighting. "You can be sure that whatever we said politically, the Karabakh Armenian and Armenian army were united in military actions." He also stated he had ordered the Armenian military into action on several occasions without advising Ter-Petrosyan. One such operation was the March 1993 attack on Kelbajar. "I presented a small part of this operation" to the president, he said. "Receiving permission for this small part, we did more."[24] The Russian peace representative Vladimir Kazimirov also reported that by 1993 the regular army of the Armenian Republic was involved in the fighting.[25]

Hot War

Armenians launched a large-scale offensive in the Mardakert area in February 1993 and reversed most of the advances the Azerbaijanis had made in 1992. Eyewitnesses such as journalist Thomas Goltz reported artillery fire falling on Kelbajar city with a trajectory originating in Armenia.[26] Human Rights Watch representatives spoke with Republic of Armenia soldiers on active duty who were transporting weapons to Karabakh Armenians fighting in Kelbajar. UN Secretary General Boutros Ghali said that the level of heavy weaponry on the Armenian side also pointed toward Armenian army involvement.[27]

[23] Goltz, Thomas. "Letter from Eurasia: The Hidden Hand," *Foreign Policy* 92 (Fall 1993). Web. Retrieved 28 May 2019. https://eds-b-ebscohost-com.libproxy.chapman.edu/ehost/detail/detail?vid=3&sid=825876a9-13c4-4a22-bab0-fbde9d80dda6%40sessionmgr120&bdata=JkF1dGhUeXBlPWlwLHVpZCxjb29raWUsdXJsJnNpdGU9ZWhvc3QtbGl2ZQ%3d%3d#AN=9309090235&db=aph.

[24] de Waal, ibid., 222, 224.

[25] Kazimirov, Vladimir. "Peace to Karabakh," 25 March 2005. Web. Retrieved 3 June 2019. http://www.vn.kazimirov.ru/x015eng.htm.

[26] Human Rights Watch, ibid., 12, 23, 115.

[27] Human Rights Watch, ibid., 115.

Baku launched a helicopter airlift of civilians, although some soldiers made their way onto the flights.[28] In the space of a week, 60,000 Azerbaijanis and Kurds living in Kelbajar district were forced to flee.[29] At first, the Armenians allowed the majority of the civilian population to flee, but all the escape routes were closed except over the Murov Mountains. Soon, the Armenians began firing on these refugees. On 31 March, men from Galaboynu village were fired upon as they tried to make their escape. In a separate incident, on 1 April Armenians attacked with automatic rifles and rocket-propelled grenades a truck carrying approximately 25 civilians.[30]

By 3 April, Armenians controlled the entire city. They captured 80 civilians to be held as hostages for exchange for Armenians in Azerbaijani captivity, and 150 soldiers.[31] Senior Armenian diplomat Jirair Libaridian admitted that, despite his government's official denials, the Republic of Armenia was providing Karabakh with military equipment, including surface-to-air missiles.[32] Throughout the entire front there were credible reports—including from the International Committee of the Red Cross—of fighting by regular army units of the Republic of Armenia.[33]

After Lachin, this was another major Armenian victory as the invasion of Kelbajar allowed Armenia to control the entire strip of land separating it from Nagorno-Karabakh. Armenians also seized the Sarsang water reservoir and hydroelectric station, an important power source. Finally, in seizing Kelbajar's eastern flank it cut off the main highway between Kelbajar and the rest of Azerbaijan.[34]

Three days later, Armenians launched another offensive, against Fuzuli, Qubadli, and Zangilan. Armenia's forces racked up victory after victory. As they invaded, they looted and burned the villages. Human Rights

[28] Human Rights Watch, ibid., 23.

[29] Human Rights Watch, ibid., 13.

[30] Human Rights Watch, ibid., 19–20.

[31] Human Rights Watch, ibid., 25.

[32] Bonner, Raymond. "War in Caucasus Shows Ethnic Hate's Front Line," *The New York Times*, 2 August 1993. Web. Retrieved 23 May 2019. http://link.galegroup.com/apps/doc/A174660379/AONE?u=chap_main&sid=AONE&xid=c37cbcf5.

[33] Human Rights Watch, ibid., 56.

[34] Human Rights Watch, ibid., 9.

Watch reported that some of the looting, such as in Aghdam, was organized and planned by the Armenian authorities in Nagorno-Karabakh.[35] It took the Armenians a month to capture Aghdam. By October 1993, 600,000 Azerbaijanis were expelled from conquered Azerbaijani territory as Armenia consolidated its hold on southwest Azerbaijan.[36] Armenians controlled forty kilometers of the Iranian-Azerbaijani border, according to Robert Kocharyan. The Russian Foreign Ministry blamed Karabakh Armenians for yet another cease-fire violation, and called on them to withdraw their troops,[37] to no avail.

Azerbaijani president Heydar Aliyev, who was elected in October 1993, said, "It must be noted that our defeats are due, on the one hand, to weakness and the Azerbaijani Army units' lack of fighting and skill…It would have been possible to create an army over two or three years (from the beginning of the conflict in 1988) and defend Azerbaijan. But this opportunity was lost, and Azerbaijan's defense has suffered rather than improved. Various groups and battalions fought independently of each other. They served various forces and goals and lacked an overall military strategy."[38]

One such individual with an individual agenda was the Azerbaijani military commander for Nagorno-Karabakh, Colonel Surat Huseynov. He had announced he would personally lead his troops into battle and supposedly headed to Aghdam. Huseynov did little to supply the city, however. Human Rights Watch reported incorrectly Huseynov was a closet supporter of former President Mutalibov and Aghdam had not supported the former president.[39] In reality, Huseynov had Russian sympathies; when he fell from power, he fled to Russia.

Baku needed some breathing room, and they got it. Alarmed by the Armenian battlefield successes, Turkey decided to provide some passive assistance. At first, in May 1992, they only threatened Armenia with military intervention. Turkey announced that it was obligated to

[35] Human Rights Watch, ibid., 48.

[36] Croissant, ibid., 95.

[37] "Daily Report," Radio Free Europe/Radio Liberty, 26 October 1993. Web. Retrieved 6 June 2019. http://www.friends-partners.org/friends/news/omri/1993/10/931026.html(opt,mozilla,unix,english,,new).

[38] Human Rights Watch, ibid., 82.

[39] Human Rights Watch, ibid., 46.

protect Nakhichevan (an Azerbaijani exclave being threatened by Armenian advances) by the Treaty of Kars (1920). Article V of the treaty states that the governments of Armenia, Azerbaijan, and Turkey agreed to create Nakhichevan to be administered by Azerbaijan.[40] Turkey took the position they were obligated by the treaty to keep Nakhichevan an Azerbaijani territory. Turkish member of Parliament Abdullatif Sener stated "The Moscow and Kars treaties make Turkey a guarantor state. Turkey should fulfill the requirements mentioned in those treaties. Volunteers who want to go there should be granted permission. Nakhichevan should be provided arms to defend itself." General Dogan Gures, chief of the Turkish General Staff, said the Turkish military was ready to carry out any mission it was assigned by the competent political authorities.[41]

Faced with the threat from Turkey, Russian Foreign Minister Andrey Kozyrev promised to protect Armenia from any Turkish threat.[42] The Turks did not engage in any fighting, but in May 1993 they amassed troops on their border with Armenia because of continued Armenian attacks on Nakhichevan. Turkey may have been dissuaded from taking further steps for fear that the neutral United States administration could tilt toward Armenia.[43] Another possible reason for their reticence to enter the battlefield was the fear of facing Russian military forces. According to the Tashkent Treaty that created the Commonwealth of Independent States, Russia committed itself to use nuclear weapons to protect any member state that is attacked. Armenia fell under the Russian nuclear umbrella. It appears that Russian military planners may have drawn up contingency plans for a nuclear attack on a US radar base near Kars using a 100-kiloton warhead.[44]

[40] Tase, Peter. "The Fate of Nakhchivan: Repeated Violations of the Moscow and Kars Treaties—Op Ed," *Eurasia Review* 23 March 2015. Web. Retrieved 30 May 2019. https://www.eurasiareview.com/23102015-the-fate-of-nakhchivan-repeated-violations-of-moscow-and-kars-treaties-oped/.

[41] Pry, Peter Vincent and D. McFerran, *War Scare: Russia and America on the Nuclear Brink* (Westport: Greenwood, 1999), 121.

[42] Pry and McFerran, ibid.

[43] Gelb, Leslie H. "Foreign Affairs: War in Nakhichevan," *New York Times*, 22 May 2019. Web. Retrieved 30 May 2019. http://link.galegroup.com/apps/doc/A174851655/AONE?u=chap_main&sid=AONE&xid=4885d258.

[44] Pry and McFerran, ibid., 126–127.

Russian defense minister Pavel Grachev declared that troops on the border of a neighboring state were a direct military threat to the Russian Federation. At Armenia's request, Moscow sent its Seventh Army to the Turkish-Armenian border. This supposedly Russian unit was controlled by an officer cadre that was 20–30% Armenian, and most of the troops were also Armenian.[45] More Turkish troops deployed when Iran began to deploy troops in September to halt refugee flows.

The Turkish troop movements meant that Armenia had to protect its rear. Turkey thus tied up some of the forces that would have been fighting Azerbaijan. This allowed the Azerbaijanis to regroup. Under the leadership of a new president, Heydar Aliyev, Azerbaijan launched a counter-offensive in December 1993. In the Republic of Armenia, there were calls for volunteers, and the maximum age of conscription in Karabakh was increased from forty-three to fifty. Regular Armenian army forces were deployed in the fighting, and President Ter-Petrosyan threatened additional Armenian intervention if Karabakh Armenians faced defeat (he used the terms "forced deportation" and "genocide",[46] calling up memories of 1915). The Armenian parliamentarian Ashot Bleyan accused Armenia of direct involvement, saying that the administration was conducting an "undeclared war" in which over 1000 Armenian youths had been killed in the previous several months.[47] Armenian military truck drivers who were captured by Azerbaijan in January 1994 said they were told by their commanders they would be picking up refugees from an Armenian town on border. Instead, they picked up a company of Armenian army soldiers (approximately 150 men) with assault rifles, light machine guns, rocket-propelled grenades, and grenade launchers to transport to the front. Another prisoner told how he was a conscript ordered to serve on the front line. A Western diplomat involved with the Minsk group said ethnic Armenians from either the Republic of Armenia or from the Russian army based in Armenia were servicing hi-tech surface-to-air anti-aircraft missiles in Nagorno-Karabakh. Human Rights Watch spent two days in Yerevan in April 1994, interviewing soldiers on the street. Perhaps 30% were draftees in the army of the Armenian Republic who had either fought in Karabakh, had orders to go to Karabakh, or had

[45] de Waal, ibid., 215.

[46] Human Rights Watch, ibid., 84.

[47] Human Rights Watch, ibid., 117.

been "volunteered" by their officers for service in Karabakh. The NGO's representatives counted five buses full of Armenian Army soldiers entering Nagorno-Karabakh on a single day, Sunday, 17 April 1994. One bus had a flat tire, and the NGO took advantage of the opportunity to speak with the officer. At first, he denied they were headed to Karabakh, but then admitted it. "Karabakh is Armenian land," he said, "and had to be defended."[48]

Russia was also supporting heavily the Armenian side. According to a political analyst with the Armenian Assembly of America, at the height of the December 1993 Azerbaijan offensive, Russian Ministry of Defense officials called Karabakh authorities regularly to inquire about weapons needs. They sent large weapons shipments via Armenia and then through the Lachin corridor to Karabakh. At peak periods, roughly forty Russian transport planes per day were landing at Yerevan's airport.[49]

After a failed mid-April Armenian offensive, a stalemate ensued that brought both sides to the table. A cease-fire was signed on 12 May 1994. The Republic of Armenia also signed the cease-fire, despite its position that it was not a party to the conflict. The war that had begun with clubs had ended with tanks. According to Human Rights Watch, since at least late 1993 troops of the Republic of Armenia participated in the fighting, both in Karabakh and in Azerbaijan itself.[50] According to Vahan Hovanessian, deputy speaker of the Armenian parliament, the death toll was 30,000. "I am proud that in the Karabakh war we killed 25,000 Azeris," he told the Russian newspaper New Times. "Only 5,000 Armenians were killed. I am proud that my friends and I took part in that war. And my son is also proud of this. And if they again start the war, they should know that the score will be the same again. And I am not proud of this secretly at night, I am openly proud of this. I think there is nothing shameful in it."[51] Even in expressing his pride, Hovanessian

[48] Human Rights Watch, ibid., 119–125.

[49] Human Rights Watch, ibid., 152.

[50] Human Rights Watch, ibid., xiii.

[51] Manucharova, Naira. "It Is Strange but We Should Fight for Democracy in Azerbaijan," Novoye Vremya (Yerevan) in Russian, 16 March 2004. English language translation found in Azerbaijan Society of America, "Is Armenia Seeking Peace?" 28 March 2014. Web. Retrieved 30 May 2019. https://groups.yahoo.com/neo/groups/RMSMC/conversations/messages/3433?guccounter=1.

became another individual who contradicted Armenia's claim that it was not a belligerent in the war.

Even as the war ended, evidence continued to amass of the Republic of Armenia's direct involvement. In an August 1994 meeting with Human Rights Watch, Armenian Foreign Minister Vahan Papazyan stated Armenia held between 18 and 22 prisoners. Shortly thereafter, eight prisoners of war were killed under suspicious circumstances during an alleged escape attempt. A Scottish forensics expert performed autopsies on the corpses and concluded that the nature of the wounds on six of them indicated summary execution.[52]

Post War Military Actions

Despite the ceasefire, Azerbaijan and Armenia continued to have low-level skirmishes along the border. There were exchanges of artillery and small arms fire across the line of contact daily. The large-scale war of 1994 degenerated into a sniper war.

At the same time, Russia and Armenia formalized the military alliance they had created on an ad hoc basis throughout the war. On 16 March 1995, Presidents Yeltsin and Ter-Petrosyan signed a bilateral defense treaty that allowed the former Soviet Red Army 261st Rifle Division to remain on Armenian soil. The 5000-man unit was renamed the 102nd Military Base of the Russian Forces in Transcaucasia located in Gyumri, about 75 miles north of Yerevan. Russia had three bases in Armenia: the 102nd base in Gyumri facing Turkey, the 426th base in Erebuni whose inhabitants participated in the second Chechen war, and one in Meghri with 5000 soldiers of which 2000 were border guards.[53]

The treaty was ratified by the Russian and Armenian parliaments in 1997. Although there is no mention of Nagorno-Karabakh or Azerbaijan in the treaty, over the years many considered the treaty to be Russia's guarantee of Armenian and Karabakhi independence. Russia, however, had a different interpretation. Foreign Minister Yevgeny Primakov specifically repudiated any idea that the treaty involved Russia in the dispute

[52] Human Rights Watch, ibid., 97.

[53] Minassian, Gaidz, "Armenia, a Russian Outpost in the Caucasus?" IFRI Russie.Nei.Visions 27, IFRI Russia/NIS Center, February 2008, 11. Web. Retrieved 23 July 2019. https://www.ifri.org/sites/default/files/atoms/files/ifri_RNV_minassian_Armenie_Russie_ANG_fevr2008.pdf.

with Baku. "I am authorized by Russian President Boris Yeltsin to state that the Treaty of the Russian Federation with Armenia is in no way targeted against Azerbaijan and will never be used in favor of those who are speaking against its territorial integrity," he said.[54]

Under the terms of the accord, which would last for 25 years but could be extended in the following five years if mutually agreed upon, Armenia would pay 30% of the cost of the base's utilities and electricity. All other expenses would be covered by Russia. An attack upon Armenia would be considered an attack upon Russia. The Armenian and Russian presidents pledged not to participate in any action or initiative which is against the sovereignty or territorial integrity of one of the signatory countries. They also agreed to coordinate military-technical policy, and to coordinate defense industries, to standardize military hardware and finance joint military projects. Besides defending the interests of the Russian Federation, the Russian military pledged to ensure security for Armenia along the entire perimeter of the Armenia-Turkey and Armenia-Iran borders.

There was real doubt that the treaty guaranteed Russian support. Former Armenian National Security Advisor Gerard Libaridian noted, "The 1995 treaty has a provision… that if there are military hostilities within Armenia's borders Russia won't automatically come to [Armenia's] aid. That is, if one party [to the treaty] is subjected to attack, there will be consultations with the other. It's the other side that will decide whether or not to participate [in the war.]" This ambiguity in interpretation allowed Russia to not intervene militarily in 2020.

The 2010 extension of the treaty was supposed to resolve the issue. The deal extended the lease on Gyumri from 2020 to 2044. It also called for Russia to provide modern weapons and equipment to Armenia's military. The defense pact expanded the Russian mission to ensuring the security of the Republic of Armenia. A spokesman for President Serzh Sargsyan's ruling Republican Party, Eduard Sharmazanov, said the new pact would not only protect Armenia's borders, but would exclude the possibility that neighboring Azerbaijan would try to settle the ongoing Nagorno-Karabakh conflict by force.

Others were not so sure. Analysts note the extended treaty only referred to defending Armenia, while Nagorno-Karabakh was legally part

[54] Walker, Edward. *No Peace, No War in the Caucasus: Secessionist Conflicts in Chechnya, Abkkazia and Nagorno-Karabakh* (Belfer Center for Science and International Affairs) (February 1988), 24.

of Azerbaijan. Any fresh fighting involving Armenian troops would likely be on the territory of Nagorno-Karabakh, not of Armenia.[55] Russian officials were careful not to specify what their reaction would be in another Armenia-Azerbaijan conflict. As the 2010 extension was being negotiated, there were reports that Russia's then-President Dmitry Medvedev received a government "protocol" stating that the troops would "protect Armenia's security together with Armenian Army units."[56] Such wording raised an interesting proposition: Armenia has consistently claimed that there are no Armenian Army units in Karabakh, meaning the Russians are not obligated to intervene in the region. Should Armenia acknowledge that it is an occupying power with troops on internationally recognized Azerbaijan territory and in violation of international law, however, the protocol would require that Russia defend the army units.

One of the more unusual incidents in the life of the conflict unfolded in September 2012. Ramil Safarov is an Azerbaijani serviceman serving a life sentence for the brutal murder of an Armenian serviceman. The two had been at a NATO Partnership for Peace event, and Safarov believed his honor had been impugned by the Armenian. Azerbaijan negotiated Safarov's return to Baku, with a promise he would complete his sentence there. Even though he had only served eight years of his sentence, President Aliyev commuted his sentence. The entire episode was the kind of ethnic paroxysm that is not understandable in the West. It was no more understandable than Armenia's decision to declare Gargarin Nzhdeh a hero of its own Republic. Nzhdeh was a Nazi collaborator who, earlier in his career, oversaw paramilitary forces who killed over 10,000 ethnic Azerbaijanis.

There were exchanges of gunfire between 30 July and 14 August 2014. 14 Azerbaijani soldiers were killed. Then, tens of thousands of Armenian and Karabakh military forces held maneuvers named Unity-2014 near

[55] O'Rourke, Breffni. "Russia, Armenia Sign Extended Defense Pact," Radio Free Europe/Radio Liberty, 19 August 2010. Web. Retrieved 7 July 2019. https://www.rferl.org/a/Russian_President_Medvedev_To_Visit_Armenia/2131915.html.

[56] "Close Military Ties with Armenia to Boost Russia's Regional Clout," Radio Free Europe/Radio Liberty, 12 August 2010. Web. Retrieved 7 July 2019. https://www.rferl.org/a/Closer_Military_Ties_With_Armenia_To_Boost_Russias_Regional_Clout/2126126.html.

the line of contact for seven days.[57] In November 2014, the Azerbaijani army shot down an MI-24 helicopter flying over Aghdam, killing three crew members. Azerbaijan said the helicopter was attacking their military positions; the Karabakh Armenian army claimed their helicopter was on a training mission.[58] According to Karabakh's "defense minister" Movses Hakobian, the Azerbaijanis used a Strela air-defense system supplied by Moscow to down the helicopter.[59] Bloomsberg labeled it the worst military incident in 20 years.[60] The wreckage fell into the buffer zone between the two sides, and the three corpses laid unclaimed for several days. To demonstrate his support of the Armenian troops, President Sargsyan flew to Stepanakert the day after the downing for an inspection tour.[61]

In January 2015, bloody fighting broke out again between the two sides. Over the weekend of 23 January, fighting killed two Armenians and three Azerbaijanis as they fought with grenades and mortar attacks.[62] In September, in the Tavush province of Armenia and at the Line of Contact, six civilians and two servicemen were wounded, and another four servicemen were killed in artillery duels. Military preparations on both sides showed that the status quo could not last forever. Armenia

[57] Harutunyan, Sargis. "Armenian Helicopter Shot Down Near Karabakh," Azatutyun, 14 November 2014. Web. Retrieved 20 June 2019. https://www.azatutyun.am/a/26687991.html.

[58] "Armenian Military Helicopter Shot Down by Azerbaijani Forces, Killing Three," *The Guardian*, 12 November 2014. Web. Retrieved 20 June 2019. https://www.theguardian.com/world/2014/nov/12/azerbaijani-forces-shoot-down-armenian-military-helicopter.

[59] Grigoryan, Marianna. "Armenia: Feeling Betrayed by Russia?" *Eurasia Review*, 24 November 2014. Web. Retrieved 28 July 2019. https://eurasianet.org/armenia-feeling-betrayed-by-russia.

[60] Agayev, Zulfikar. "Aliyev Hails Armenian Helicopter Downing, Vows More Action," Bloomsberg.com, 16 November 2014. Web. Retrieved 30 May 2019. https://www.bloomberg.com/news/articles/2014-11-16/aliyev-hails-armenian-chopper-downing-vows-more-military-action

[61] "Sarkisian Arrives in Karabakh landing at Stepanakert Airport," Asbarez, 13 November 2014. Web. Retrieved 20 June 2019. http://asbarez.com/128840/sarkisan-arrives-in-karabakh-landing-at-stepanakert-airport/.

[62] Herszenhorn, David M. "Clashes Intensify Between Armenia and Azerbaijan Over Disputed Land," *New York Times*, 1 February 2015. Web. Retrieved 23 May 2019. , http://link.galegroup.com/apps/doc/A399621804/AONE?u=chap_main&sid=AONE&xid=dbe4e18e.

announced military exercises, Shant-2015.[63] Azerbaijan announced it also was exercising its military, involving 65 thousand men, some 700 armored vehicles, more than 500 rockets and artillery units, 40 planes and 50 helicopters of the Air Force, 20 ships and boats of the Navy, as well as air defense units armed with modern antiaircraft systems. Unmanned aerial vehicles were also used. To test the level of preparedness of the mobilization of resources, more than 6 thousand reservists were scheduled to participate.[64]

Azerbaijan shot down an unmanned drone near Aghdam on 29 January, as new weapons were introduced to the zone of conflict.[65] Another Azerbaijani exercise featured 20,000 soldiers, 300 armored vehicles, 200 missile launchers and artillery units, and up to 20 military jets.[66]

Armenia launched large-scale military exercises in September 2015 and Azerbaijan did the same in response. Two large, hostile armies were engaged in these maneuvers in a limited space. Dozens of soldiers and civilians were killed or wounded on both sides of the line of contact, many from exchanges of artillery fire.[67]

Fighting broke out on 2 April 2016, as Presidents Aliyev and Sargsyan were returning home from the Nuclear Security Summit in Washington, DC. Who initiated the attacks is uncertain. Armenia claimed that at 2 am Azerbaijan launched a surprise attack with an artillery barrage, followed by tanks and aircraft. Azerbaijan said their troops responded to

[63] "Shant-2015: Large-Scale Drills Simulate Armenia's Response to Different Military Situations," Armenianow.com, 8 September 2015. Web. Retrieved 1 June 2019. https://www.armenianow.com/news/66070/armenia_shant_2015_military_exercises.

[64] "Azerbaijani Army Conducts Large Scale Military Exercises," Contact.az, 6 September 2015. Web. Retrieved 1 June 2019. http://www.contact.az/.

[65] Herszenhorn, David M. "Clashes Intensify Between Armenia and Azerbaijan Over Disputed Land," *The New York Times*, 1 February 2015. Web. Retrieved 23 May 2019. http://link.galegroup.com/apps/doc/A399621804/AONE?u=chap_main&sid=AONE&xid=dbe4e18e.

[66] "Azerbaijan Launches Military Exercises Amid Tensions with Armenia," Radio Free Europe/Radio Liberty, 2 February 2015. Web. Retrieved 31 July 2019. https://www.rferl.org/a/azerbaijan-launches-military-maneures-amid-tensions-witjh-armenia/26826334.html.

[67] Keshishyan, Manvel. "An Unending Cycle of Violence," Near Eastern Europe, 10 November 2015. Web. Retrieved 20 June 2019. http://neweasterneurope.eu/old_site/articles-and-commentary/1788-an-unending-cycle-of-violence.

intensive fire from the Armenians.[68] Backed by heavy tanks and heavy artillery, Azerbaijan seized strategic heights in both the north and south of the disputed region. When Armenians fired, Azerbaijan replied with the Russian-made TOS-1 heavy flamethrower system. Azerbaijan's Defense Ministry spokesman Vagif Dargahly warned, "in the event of continued Armenian provocations, we will launch a full-scale operation along the entire line, using all kinds of weapons."[69] At least 64 people were killed in the four days of fighting, and Azerbaijan lost at least one helicopter.

The Armenian front line forces had been defeated leaving little between the Azerbaijani armored columns and Stepanakert. Azerbaijan did not seek to exploit the opening further, probably for fear of triggering a Russian response. As soon as the fighting began, President Putin called for an immediate cease-fire. When the Azerbaijan Defense Ministry indicated they might move beyond defensive positions and move further into Nagorno-Karabakh, analysts such as Cliff Kupchan at the Eurasia Group were convinced Russia would halt an offensive. "There's real doubt whether Putin will let it stand," he said. "If we see this (fighting) last a few days, then we have a new Nagorno-Karabakh war."[70] In Armenia, hundreds of veterans of the 1992–1994 war rushed to the front lines, where Armenia tried to launch a counterattack.[71]

The victory helped restore the morale of the Azerbaijan army, and shocked Armenia who considered their army to be the descendent of Soviet generals while Azerbaijan's came from cooks and dishwashers. Azerbaijan called a unilateral cease-fire after the first day's fighting, but the fighting did not stop until 6 April. For Azerbaijan, the fighting had achieved its objectives: strategic territory on the ground, and a change in attitude on both sides of the line of contact.

[68] Kramer, Andrew. "Ethnic Tinderbox Flares in Nagorno Karabakh," *The New York Times*, 3 April 2016. Web. Retrieved 23 May 2019. http://link.galegroup.com/apps/doc/A448223308/AONE?u=chap_main&sid=AONE&xid=102569a2.

[69] "Armenia Warns of Full-Scale War Amid Fresh Casualties in Karabakh Fighting," Radio Free Europe/Radio Liberty, 04 April 2016. Web. Retrieved 30 May 2019. https://www.rferl.org/a/nagorno-karabakh-fighting-fresh-casualties-aremenia-azerbaijan/27653202.html.

[70] Kramer, Andrew E. "Ethnic Tinderbox Flares in Nagorno-Karabakh," *The New York Times*, 3 April 2016, 10.

[71] "Baku Announces Cease-Fire Amid Continued Karabakh Fighting," Radio Free Europe/Radio Liberty, 3 April 2016. Web. Retrieved 30 May 2019. https://www.rferl.org/a/azerbaijan-armenia-nagorno-karabakh-violence-erupts/27651414.html.

In Armenia, the results of the fighting caused wide consternation. By the end of the month, President Sargsyan fired three senior military officials: Deputy Defense Minister Alik Mirzabekian, military intelligence chief General Arshak Karapetian, and General Komitas Muradian, the commander of the Armenian army's communication units. The chairman of the parliamentary committee on defense and security confirmed that they had been relieved of duty because of "shortcomings" in the Armenian military's performance. President Sargsyan admitted military intelligence had not prepared the army for the battle. "Had we had [such intelligence] the Azerbaijanis would have suffered much greater losses and failed to seize those several meters [of land]," said the president.[72]

The conflict resolved the question of whether Russian security guarantees to Armenia extended to Karabakh: they did not. With the Russian army overextended on the borders of Ukraine and fighting in Syria, its security guarantees were subject to the Kremlin's interpretation—not Yerevan's. Despite Armenians believing the Russian military would defend Armenians in Karabakh, Moscow provided no military support to the separatists. Instead, they put Foreign Minister Lavrov in front of a microphone to announce there was no military solution to the conflict. "It is inadvisable to change the format of the OSCE Minsk Group," he said.[73]

Russia's utilitarian view of its relationship with Armenia was on full display when ultra-nationalist Vladimir Zhirinovsky discussed the country. "I could spit on Armenia and never look back," he said. "If Armenians try to find another ally we will cut ties with them. If Armenians get in the way, Russia will let Turkey and Azerbaijan run over Armenia.[74]

While Russia had not supported Armenia in the 2016 military exchange, it did lay down some red lines that Azerbaijan could not cross. Moscow signaled to Baku that military action concerning Karabakh could not expand into Armenia, and Russia would oppose Baku obtaining military superiority over Armenia. What this meant was that while Azerbaijan could destroy Armenian weaponry once it was in Karabakh, it could take

[72] "Senior Armenian Military Officials Sacked," Azutuyun, 26 March 2016. Web. Accessed 1 June 2019. https://www.azatutyun.am/a/27699843.html.

[73] "Lavrov: No Military Solution to the Nagorno-Karabakh Conflict," News.Az, 4 April 2016. Web. Retrieved 7 July 2019. http://news.az/articles/karabakh/106259.

[74] "Armenia and Azerbaijan Are Stuck with Russia and the U.S," *International Policy Digest*, 13 September 2017. Web. Retrieved 23 July 2019. https://intpolicydigest.org/2017/09/13/armenia-and-azerbaijan-are-stuck-with-russia-and-the-u-s/.

no action to prevent the weaponry from entering the enclave in the first place. Further, even if Armenia shelled villages in Nakhichevan and western Azerbaijan, Baku could not retaliate. As for further military action against Karabakh itself, Russian Foreign Minister Lavrov ambiguously warned that an Azerbaijani counterterrorist operation in the occupied territories would not be merely an issue of Azerbaijan exercising its rights over internal affairs. The statement sparked outrage in Azerbaijan,[75] because the implication was that any efforts to regain control of Karabakh militarily would be considered an international incident.

In November 2016 Russian President Vladimir Putin approved a proposal to form a permanent joint Russian-Armenian force in the Caucasus. In the case of an attack against one of the parties, troops from the two countries would jointly counter the threat. In peacetime, the Caucasus forces would be commanded by the Armenian General Staff. "From now on, the General Staff of Armenia has the ultimate authority to plan joint activities in the region: exercises, command and staff trainings, and so on," Pavel Zolotarev, military analyst and deputy director of the Institute for US and Canadian Studies at the Russian Academy of Sciences, said. The agreement contained an important element in Armenia's efforts to modernize its army. "In addition to the development of joint plans for training and combat use of troops, Armenia will be able to buy Russian weapons at domestic prices, rather than as a foreign customer," said Dmitry Safonov, military columnist for the Russian daily newspaper Izvestiya.

During hostilities, the leadership would be transferred to Russia's Southern Military District, stationed in Rostov-on-Don (670 miles south of Moscow). The proposal was for a five-year agreement with an automatic extension option if neither of the parties wishes to terminate the cooperation. As for Nagorno-Karabakh, "Russia abstracts itself from this conflict," said Zolotarev. "Under the new agreement, our troops cannot be used in the fighting in this area. Nagorno-Karabakh will be defended only by the Armenian armed forces."[76]

[75] Valiyev, Anar. "The Kremlin's Security Strategy in the South Caucasus: Implications for Baku," CACI, 7 March 2017. Web. Retrieved 29 July 2019. https://www.cacianalyst.org/publications/analytical-articles/item/13431-the-kremlin-security-strategy-in-the-south-caucasus-implications-for-baku.html.

[76] Litovkin, Nikolai. "Russia and Armenia to Create a Joint Defense Force in the Caucasus," Russia Beyond, 16 November 2016. Web. Retrieved 7 July

Azerbaijan increased the pressure on Armenia in May 2018 by moving troops in Nakhichevan closer to the international border with Armenia. There was no fighting involved in the troop movements. Azerbaijani troops stayed on their side of the border. With the new positions they could control the Yerevan-Goris-Gafan-Lachin highway in the event of hostilities.[77]

With the coming of power of the Pashinyan government in Armenia in April 2018, tensions arose in the Armenian-Russian military alliance. In July 2018, Russian military forces conducted snap drills near the Armenian village of Panik, precipitating protests by residents and drawing a reprimand from Nikol Pashinyan who chided Moscow for not giving locals advance notice of the exercises. Small demonstrations against Russia's military activities became increasingly frequent, particularly after a Russian soldier was accused of killing an Armenian woman in Gyumri.

The United States tried to capitalize on the strain in Armenian-Russia relations. During a visit to Yerevan in October 2018, US national security adviser John Bolton said the United States would consider the possibility of selling weapons to Armenia. He said such a sale "… increases Armenia's options when it's not entirely dependent on one major power." Russia promptly condemned the statement and called on the United States to refrain from interference in its affairs. Pashinyan, meanwhile, told Bolton that Yerevan was open to discussing an arms deal.[78]

Russian President Vladimir Putin instructed the government to sign an agreement with Armenia on the creation of a joint regional missile defense system in the Caucasus, according to the decree published 11 November 2015. "Accept the proposal by the government of the Russian Federation on signing an agreement between the Russian Federation and the Republic of Armenia on creating a Joint Regional System of Anti-Air Defense in the Caucasus region of collective security," Putin instructed

2019. https://www.rbth.com/defence/2016/11/16/russia-and-armenia-to-create-joint-defense-force-in-caucasus_648317.

[77] Kucera, Joshua. "Azerbaijani Military Advances on Tense Nakhichevan-Armenia border," Eurasianet, 30 May 2018. Web. Retrieved 31 July 2019. https://eurasianet.org/azerbaijani-military-advances-on-tense-nakhchivan-armenia-border.

[78] "What the Chill in Russian-Armenian Relations Means," STRATFOR, 21 January 2019. Web. Retrieved 7 July 2019. https://worldview.stratfor.com/article/what-chill-russian-armenian-relations-means.

the Russian Defense Ministry.[79] This agreement, ratified by the Armenian parliament after the April 2016 fighting in Karabakh, integrated the Russian Air Force's full range of capabilities, including multifunction fighter jets, into joint regional air defense. "It will allow us to have serious reconnaissance data, which will be in the common informational field and will prevent all violations by adversaries," said Armenian Defense Minister Seyran Ohanyan. The Russians carefully excluded Nagorno-Karabakh from the agreement.[80] This meant that if Armenia were attacked by NATO member Turkey (not a likely scenario but one the Armenians feared the most), or if Azerbaijan attacked Armenia proper, the Russian air defense system would be implemented.

Azerbaijan continued its military exercises. As an example, during March 2019, it held a four-day exercise that included 10,000 military personnel, up to 500 tanks and other armored vehicles, up to 300 missiles and artillery systems of different caliber, multiple launch rocket systems, mortars, and up to 20 army and frontline aviation for various purposes.[81] They had two additional late-spring exercises: around Baku (1–3 May) and in the exclave of Nakhichevan (7–11 June). Both exercises were joint exercises with Turkey to increase coordination and interoperability between the two forces, building on seven joint exercises the two countries held in 2018. The Ministry of Defense envisioned an additional 13 joint exercises for 2019.

Armenia held joint exercises with Russia's 102nd Military Base in April. In June, according to the Nagorno-Karabakh "ministry of defense," there was another exercise in which about 10 thousand troops, more than 200 artillery systems, about 150 armored vehicles, more than 50 air defense systems, more than 400 vehicles and other units of mobile units were scheduled to participate.[82]

[79] "Armenia Relations with Russia," GlobalSecurity.org, undated. Web. Retrieved 7 July 2019.https://www.globalsecurity.org/military/world/armenia/foreign-relations-ru.htm.

[80] "Armenia Ratifies Agreement on Joint Air Defense System with Russia," Reuters, 30 June 2016. Web. Retrieved 8 July 2019. https://www.reuters.com/article/us-armenia-russia-defence/armenia-ratifies-agreement-on-joint-air-defense-system-with-russia-idUSKCN0ZG2AS.

[81] "Azerbaijani Army to Conduct Large Scale Exercises," Azernews, Trend. 8 March 2019. Web. Retrieved 1 June 2019. https://www.azernews.az/nation/146965.html.

[82] "Large-scale Military Exercises Started in Artsakh (Video)," News Armenia, 17 June 2019. Web. Retrieved 16 July 2019. http://newsarmenia.am/news/nagorno_karabakh/krupnomasshtabnye-voennye-ucheniya-startovali-v-artsakhe-video/.

Following the June exercises, the Defense Minister of Georgia joined the ministers from Azerbaijan and Turkey to discuss the regional military-political situation. Georgian Minister Levan Isoria said Georgia might join the two Turkic countries in future joint exercises. An Azerbaijani opinion piece speculated that the agreements signed in Gabala by the defense ministers denoted a significant rapprochement between the three countries in the military sphere. They noted that trilateral military exercises had occurred previously, but they were special exercises for protecting pipelines and railways. These talks were held, however, after a series of Azerbaijan-Turkish tactical exercises, and the implication was that it was these exercises that Georgia would be joining.[83]

Outside of the cycle of exercises, low-level hostilities resumed along the line of contact. On the eve of foreign ministers' meeting with the Minsk co-chairs in June 2019, Armenian snipers shot two Azerbaijani service members. To emphasize the point that this was an intentional act, the Armenian Ministry of Defense awarded medals to the snipers. Armenia said the killings were in retribution for an Azerbaijani shooting of an Armenian soldier. Military commentator Leonid Nersisyan stated, "In case of any Azerbaijani provocation or murder of an Armenian soldier, some answer will be given, moreover publicly." The timing of the shootings raised the question, however, if this was not a ploy to increase tensions and make diplomacy more difficult to achieve.

While it was unclear as to whether these retribution shootings were a new tactic, they corresponded to Armenia's emerging defense policy. Armenian Defense Minister David Tonoyan and other defense officials said there would be strategic changes in the country's defense policy, that the Armenian Armed Forces were moving from a passive to an active defense. Tonoyan said Yerevan had deployed special forces units along

[83] Nurani. "What Threatens Armenia with Georgia's Accession to the Alliance of Azerbaijan and Turkey?" Minival.az, 13 June 2019. Web. Retrieved 16 July 2019. https://minval.az/news/123894519.

the front line,[84] and this more kinetic stance could be implemented by the special forces.[85]

2020

On 12 July 2020, firefights broke out between the two sides, including the use of artillery, tanks, and armed drones. Soldiers on the front line awoke to find the status quo had been altered: Armenia installed a new military position on the border near the town of Tovuz, that gave them a tactical advantage in the area.

According to Armenia, Azerbaijan was unwilling to accept this unilateral change outside of the Minsk Peace Process and its forces pushed back. According to Azerbaijan, Armenia launched an unprovoked attack across the international border.

The fighting resulted in at least 16 fatalities, including an Azerbaijani major general who was second in command to its Third Army Corps. Eleven of the dead were Azerbaijani soldiers, four were Armenian soldiers, and one was a 76-year-old Azerbaijani civilian.[86] What made the fighting unique compared to other cross-border clashes was that it did not take place along the Nagorno-Karabakh line of contact, but across the Armenian-Azerbaijan international border. Tovuz is near the Caspian oil and gas pipelines to Western Europe.

Russian Foreign Minister Sergei Lavrov reportedly called the leaders of both countries, and his foreign ministry issued a news release urging restraint by both sides. Other than words, however, as of 20 July 2020 Moscow had taken no steps to stop the fighting. The Kremlin-dominated Collective Security Treaty Organization, of which Armenia is a member, was supposed to discuss the violence but the meeting was canceled for unknown reasons.

[84] Gurbanov, Ilgar. "Azerbaijan's Military Exercises Send Defiant message to Armenia," *Eurasian Daily Monitor* 16/99, Jamestown Foundation, 11 July 2019. Web. Retrieved 16 July 2019. https://jamestown.org/program/azerbaijans-military-exercises-send-defiant-message-to-armenia/.

[85] "Armenian Armed Forces Revenge for Dead Soldier: Not a Single Provocation of the Enemy Will Remain Unanswered," 14 June 2019. Web. Retrieved 16 July 2019. https://ru.1in.am/1261266.html.

[86] "Azerbaijani MFA: Murder of Azerbaijani Civilian by Armenian Armed Forces Is a Bloody Crime," 14 July 2020. Web. Retrieved 17 July 2020. https://en.trend.az/azerbaijan/politics/3269445.html.

Fighting broke out again on 27 September. In the six week war that followed, Azerbaijan recaptured three of the seven provinces surrounding Karabakh, as well as Shusha. Russia brokered a ceasefire in November that solidified an Armenian retreat. It also introduced 2000 Russian peacekeepers to the war zone.

Weapons Purchases

The Nagorno-Karabakh conflict led to a regional arms race. With its oil wealth, Azerbaijan purchases weapons from Russia at market price; Armenia, by contrast gets Russian weaponry as either military aid or at discretionary prices. Armenian Defense Minister Vazgen Sargsyan boasted that Armenia's defense capability had doubled at no cost to the country's budget. In early 1997, Russian newspapers reported the Kremlin had delivered to Yerevan some $1 billion in military hardware, despite a Yeltsin directive of September 1993 banning arms sales to either Armenia or Azerbaijan until they settled the dispute over Karabakh.[87]

Karabakh was not left out. In 2012, it formed a new tank brigade and received additional heavy artillery. In late 2013, it announced the provision of another 33 Russian-made tanks to its forces. (Russia also reportedly delivered 110 armored vehicles and 50 rocket systems to the Armenian military during the same period).[88]

Russia has felt no compunction in arming both sides in the conflict. When it negotiated the 2010 extension of the Gyumri basing agreement, it also negotiated the sale of an S-300 air-defense system to Azerbaijan. Dashnak international bureau leader Giro Manoyan was outraged. "It is incomprehensible and worrisome that our strategic partner has entered into such a deal with our opponent," he commented. "We have to express our concern and dismay that such a step would encourage Azerbaijan to be more bold, more self-confident, and brazen. And that can bring unpredictable consequences for the entire region."[89]

[87] Walker, Edward, ibid., 23–24.

[88] Danielyan, Emil. "Why Armenia's Military Alliance with Russia Is Not at Risk," Radio Free Europe/Radio Liberty, 7 November 2015. Web. Retrieved 16 July 2019. https://www.rferl.org/a/caucasus-report-armenian-russia-military-alliance/27351046.html.

[89] "AFRF-D Leaders Discuss Latest Armenia-Russia Military Agreement," Armenian Revolutionary Federation-Dashnaktsutyum, 25 August 2010. Web. Retrieved 7

Azerbaijan did not have to limit its arms purchases to Russia. In 2012, Israeli defense officials confirmed the state-run Israel Aerospace Industries had a $1.6 billion deal to sell drones, anti-aircraft and missile defense systems to Baku.[90] This would grow to almost $5 billion in arms purchases by 2016. In one instance, however, the Israeli Ministry of Defense suspended the export license of an Israeli drone manufacturer in 2017 when the company was involved in a live-fire demonstration of its equipment that targeted Armenian troops.[91]

President Aliyev described Azerbaijan's relationship with the Jewish state as like an iceberg, nine-tenths of it below the surface. Israel purchased 40–50% of its oil from Azerbaijan, and much of the revenue was funneled back to the Jewish state in the form of weapons purchases.[92] In 2016, President Aliyev said his country had purchased $4.85 billion in military equipment from the Jewish state. Israel sold Azerbaijan radar systems and drones, and collected intelligence on Iran from this Caucasus nation. According to other reports, an Israeli self-destructing killer drone—Israel Aerospace Industries' Harop—was seen operating in Nagorno-Karabakh. Azerbaijani soldiers are armed with Israeli Tavor rifles.[93]

Moscow lent the Armenian government $200 million for arms acquisitions in 2015. The weapons provided to the Armenian military under that deal included, among other things, multiple launch rocket systems, anti-tank rockets, and shoulder-fired surface-to-air missiles. "The arms provided under the $200 million contract are advanced and modern, and

July 2019. https://old.arfd.info/2010/08/25/arf-d-leaders-discuss-latest-armenia-russia-military-agreement/.

[90] "Israel Signs $1.6 Billion Arms Deal with Azerbaijan," *Haaretz*, 26 February 2012. Web. Retrieved 15 July 2019. https://www.haaretz.com/1.5190757.

[91] Gross, Judah Ari. "Drone Sale to Azeris Halted as Maker Accused of Bombing Armenia in Demo," *Times of Israel*, 29 August 2017. Web. Retrieved 30 August 2017. https://timesofisrael.com/suicide-drone-sales-to-azeris-blocked-after-claim-it-hit-armenians-during-show.

[92] Agayev, Zulfugar. "Israel's Top Oil Supplier Endures Gaza as Azeri Ties Grow," Bloomberg, 28 September 2014. Web. Retrieved 26 June 2019. https://www.bloomberg.com/news/articles/2014-09-28/israel-s-top-oil-supplier-endures-gaza-as-azeri-ties-grow.

[93] Cohen, Gili. "Azerbaijan's President: We've Bought Almost $5 Billion in Israeli Military Goods," *Haaretz*, 14 December 2016. Web. Retrieved 26 June 2019. https://www.haaretz.com/israel-news/.premium-azerbaijan-has-bought-5-billion-in-israeli-military-goods-1.5473569.

are not even in service yet in Russia," said Armenia's Defense Minister David Tonoyan.[94] Yerevan secured another Russian loan in 2017, worth $100 million, for further arms purchases.

Immediately after the April 2016 fighting, Russia announced it was continuing its policy of selling weapons to Azerbaijan. On 8 April, both Russian Prime Minister Dmitry Medvedev and Deputy Prime Minister Dmitry Rogozin visited Baku. Rogozin announced Russia would fulfill its weapons contract. This agreement, first announced in 2015, was to sell Azerbaijan a billion dollars of new weaponry. It included three battalions of T-90S tanks, and three battalions of BMP-3 (about 100 cars), as well as self-propelled artillery, multiple rocket launchers, and a heavy flame thrower system.[95] Russia's continued sale of weaponry to Azerbaijan, was met with considerable hostility in Armenia. The visit of Russia's foreign minister to Yerevan in summer 2016, as well as one by Vladimir Putin in October 2016, were both met with widespread anti-Russian demonstrations.[96]

Russian weapon sales to Azerbaijan did not mean a lessening of defense commitments to rival Armenia. It sold Armenia 9K720 Iskandar short-range ballistic missiles, with a range of about 280 kilometers. Armenia made a public display of their arrival, by placing them prominently in a military parade marking that country's twenty-fifth independence anniversary. Several Russian media outlets reported that Armenia had purchased at least one division, including a minimum of four launchers, of the Iskandar system, adding that this acquisition was outside the terms of 2015's Armenian-Russian arms deal. It was also emphasized that these systems are not the same as the Iskandar-M systems dispatched to Armenia in 2013 as reinforcement for Russia's 102nd Military Base in

[94] "Russia Ships $200 Million in Military Arms to Ally Armenia," *The Moscow Times*, 23 July 2018. Web. Retrieved 7 July 2019. https://www.themoscowtimes.com/2018/07/23/russia-ships-200-million-military-arms-ally-armenia-a62318.

[95] "Rogozin: Russia Will Continue to Supply Weapons to Azerbaijan," Contact.az, 8 April 2016. Web. Retrieved 1 June 2019. http://www.contact.az/.

[96] Balsyte, Erika. "Armenia: Russia First, EU Second?" European Union Institute for Security Studies, March 2017. Web. Retrieved 23 July 2019. https://www.iss.europa.eu/sites/default/files/EUISSFiles/Alert_6_Armenia.pdf.

Gyumri.[97] In May 2017, former US State Department deputy spokesman Adam Ereli noted, "Over the last six months—as Russia's war in Syria and pressure on Turkey has intensified—the flow of its arms and personnel into Armenia has escalated to include advanced Navodchik-2 and Takhion UAV drone aircrafts, MI-24 helicopter gunships and Iskandar-M ballistic missiles."[98]

Azerbaijan responded to Armenia's new weapons systems with purchases of its own. To counter the Armenian Iskandar, Baku purchased the Belarusian Polonez multiple rocket launcher system and the Israeli LORA tactical ballistic missile system. Neither missile was comparable to the Iskandar, but the Polonez had a range of 200 kilometers, and the LORA had 300 kilometers. Now, neither side could use their newly acquired missiles without suffering a crippling reprisal in return.

Armenia tried to prevent Belarus from making the arms sale. "Considering that Belarus is a friendly nation, participates with us in many multilateral formats and has treaty obligations toward us, it's insulting that Belarus would sell weapons to a state in conflict with us," said Ruben Rubinyan, a deputy Armenian foreign minister. "And we will, as before, and in the future, raise these issues in the corresponding manner. I think it's not entirely logical, considering the friendly alliance between Armenia and Belarus." Belarus President Alexander Lukashenko was unrepentant, and even took a slightly offensive tone by reminding the Armenians they were in violation of UN Security Council resolutions. "I just want to say that our relations in no way violate any international treaty, any resolution of the UN Security Council," he said. "We are a sovereign and independent state, and we are competent to determine the direction of our cooperation. We don't have any problems with Azerbaijan at all, and

[97] Abrahamyan, Eduard. "Armenia's New Ballistic Missiles Will Shake up the Neighborhood," *The National Interest*, 12 October 2016. Web. Retrieved 7 July 2019. https://nationalinterest.org/feature/armenias-new-ballistic-missiles-will-shake-the-neighborhood-18026.

[98] Murinson, Alexander. "With Russia Strengthening Its Alliance with Armenia, It's Time to Cut off Foreign Aid to Armenia," *Washington Examiner*, 9 May 2017. Web. Retrieved 16 July 2019. https://www.washingtonexaminer.com/with-russia-strengthening-its-alliance-with-armenia-its-time-to-cut-off-foreign-aid-to-armenia.

we very well remember how the President of Azerbaijan helped us in the difficult times for Belarus."[99]

Moscow was quite happy with its role as principal arms supplier to both sides in the Karabakh dispute, even though Yerevan frequently complained about the Kremlin giving aid to the enemy. Manvel Sargsyan, Director of the Armenian Center for National and International Studies, commented in 2015 that the military sales to Azerbaijan were the beginning of a military-political alliance with Baku. "Russia is trying its best to assure that the sale of weapons is just business," he said. "But in the end it became clear that it is a new strategy of Russia." Sargsyan observed that Moscow was keeping the two South Caucasus states locked in conflict over Karabakh, so that both could be dependent on Russian weapons.[100]

While Russia's principal allies in the Armenian government lost power in 2018, it did not stop Moscow from continuing to be Armenia's primary arms supplier. In February 2019 the Armenian Ministry of Defense confirmed it was expecting delivery of four Sukhoi SU-30SM multi-role fighter jets. The Sargsyan administration had originally negotiated the deal in 2012 but were unable to complete the transaction because of lack of funds. Under Pashinyan, Yerevan would purchase the jets at CSTO concessionary prices with money borrowed from Russia. The Ministry also agreed to become the first foreign purchaser of the Russian AK-12 infantry assault rifle.[101] Defense Minister Davit Tonoyan stated Yerevan would seek to acquire more such aircraft after receiving their first batch by "the beginning of next year." Russian Defense Ministry officials announced additional contracts signed in Moscow by Armenia's Deputy Defense Minister Davit Pakhchanyan and top Russian defense industry executives. The Armenian Defense Ministry confirmed the information

[99] Buniatyan, Heghine. "The Sale of Weapons by Belarus to Azerbaijan 'Is Not Entirely Logical'—Armenian Deputy Foreign Minister," Azatutyun, 11 June 2018. Web. Retrieved 7 July 2019. https://rus.azatutyun.am/a/29283647.html.

[100] Hayrumyan, Naira. "Allies and Allegiances: Armenia takes Russian-Azerbaijani Military Ties in Stride," ArmeniaNow.com, 14 October 2015. Web. Retrieved 22 July 2019. www.armenianow.com/commentary/analysis/57619/armenia_azerbaijan_military_cooperation.

[101] Elliott, Raffi. "Russia to Boost Armenian Military, Fighter Jets Approved," *Armenian Weekly*, 5 February 2019. Web. Retrieved 22 July 2019. https://armenianweekly.com/2019/02/05/russia-to-boost-armenian-military-fighter-jets-approved/.

but did not divulge financial details of the contracts or specify the types of weapons covered by them.[102]

The weapons balanced was overturned in 2020 when Azerbaijan began purchasing Bayraktar drones from Turkey. These weapons proved decisive in the Autumn 6 week war.

Conclusion

During the Soviet era Armenian nationalists used the cause of Nagorno-Karabakh to build a sense of Armenian nationalism. As the USSR collapsed, these nationalists acquired arms through illicit purchases and by raiding Soviet military bases. They began to use the arms against Soviet security forces, and the troops of the Azerbaijan SSR Ministry of Interior. Eventually, these defenders joined together in Operation Ring—an attempt to eliminate secessionists from Nagorno-Karabakh.

When the Soviet Union dissolved, open fighting broke out between Armenia and Azerbaijan. Russian military units fought on both sides of the conflict in the beginning, meaning Russia could benefit regardless of who emerged the victor. This quickly changed, as Russian support for Armenia grew. During the 1992–1994 war, Russia provided Armenia with the armaments it needed to seize Nagorno-Karabakh and the seven surrounding provinces of Azerbaijan. Today, there are over 5000 Russian troops based in Armenia, Russian border guards patrol the borders of Armenia, and Armenia's air defenses are integrated into the Russian military command.

At the same time, the Russian armaments industry has benefited tremendously from the ongoing unrest. In addition to the billion dollars in illegal arms transfers to Armenia in the 1990s, Russia lent $300 million to Yerevan for Russian weapons purchases, and it has sold billions of dollars of weapons to Azerbaijan. The military conflict has decimated the land Armenia claimed it was saving, and caused Azerbaijan to lose control over 16–20% of its national territory. The only country to benefit has been the Russian Federation.

[102] "Armenia, Russia Sign More Arms Deals," Asbarez, 1 March 2019. Web. Retrieved 7 July 2019. http://asbarez.com/178042/armenia-russia-sign-more-arms-deals/.

CHAPTER 3

The Politics of Frozen Conflict

Political figures in both Armenia and Azerbaijan have paid a heavy cost for the war over Karabakh. In Armenia, a president had to resign because he was perceived as too willing to compromise for peace. In Azerbaijan, two presidents lost their jobs because of their inability to defend their country adequately. Modern politics in both countries takes no prisoners.

Armenia

As the Soviet Union began its slow collapse throughout the late 1980s, members of the Armenian political elite created the Karabakh Committee, which evolved into the Armenian National Movement (ANM).[1] They rapidly perceived that they needed an issue around which the Armenian people could rally, and they settled on the status of Nagorno-Karabakh. In addition to passing numerous calls for Karabakh's secession from the Azerbaijan SSR and/or unification with the Armenian SSR, the ANM organized mass demonstrations and work stoppages in solidarity with Armenian ethnic kin in Karabakh. These mass actions raised popular support for the ANM itself, and for its desire to be independent of the Kremlin. Azerbaijan SSR's supposed threat to the Armenian inhabitants of Karabakh was cited as an existential threat to all Armenians; after 1991,

[1] Human Rights Watch, ibid., 3.

J. J. Coyle, *Russia's Interventions in Ethnic Conflicts*,
https://doi.org/10.1007/978-3-030-59573-9_3

the Republic of Azerbaijan's military superiority was cited as the threat. "A few words about Armenia's perception of its own security, or rather its perceived threats to its security. Our geographic position and our long history have contributed to our desire to define our security needs in terms which takes into account very carefully the behavior and intentions of our immediate neighbors," said Minister of Foreign Affairs Vartan Oskanian in 1998. "Our own resources are objectively speaking no match to the size, strength or military capabilities of our neighbors."[2]

Papazian writes that when the Karabakh issue re-emerged in February 1988 in Karabakh and Armenia, only the intelligentsia was aware of the persistence since Tsarist times of this bone of contention between Armenians and Azerbaijanis.[3] They turned the Karabakh issue into an instrument of nation building. This gave the Karabakh Committee, ethnic Armenians who wanted to seize control of Karabakh from Baku and/or Moscow, an inordinate role in the mobilization of Armenian nationalism. Eventually, members of the Karabakh political elite seized control of the Republic of Armenia. Stepanakert controlled Yerevan rather than Yerevan controlling Stepanakert.

Levon Ter-Petrosyan joined the ANM in May 1989 and subsequently became chairman. As an Orientalism scholar before joining the movement, he had written extensively on medieval topics; but he also touched on Armenian politics, history, and nationalism.[4] He had been involved in political movements since at least 1966 when he was arrested for his participation in a 24 April demonstration (Armenian Genocide Remembrance Day). As a senior researcher at Matenadaran, the Mesrop Mashtots Institute of Ancient Manuscripts, he led the Matenadaran Karabakh Committee. After joining the ANM, he spent six months in jail for his nationalist activities, from December 1988 to May 1989. These activities include his command of the Armenian National Army, a banned paramilitary group that patrolled the borders of Nagorno-Karabakh. Upon his

[2] "Address by Vartan Oskanian Minister of Foreign Affairs of the Republic of Armenia to the Permanent Council Meeting of the OSCE," 8 October 1998. Web. Retrieved 31 May 2019. https://www.mfa.am/en/speeches/1998/10/08/osce/1589.

[3] Papazian, Taline. "State at War, State in War: The Nagorno-Karabakh Conflict and State-Making in Armenia, 1991–1995," *The Journal of Power Institutions in Post-Soviet Republics* 8 (2008). Web. Accessed 31 May 2019. https://journals.openedition.org/pipss/1623.

[4] Papazian, ibid.

release, he was elected in May 1990 as a deputy to the Supreme Soviet of the Armenian SSR.

In these elections, Armenia sent ballots and ballot boxes to Nagorno-Karabakh, so the inhabitants could participate in the election. While most of the oblast could not participate because it was under military rule, eleven districts held elections, choosing 11 representatives to the Armenian Supreme Soviet.[5] There could be no clearer signal as to the Armenian belief that Karabakh was an integral part of Armenia.

On 4 August 1990, Ter-Petrosyan became the first non-communist Chairman of the Supreme Council of the Armenia SSR. He was elected in 1991 as the first president of an independent Armenia with 83% of the vote. In September 1993, he appointed Serzh Sargsyan as his Minister of Defense and special representative for negotiating a cease-fire. Sargsyan was not a politician from the Republic of Armenia; rather he was Karabakh's director of defense forces. By May 1995, he was the Minister of National Security. This made room for Vazgen Sargsyan (no relationship to Serzh) to be the Minister of Defense.

The Ministers of Interior, Defense and National Security often found themselves in opposition to the president. Ter-Petrosyan adopted a number of measures to keep these powerful individuals under his control. As an example, in 1994 he ended their special economic privileges and disqualified army officers, Interior Ministry officers, and members of the cabinet from being eligible to be members of parliament.[6] These moves did little to halt the opposition. In the parliamentary elections of 1995, the opposition Republicans gained majority control. This party was loyal to Defense Minister Vazgen Sargsyan.[7] The ANM placed a close second. The Republicans were allied with a group comprised principally of veterans of the Karabakh war, the Yerkrapah (Guardians of the Land).

The president faced more than internal challenges, he faced external ones from the Armenian diaspora. The Armenian Revolutionary Federation (ARF), the old Dashnak party, was against anything that even hinted at compromise over Karabakh. At the end of 1994, Ter-Petrosyan suspended the Dashnak party in the republic and ordered the closure of 12 media outlets allegedly associated with it. He claimed that the ARF

[5] Balukbasi, ibid., 151.

[6] Papazian, ibid.

[7] Papazian, ibid.

had become a cover for a secret organization allegedly responsible for terrorism, drug trafficking, and illegal arms trading. In January 1995 the Supreme Court upheld the ARF's suspension for a six-month period. The Court's reason was not a threat to national security, but the presence of foreigners (members of the diaspora) on the party's board. The government allowed individual ARF members to run for parliament in 1996, but the party's absence paved the way for a resounding victory of Ter-Petrosyan's ANM.[8] Despite the victory, Dashnak supporters continued to give him trouble.

Ter-Petrosyan realized he needed to expand his base of support or rule as a minority president. In December 1995 at the ANM's seventh congress, he called for an alliance of liberal democratic forces with right-wing forces, but he excluded Yerkrapah from the proposed coalition.

His own reelection in 1996 was marred by charges of vote rigging. Minister of Interior Vano Siradeghian claimed that it was obvious a month before the elections that the president would not win reelection, so he fixed the election. He said that the political leadership of Armenia and Nagorno-Karabakh were at Ter-Petrosyan's headquarters when they learned he would need to face a runoff election because he had not received a majority of the votes.[9] The second round never took place. Dashnaks organized street protests, and the president ordered the army into the street to prevent the opposition from seizing power.[10] According to Siradeghian, Ter-Petrosyan started planning his resignation at that time.

To shore up his declining political base, Ter-Petrosyan turned to the recently elected "president" of Nagorno-Karabakh, Robert Kocharyan, and named him prime minister of Armenia in March 1997. For most of the next two decades, the tail would wag the proverbial dog. The political elite of Nagorno-Karabakh would control Yerevan and its policies.

In September 1997, Ter-Petrosyan gave a press conference in which he said he accepted a peace plan known as the phased approach as a

[8] "Democracy on Rocky Ground," Human Rights Watch, 25 February 2009. Web. Retrieved 1 July 2019. https://www.hrw.org/report/2009/02/25/democracy-rocky-ground/armenias-disputed-2008-presidential-election-post-election.

[9] Danielyan, Emil. "Armenia: 1996 Presidential Election Was Rigged, Aide Suggests," Radio Free Europe/Radio Liberty, 9 January 1999. Web. Retrieved 1 July 2019. https://www.rferl.org/a/1090270.html.

[10] Papazian, ibid.

basis for negotiations with Azerbaijan. He was immediately savaged by the opposition. National Democratic Union leader Vazgen Manukyan rejected Ter-Petrosyan's position as "capitulation" and "treason," saying the president's arguments "substantially undermine Armenia's negotiating position." Manukyan said Ter-Petrosyan "should be barred from leading a country" and warned that "aggressive haste" in seeking to resolve the Karabakh conflict could prove counter-productive.[11] Ter-Petrosyan also found himself fighting members of his own cabinet. Prime Minister Robert Kocharyan and Minister for National Security Serzh Sargsyan were both former officials in Karabakh. They were joined by Armenia's Minister of Defense, Vazgen Sargsyan, in opposing the president.[12]

It was the beginning of the end for Ter-Petrosyan's presidency. The people of Armenia had not been prepared for a peace proposal. The criticisms of the president fell on fertile ground. Within the elite, Prime Minister Kocharyan united with National Security's Sargsyan and Defense Minister Sargsyan to force Ter-Petrosyan to resign. "I have faced demands to resign," he said in a statement. "Considering that, in this situation, exercising the President's constitutional powers may cause a serious destabilization of the situation, I accept this demand and announce my resignation."[13]

In Karabakh, the news was well-received. "We were in despair with Ter-Petrosyan," said Karabakh MFA spokesman Janna Grikorova. "We think Kocharyan will take a firm line."[14] Kocharyan had little room to maneuver. He had come to power with the backing of the Dashnaks and the power ministers. Dependent on them and their military supporters to stay in power, he adopted a hard-line nationalist policy.[15] He was then

[11] "Newsline-October 1, 1997," Radio Free Europe/Radio Liberty, 1 October 1997. Web. Retrieved 5 June 2019. https://www.rferl.org/a/1141506.html.

[12] Cornell, ibid., 128.

[13] "Armenian Chief Quits in Dispute Over a Region," *The New York Times*, 4 February 1998. Net. Retrieved 23 May 2019. *Academic OneFile*. http://link.galegroup.com/apps/doc/A150238209/AONE?u=chap_main&sid=AONE&xid=62d0cb89.

[14] Williams, Daniel. "Karabakhis Defend Independence Fight," *Washington Post*, 2 August 1998, A29. Web. Retrieved 7 June 2019. http://www.washingtonpost.com/wp-srv/inatl/longterm/postsoviet/nagorno080298.htm?noredirect=on.

[15] Laitin and Suny, ibid.

elected president in the second round of elections in March 1998, in a vote criticized by international observers.

In the parliamentary elections of 1999, Vazgen Sargsyan and his Republican Party won the elections. Together with his coalition partner Karen Demirchian's People's Party, they took over the legislative body. Ter-Petrosyan's ANM failed to win a single seat. When the politicians divided up the spoils Sargsyan became Prime Minister, and Demirchian speaker of the parliament.

The new political structure was shattered on 27 October 1999 when armed gunmen burst into the parliament, killing Vazgen Sargsyan and the speaker. President Robert Kocharyan personally took control of the surrender negotiations. The gunmen demanded the right to make a public statement on television. They cited a laundry list of complaints against Vazgen Sargsyan. The gunmen blamed him for a loss of national pride, corruption, and economic decline.[16] The official government line was that the gunmen were individuals in need of psychiatric care, with no known political affiliation. Onlookers, however, said that from the slogans being shouted the attackers were nationalists unhappy about the possibility of a negotiated settlement in Karabakh. "This is a patriotic action," said their spokesman. "This shake-up is needed for the nation to regain its senses." An Armenian journalist who was in the chamber at the time said one of the men cried that they had "come to avenge those who have drunk the blood of the nation."[17] Republican Party of Armenia's Aram Sargsyan was named prime minister (later to be replaced by Andranik Margaryan), but Kocharyan and Serzh Sargsyan now controlled the Armenian government.

In Karabakh, Samvel Babayan had been the top commander of ethnic Armenian forces from 1993 to 1999. In 2000, he was arrested and sentenced to 14 years in prison for masterminding a failed attempt on the

[16] "Armenia's Tragedy," *The New York Times*, 30 October 1999. Web. Retrieved 23 May 2019. *Academic OneFile*. http://link.galegroup.com/apps/doc/A149773974/AONE?u=chap_main&sid=AONE&xid=a1859d16.

[17] Wines, Michael. "Prime Minister and Others Slain in Armenian Siege," *The New York Times*, 28 October 1999. Web. Retrieved 23 May 2019. *Academic OneFile*. http://link.galegroup.com/apps/doc/A149773586/AONE?u=chap_main&sid=AONE&xid=c1fb7eeb.

life of the "president" of Nagorno-Karabakh Arkady Ghukasian. Babayan was released in 2004 after Ghukasian pardoned him.[18]

In the Spring of 2002, Kocharyan was rocked by a series of opposition demonstrations calling for his impeachment. The issue was the closing of opposition media outlets. Kocharyan detained a number of the rank and file demonstrators using the power of administrative detention, but he took no action against the demonstrations' leaders.[19]

During the first round of voting in the February 2003 presidential election, more than 250 opposition activists, supporters and observers were detained. The opposition held large unsanctioned rallies in Yerevan between the first and second rounds. At least 200 individuals were detained including many opposition staff. Many were sentenced to up to 15 days of administrative detention, probably an attempt to hurt the opposition in the runoff election of 5 March. They noted, "The failure of the 2003 presidential election to meet international standards lay not in technical or procedural lapses, but in a lack of sufficient political determination by the authorities to ensure a fair and honest process."

Losing candidate Stepan Demirchyan challenged the results in the Constitutional Court. While the Court did not rule in his favor, it did strike down results in 40 polling stations. A year later, the opposition held mass peaceful protests to force a "referendum of confidence" on President Kocharyan and to call for his resignation. The government dispersed the demonstrators with force. The authorities again arrested opposition members, violently dispersed demonstrators, raided political party headquarters, and attacked journalists.[20]

The right-leaning Republican Party of Armenia emerged from the parliamentary elections of 2003 with the largest bloc, supporters of the president. Outside observers criticized both elections as failing to

[18] "Ex Karabakh Military Leader Warns of Another War," Radio Free Europe/Radio Liberty, 10 March 2010. Web. Retrieved 22 July 2019. https://www.rferl.org/a/ExKarabakh_Military_Leader_Warns_Of_Another_War/1999201.html.

[19] "An Imitation of Law: The Use of Administrative Detention in the 2003 Armenian Presidential Election," Human Rights Watch Briefing Paper, 23 May 2003, 6. Web. Retrieved 1 July 2019. http://hrlibrary.umn.edu/research/armenia/HRW%20Briefing%20Paper%202003.pdf.

[20] "Democracy on Rocky Ground," ibid.

meet international standards.[21] By the 2007 parliamentary elections, the Republicans had secured their hold on the legislature. The CSCE noted significant improvement in the electoral process, but it still failed to meet international standards.[22] Samvel Babayan ran for election with the Alliance Party from Nagorno-Karabakh, but the party failed to pass the 5% bar to be represented in parliament. The party announced it would create an opposition by uniting with two other parties who also failed to reach the 5% mark.[23] After failing as an opposition leader, Babayan emigrated to Russia in 2011.

All eyes now turned on the presidential elections of 19 February 2008, when Robert Kocharyan would not stand for reelection. Serzh Sargsyan won handily with 52.8% of the vote. An international observer mission initially endorsed the election as mostly in line with the country's international commitments. On 3 March, however, the OSCE issued a harsher statement, claiming that there had been irregularities including implausibly high voter turnout at some polling stations, high numbers of invalid ballots at some Yerevan polling stations, and significant procedural errors and irregularities in the vote counting and tabulation.

The losing candidate was former president Levon Ter-Petrosyan who accused the government of stealing the election. He said that he, and not Sargsyan, had won the election.[24] Riots broke out after the election. A group of protestors claiming that Sargsyan's victory was the result of fraud established a continuous protest with daily rallies and a camp on a city center square. Initially, the authorities tolerated the protestors, but police staged a pre-dawn raid on the camp on March 1, claiming to search for weapons. The police dispersed and dismantled the protestors'

[21] "Report on the 2003 Presidential and Parliamentary Elections in Armenia," Commission on Security and Cooperation in Europe, 2004. Web. Retrieved 1 July 2019. https://www.csce.gov/sites/helsinkicommission.house.gov/files/2003%255FArmenia%255Felections.pdf.

[22] Office for Democratic Institutions and Human Rights, Organization on Security and Cooperation in Europe. "Republic of Armenia: Parliamentary Elections 2007," OSCE/ODIHR Election Observation Mission Report, 10 September 2007. Web. Retrieved 1 July 2019. https://www.osce.org/odihr/elections/armenia/26606?download=true.

[23] Saghabalian, Anna and Liz Fuller. "Three Armenian Parties to Merge in Opposition," Radio Free Europe/Radio Liberty, 24 August 2007. Web. Retrieved 22 July 2019. https://www.rferl.org/a/1347626.html.

[24] "Democracy on Rocky Ground," ibid.

camp, beating protest participants including people who were entangled inside collapsed tents. This triggered a much larger, violent demonstration elsewhere in the city center. By evening, outgoing President Robert Kocharyan declared a 20-day state of emergency during which public gatherings and strikes were banned. Riot police returned in force, firing tracer bullets and using teargas. According to witnesses interviewed by Human Rights Watch, there had been no verbal directives to disperse. Protestors who had armed themselves with metal rods, sticks, paving stones, and even Molotov cocktails repulsed the police attack, and the police withdrew to a road junction a few hundred meters away. While the main demonstration continued peacefully behind the barricades, a group of protestors began attacking the police. Approximately 10 people were killed. In the aftermath of the violence, there were more than 100 arrests. Armenian authorities investigated, prosecuted, and convicted dozens of opposition members, sometimes in flawed and politically motivated trials, for organizing the demonstration and participating in violent disorder. They did not prosecute a single representative of the authorities for excessive use of force.[25]

Street protests entered a relatively calm period until early 2011. On 13 March, the three parties in the ruling coalition signed a compact to not attack one another in the upcoming 2012 parliamentary and 2013 presidential elections. The following week, Ter-Petrosyan and the ANC organized protests attended by tens of thousands. The opposition concentrated on the failure of the government's economic policies, but they also criticized the government for its submissiveness on Nagorno-Karabakh.[26]

Ter-Petrosyan had a long list of economic and political demands that he claimed President Sargsyan had ignored. Ter-Petrosyan said he and his political team remained ready to start a "dialogue" with the government but "I absolutely don't doubt that what has happened in Tunisia, Egypt, and elsewhere will also happen in Armenia. That is, the authorities will after all submit to the will of the people."[27]

[25] "Democracy on Rocky Ground," ibid.

[26] "Protests in Armenia," Center for Eastern Studies, Warsaw, 23 February 2011. Web. Retrieved 3 July 2019. https://www.osw.waw.pl/en/publikacje/analyses/2011-02-23/protests-armenia.

[27] "Armenian Opposition Reoccupies Key Square as Protests Grow in Strength," Radio Free Europe/Radio Liberty, 18 March 2011. Web. Retrieved 3 July 2019. https://www.rferl.org/a/armenian_opposition_rally_new_elections/2341470.html.

Ter-Petrosyan convened a total of four protest demonstrations that year to demand new elections. He never accepted the legality of his defeat at the hands of President Sargsyan. The protests mobilized up to 35,000 people but Ter-Petrosyan failed to capitalize on the mass support: He advocated "caution" rather than "pushing the authorities into a corner." Interparty talks followed, but they ended in deadlock.[28]

Sargsyan was reelected in 2013. The parliamentary opposition issued a series of demands for change and set a deadline of 30 September 2014 for meeting them. Most of the demands focused on the socioeconomic situation, but they included a ban on the signing of any document that could pose a threat to the continued existence of the unrecognized Nagorno-Karabakh Republic. The authorities failed to agree to any of them, causing a new wave of demonstrations. Only 2000 people showed up for the first rally, held in a town 15 km north of Yerevan.[29] Crowds swelled to over 10,000 when the demonstrations finally moved to the capital.[30]

In 2015, the protests were over the price of electricity. Dubbed the "Electric Yerevan" movement, it failed to dislodge the government any more than the previous street protests. It was caused by the state utilities commission agreeing to a 17–22% hike in the price the Electric Networks of Armenia would charge the public. This utility was 100% owned by Inter RAO, a Russian company run by Kremlin insider Igor Sechin.[31]

In 2016, protests were led by veterans of the war in Karabakh. The gunmen seized a police station, taking eight hostages to include the country's deputy chief of police. One policeman was killed and two wounded while two others were released early for medical conditions. Media reports said the group was demanding the release of Zhirair Sefilyan, an opposition politician who had been arrested the month before for alleged firearms offenses.

[28] Fuller, Liz. "Armenian Opposition Launches New Wave of Protests," Radio Free Europe/Radio Liberty, 28 September 2014. Web. Retrieved 3 July 2019. https://www.rferl.org/a/caucasus-report-armenia-opposition-protests/26610291.html.

[29] Fuller, Liz, 28 September 2014, ibid.

[30] "Thousands Protest Against Government in Armenia," *The Guardian*, 10 October 2014. Web. Retrieved 3 July 2019. https://www.theguardian.com/world/2014/oct/10/thousands-protest-against-government-armenia.

[31] Luhn, Alec. "Armenia Protests Escalate After Police Turn on Demonstrators," *The Guardian*, 25 June 2015. Web. Retrieved 3 July 2019. https://www.theguardian.com/world/2015/jun/24/armenia-yerevan-protests-electric-prices-russia.

Sefilyan had previously been arrested in 2006 for calling for "a violent overthrow of the government." He was jailed for 18 months and released in 2008. In 2015, he and several of his supporters were arrested again on suspicion of preparing a coup but were released shortly afterward. In June 2016 he and six members of his small opposition group, the New Armenia Public Salvation Front, were arrested after authorities claimed they were preparing a plot to seize several government buildings and telecommunications facilities in Yerevan.[32]

Police scuffled with the hostage takers several times, and the original hostages were released. One of the gunmen was wounded, and the Ministry of Health sent medical personnel to look after him. The gunmen seized the health workers as new hostages. The gunmen were supported by street demonstrations.[33] More than 1500 anti-government protesters rallied in the capital to call for a bloodless resolution to the crisis.[34] The gunmen finally surrendered after two weeks, and twenty were arrested.[35]

Karabakh's Samvel Babayan made headlines in 2016 when he returned from his voluntary exile in Russia because, as he explained, of Azerbaijan's continued hostility and the need to defend the Nagorno-Karabakh. "Azerbaijan will not make compromises during negotiations," he said. "It wants everything and we can restrain it only by maintaining the military balance in favor of Armenia." Babayan estimated it would take at least ten months to bring the military back to its required strength. "My key mission is to be conducted in Artsakh (the Armenian name for Nagorno-Karabakh). The rest should be decided by the people."[36]

[32] "Armenian Opposition Group Takes Hostages in Yerevan Police Building," *The Guardian*, 17 July 2016. Web. Retrieved 16 July 2019. https://www.theguardian.com/world/2016/jul/17/armenia-opposition-group-hostages-yerevan-police-building.

[33] Lomsadze, Georgi. "Armenia: Yerevan Gunmen Grab More Hostages at Police Station," Eurasianet, 27 July 2016. Web. Retrieved 16 July 2019.https://eurasianet.org/armenia-yerevan-gunmen-grab-more-hostages-police-station.

[34] "Rioting in Armenian Capital Yerevan as Hostage Crisis Enters Fifth Day," *The Telegraph*, 21 July 2016. Web. Retrieved 16 July 2019. https://www.telegraph.co.uk/news/2016/07/21/rioting-in-armenian-capital-as-hostage-crisis-enters-fifth-day/.

[35] "Gunmen Surrender in Armenia Police Station Siege," Deutche Welle, 31 July 2016. Web. Retrieved 16 July 2019. https://www.dw.com/en/gunmen-surrender-in-armenia-police-station-siege/a-19440599-0.

[36] "Main Mission of My Return Is Karabakh: Samvel Babayan." 168 Hours, 26 May 2016. Web. Retrieved 22 July 2019. https://en.168.am/2016/05/26/7452.html.

While Babayan claimed he would not be joining a political party, Sargsyan's government was suspicious of his return. Two weeks before the 2017 parliamentary elections in which Babayan voiced support for an opposition alliance led by former Defense Minister Seyran Ohanian and two former foreign ministers, the government arrested Babayan on weapons smuggling and money laundering charges. He was sentenced to six years in prison for allegedly securing a man-portable Igla surface-to-air missile system. Prosecutors claimed that Babayan had been prepared to pay $50,000 for delivery of the system.[37]

Inside the government, faced with the approaching end of his two, five-year terms in office, Serzh Sargsyan passed a constitutional amendment by referendum in 2015 transferring most presidential power to the office of the prime minister. To secure passage, he assured the public that he would "not aspire" to be named prime minister when his presidential term expired. The individual who emerged as a powerful opposition figure was not Babayan or Ter-Petrosyan, however, but another former president: Sargsyan's patron Robert Kocharyan. He created the Prosperous Armenia Party (PAP) to keep a hand in the Armenian political scene. The new party was led by a man who became wealthy during Kocharyan's presidency, Gagik Tsarukian. When Tsarukian's criticisms of Sargsyan's constitutional amendments became too loud, the president ordered tax authorities to audit Tsarukian's business interests-effectively silencing him.[38]

Sargsyan's allies maintained their hold on parliament in the April 2017 elections. On 17 April 2018, Sargsyan stepped down and his hand-picked successor Armen Sargsyan (no relation) was sworn in as president. Despite his promise to withdraw quietly, eight days after his presidency ended, Serzh's allies in the parliament elected him Prime Minister by a 76–17 vote. He argued that in a democracy it was only right that the leader of the majority party to serve as prime minister. "I have enough influence

[37] "Armenian Court Sentences Former Karabakh Commander Babayan to Six Years in Prison," Radio Free Europe/Radio Liberty, 28 November 2017. Web. Retrieved 22 July 2019. https://www.rferl.org/a/armenia-babayan-nagorno-karabakh-jailed-six-years-opposition/28883607.html.

[38] "Armenian President Cracks Down on Main Rival," *The Economist*, 17 February 2015. Web. Retrieved 22 July 2019. http://country.eiu.com/article.aspx?articleid=1332604117&Country=Armenia&topic=Economy&subtopic=Forecast&subsubtopic=International+assumptions&oid=122531596&flid=1332842717.

and power to make the executive and legislative branches of power work effectively," he declared to the parliament.[39]

This prompted thousands to take to the streets to protest the power grab. Opposition leader Nikol Pashinyan gave the opposition movement a new name: The Velvet Revolution. "I declare today the launching of a velvet [revolution], a peaceful people's revolution," he told the parliament. "A revolutionary situation is brewing across the country. Demonstrators are blocking streets and... highways in the cities of Gyumri, Ijevan, Vanadzor, Kapan, and Metsamor. People are not going to work; mass strikes have begun."[40]

More than 180 people were arrested as the protests forced the new prime minister to postpone his first cabinet meeting for several hours. President Armen Sargsyan called for "dialogue and mutual respect" to solve the crisis. The Dashnaks called on political factions to "jointly find solutions." [41] Finally, as the crowds continued to swell, Sargsyan resigned as prime minister after a mere eleven days in office.

This led to a political crisis. Karen Karapetyan of the Republican Party stepped in as acting prime minister while parliament decided what to do next. Karapetyan was a top executive at the Russian gas giant Gazprom (he ran Gazprom Armenia and later Gazprombank). The only candidate for prime minister was the parliamentary leader of the opposition, Nikol Pashinyan—but Sargsyan's Republican Party held the majority and refused to ratify him. He needed 53 votes to get elected, but only secured 45. In reply, Pashinyan called for a day of protest. The demonstrators

[39] Mkrtchyan, Hasmik. "Thousands Protest in Armenian Capital as Sarkisyan Approved as PM," Reuters, 17 April 2018. Web. Retrieved 22 July 2019. https://www.reuters.com/article/us-armenia-politics/thousands-protest-in-armenian-capital-as-sarksyan-approved-as-pm-idUSKBN1HO2HW.

[40] "Tens of Thousands Protest in Yerevan, Other Armenian Cities Against Sarkisian as New Prime Minister," Radio Free Europe/Radio Liberty, 17 April 2018. Web. Retrieved 3 July 2019. https://www.rferl.org/a/armenia-opposition-protests-parliament-vote-sarkisian-prime-minister/29172095.html.

[41] "Almost 200 Arrests in Yerevan as Anti-Sarkisian Protests Continue," Radio Free Europe/Radio Liberty, 20 April 2018. Web. Retrieved 22 July 2019.https://www.rferl.org/a/more-arrests-in-yerevan-as-armenian-opposition-protests-resume-/29180654.html.

paralyzed the road network in Yerevan, and travelers seeking international flights had to walk to the airport terminals after abandoning their cars.[42]

Pashinyan won a second vote 59–42, with members of Sargsyan's own party turning to him to end the political stalemate. Russian President Vladimir Putin immediately issued a statement congratulating him on his victory, and that he looked forward to continuing "friendly relations."[43] Pashinyan promised there would be no new directions in Armenian foreign policy, and Armenia would stay close to Russia. He also said he would not change any policies concerning Nagorno-Karabakh.[44]

He never forgot his arrest protesting the 2008 election results. With Sargsyan out of power and Pashinyan in charge, the courts in July ordered the arrest of Robert Kocharyan on charges of attempting to overthrow the constitutional order. The courts ruled that he could be detained while charges were investigated that he ordered the illegal violent dispersal of 2008 post-election protestors. Also arrested were Yuri Khachaturov, the Armenian chief of the Russia-led Collective Security Treaty Organization (CSTO), who was recalled to Yerevan to face the charges. Khachaturov, who was Armenia's deputy defense minister at the time, denied any wrongdoing in comments to reporters. Officials said he would be released after paying a bail of about $10,000. Authorities also issued an arrest warrant for retired General Mikael Harutiunian, who served as defense minister during the 2008 unrest.[45]

Yerevan's recall of CSTO Secretary-General Khachaturov to face charges on trying to subvert the constitutional order in 2008 (Khachaturov ordered troops to oppose post-election demonstrators) annoyed Russia. Kremlin insiders warned the criminal prosecution of former Armenian president Robert Kocharyan and Khachaturov could

[42] Smith-Spark, Laura. "Armenia Protests: What Happens Next?" CNN News, 2 May 2018. Web. Retrieved 3 July 2019. https://edition.cnn.com/2018/04/26/europe/armenia-protests-explainer-intl/index.html.

[43] "Armenia Protest Leader Pashinyan Wins PM Vote," BBC, 8 May 2018. Web. Retrieved 22 July 2019. www.bbc.com/news/world-europe-44037727.

[44] "Armenian Election Tests Revolution's Power," *New York Times*, 10 December 2018, p. A10(L). Web. Retrieved 23 May 3019. *Academic OneFile*. http://link.galegroup.com/apps/doc/A565023587/AONE?u=chap_main&sid=AONE&xid=6ad34d95.

[45] "Armenia's Ex-President Kocharyan Taken into Custody Over 2008 Crackdown," Radio Free Europe/Radio Liberty, 27 July 2018. Web. Retrieved 1 July 2019. https://www.rferl.org/a/armenia-s-ex-president-Kocharyan-taken-into-custody-over-2008-crackdown/29394682.html.

result in discord between the two capitals.[46] Kocharyan was released on appeal in August 2018, sparking protests. He was rearrested on 7 December, three days before new parliamentary elections.

In October 2018, Pashinyan's reformist party won an overwhelming victory in the mayoral election in Yerevan. Seeking to capitalize on the momentum and to consolidate his power, Pashinyan called for snap parliamentary elections. He resigned his office so the parliament could be dissolved. The ploy worked: the centrist My Step Alliance, which includes Pashinyan's Civil Contract Party, won 70.4% of the vote.[47] International observers said the elections respected fundamental freedoms and were characterized by "broad public trust" and "genuine competition."[48]

On 18 May 2019, a Yerevan court said the 64-year-old Kocharyan, who had been in pretrial detention since his arrest in December, could be released after leaders from Nagorno-Karabakh said they would vouch for him and guaranteed that he would appear in court when the trial resumed. Given the fact that Armenia claims that Nagorno-Karabakh is not part of Armenia, it is interesting that the Yerevan court was willing to accept the word of foreign nationals as a fealty bond for Kocharyan. Two days later, the court suspended the criminal proceedings, saying it was sending the case to the Constitutional Court over Kocharyan's status as either a private person or a president. Pashinyan called for street protests to block access to the courts and branded the judiciary as the only remaining corrupt branch of government. He said it was time for a second phase in his revolution, to clean out the court system—including the dismissal of any judge who was overruled by the European Court of Human Rights. "The time has come for surgical intervention," he said.[49]

[46] "Armenia Recalled an Official Accused of a coup d'etat from CSTO Secretary General," Lenta.ru, 2 November 2018. Web. Retrieved 7 July 2019. https://lenta.ru/news/2018/11/02/odkb/.

[47] "Armenia Election: PM Nikol Pashinyan Wins in Landslide," BBC News, 10 December 2018. Web. Retrieved 2 July 2019. https://www.bbc.com/news/world-europe-46502681.

[48] "Monitors Hail Armenian Vote, Call for Further Electoral Reforms," Radio Free Europe/Radio Liberty, 10 December 2018. Web. Retrieved 2 July 2019. https://www.rferl.org/a/monitors-hail-armenia-s-snap-polls-call-for-further-electoral-reforms/29647816.html.

[49] "Armenian PM Calls for Radical Justice Reform As 'Second Phase of the Revolution'," Radio Free Europe/Radio Liberty, 20 May 2019. Web. Retrieved 3 July 2019. https://www.rferl.org/a/armenians-heed-call-to-block-courts-pashinian-to-speak-on-second-phase-of-revolution/29952220.html.

On 25 June, a Court of Appeal reversed the lower court's ruling and Kocharyan was returned to custody.[50]

Another oppositionist benefited from the court's decisions. In June 2018, the Court of Cassation reversed Samvel Babayan's conviction on weapons smuggling and ordered his release from prison.[51] Within a year, Babayan announced he would be a candidate for the Armenian presidency in 2020. According to the head of national security for Karabakh Babayan advocated the return of the five provinces surrounding Karabakh to Azerbaijan. In return, Babayan wanted Karabakh to be an independent state under the tutelage of Russia.[52]

Pashinyan's hold on the country was shaken in November 2020, when he agreed to a Russian-brokered ceasefire with Azerbaijan that ratified the loss of most occupied lands in and around Karabakh. To avoid crowds of demonstrators, Pashinyan retreated to a hidden bunker.

Azerbaijan

As in Armenia, the Karabakh issue helped create a nationalist movement in Azerbaijan. The political leaders emerged from the various political movements of the late Soviet period. Ayaz Mutalibov was appointed first secretary of the Communist Party after the events of Black January in 1990. Mutalibov was a bold choice. Although he was a Moscow protégé and the informal leader of the Baku political clan, he belonged to neither the more powerful Karabakh clan or Nakhichevan clan of politicians.[53]

In August 1989, the Azerbaijan Popular Front (APF) declared a boycott of Armenia and a railway blockade of Armenia and Karabakh. The economic blockades would continue sporadically until the summer

[50] "Armenian Ex-President Kocharyan Back in Custody," Radio Free Europe/Radio Liberty, 25 June 2019. Web. Retrieved 3 July 2019. https://www.rferl.org/a/order-for-former-armenian-president-Kocharyan-to-be-arrested/30019317.html.

[51] "Former Karabakh Commander Samvel Babayan Freed by High Court," *Asbarez*, 15 June 2018. Web. Retrieved 22 July 2019. http://asbarez.com/172813/former-karabakh-commander-samvel-babayan-freed-by-high-court/?utm_source=feedburner&utm_medium=feed&utm_campaign=Feed%3A+Asbarez+%28Asbarez+News%29.

[52] "Tensions in Karabakh between Balasanyan and Babayan," Turan, 17 May 2019. Web. Retrieved 22 July 2019. http://www.turan.az/ext/news/2019/5/free/politics%20news/en/81067.htm.

[53] Remler, ibid., 34.

of 1991, when they were imposed permanently.[54] The APF was acquiring legitimacy as the Soviets cracked down on them in January of 1990, but they were not fast enough to defeat the entrenched elite in the Communist Party. Since Ayaz Mutalibov was the communist leader of the Azerbaijan SSR when the USSR collapsed, he was able to maintain his control on the reins of power as the new republic's first president until he bungled the government response to the Khojaly massacre of February 1992.

News of the massacre stunned the Azerbaijan capital of Baku. At first, the Mutalibov regime joined the Russians and Armenians in denying that a massacre had occurred. It would have been political suicide for President Mutalibov to admit he was incapable of stopping such an event. The Azerbaijani government delayed announcing the tragedy for two days. Finally, after eyewitness accounts began to surface, including video footage shown to the parliament of the body-strewn killing fields, the president was forced to resign.

Months later, Mutallibov acknowledged that one of his decisions had indirectly contributed to Khojaly: his refusal to create an Azerbaijan national army. He had been counting on the Kremlin creating an army with units from throughout the former Soviet Union, and hoped this central military force would restore order in the Caucasus.[55]

Parliament chose "Dollar Yaqub" as Mutallibov's successor. Yaqub Mammadov, rector of the state medical school, earned the sobriquet for his reputation of corruption. The speaker of the parliament called for new elections, scheduled for three months later.[56]

The fall of the Azerbaijani-inhabited Shusha on 8 May 1992, was a major event for Azerbaijan. Not only was it an important strategic town in Karabakh, it was the birthplace of much of Azerbaijani culture. Mutalibov took advantage of the situation and overthrew Mammadov. "If the times demand a dictator," he announced, "I will be that dictator." His second time in office lasted barely 24 hours. The following day, the ANF-controlled militia launched a countercoup and ended Mutalibov's attempt to regain power.

[54] Human Rights Watch, ibid., 2.

[55] Bolukbasi, ibid., 183.

[56] Laitin and Suny, ibid.

Parliament chose Isa Gamber as interim president and dissolved itself in anticipation of a new vote. Its powers were transferred to a new national council dominated by the APF. The council demanded the politicians fall in line. "Perhaps there are some deputies here from the provinces who do not understand what has transpired in Baku over the past few days," said Arif Hajiyev, a Popular Front deputy. "There has been a revolution here by the Popular Front. We are in control of the city and the country, so stop playing games and get down to work." As a face-saving concession, some members of the former Government were named to the National Council. But they were expected to remain only until a new government was formed.[57]

When the elections were held, the winner was a reluctant Abulfaz Elchibey.[58] At first, Elchibey had the support of the country's leaders. He was distinctly pro-Turkish and anti-Russian, sentiments that aligned well with Azerbaijan's position in the Karabakh war. He took Azerbaijan out of the Russian-dominated Commonwealth of Independent States (CIS). The rapid military losses in February 1993, however, caused a political crisis on the home front. Elchibey accused the area commander, Colonel Surat Huseynov, of ordering the withdrawal of heavy weapons and units from the Mardakert region, leaving the area inadequately defended. "The main reason for Kelbajar's surrender to the enemy was the failure of the troops to comply with the command headquarters orders to defend the city," declared the presidential press office.[59] Elchibey stripped Huseynov of his title of "Plenipotentiary Presidential Representative" and dismissed him from military service.[60]

Huseynov did not surrender his military power. He had previously moved his 709th Brigade to his native Ganja, and the troops under his command remained loyal to him. He was supported by the Russian 104th Airborne Regiment. When that unit announced in May 1993 that it was withdrawing from Azerbaijan, they left their weapons and munitions to Huseynov rather than to the central government in Baku.

57 "Azerbaijan Communists Yield to Nationalists," *The New York Times*, 20 May 1992. Web. Retrieved 23 May 2019. *Academic OneFile*, http://link.galegroup.com/apps/doc/A174868221/AONE?u=chap_main&sid=AONE&xid=0335bf1d.

58 Remler, ibid., 43.

59 Human Rights Watch, ibid., 27.

60 Human Rights Watch, ibid., 10.

His hold on Ganja was solid. When President Elchibey sent forces to disarm Huseynov, the commander of the Baku forces was set upon and beaten. With nothing holding him back, Huseynov marched on Baku. Shortly thereafter, in Lankaran region, military commander Aliakram Humbatov staged a rebellion and proclaimed a separatist "Talysh-Mugham Republic." He was supported by former defense minister Rahim Gaziev, who swore allegiance to Mutalibov. Any efforts to bring the first president back to power were short circuited, however, when Heydar Aliyev returned to the national scene. The Talysh-Mugham Republic collapsed within months without bloodshed.[61]

As Huseynov marched on the capital, Elchibey realized he needed a strongman to run the government. He turned to the man who had run Azerbaijan during the Soviet era, former Azerbaijan KGB Major General Heydar Aliyev. Over his career, Aliyev had been first secretary of the Central Committee of the Azerbaijan Communist Party, a member of the Soviet Politburo, and First Deputy Chairman of the Council of Ministers of the USSR. He was a power broker in both Baku and in Moscow. When Mikhail Gorbachev became Soviet Premier, he forced Aliyev into retirement in 1987. He remained in Moscow for three years before resigning from the Communist Party and returning to his native Nakhichevan in 1990. He was elected chairman of the Supreme Soviet of the Nakhichevan Autonomous Region. To the reformers of the APF, Aliyev represented a return to the Soviet era they had fought so hard to escape. But he also represented their best hope of holding the country together.

On 15 June, Aliyev was elected speaker of the Azerbaijan parliament. Three days later, Elchibey recognized that Huseynov would target him first for trying to strip him of his military post. Elchibey fled the capital for his native Nakhichevan. Parliament deposed Elchibey and Aliyev assumed the presidency. "Due to the inexplicable and unwarranted absence of the president and the severance of his connections with the state apparatus, I have assumed the duties and responsibilities of the presidency of Azerbaijan in accordance with the Constitution," Mr. Aliyev said in an address televised live to the nation. "I appeal to all citizens for unity and patience so that we together can seek a way out of the disaster facing our country." He appointed Huseynov as his new prime minister. A "no confidence" referendum removed Elchibey from his position. Then, on 3 October

[61] de Waal, ibid., 227.

1993 new presidential elections were held and Aliyev was elected the third president of Azerbaijan.

Aliyev used his extraordinary powers to disband 33 battalions loyal to the APF and turned to conscription to replace the lost manpower.[62] As for Huseynov himself, after running the power ministries of defense, internal affairs, and national security from his post as prime minister, he staged a failed coup in October 1994 and was consequently removed from power. He fled to Moscow accompanied by another imprisoned official, former Defense Minister Rahim Gaziev. They arrived in Moscow, where they declared their support for former president Mutalibov. Eventually, both men were extradited to Azerbaijan and given long prison sentences.[63]

There was another coup attempt on 13 March 1995, this time by Deputy Minister of the Interior Rovshan Javadov and a paramilitary group under his control, the OMAN. His brother Mahir, a prosecutor of one of Baku's districts, joined the coup attempt. Rovshan was killed and Mahir fled to Austria.

Aliyev enjoyed the support of the people, who respected him as an experienced politician. He signed a cease-fire with Armenia on 14 May 1994. This allowed Azerbaijan to focus on bringing stability to the country after years of chaos. His emphasis on economic development led to the September 1994 signing of the "Contract of the Century" with western energy companies. Azerbaijan also renewed its ties with Russia and rejoined the CIS.

Aliyev was reelected in October 1998. In July 2003, Aliyev was taken to a hospital in Turkey. He was transferred to Cleveland in August. On 4 August, the Azerbaijani parliament approved the appointment of Heydar Aliyev's son, Ilham, as prime minister. Ilham was then elected president in October with almost 80% of the vote. His father passed away two months later on 12 December 2003.

The Ilham Aliyev years have been mostly peaceful on the domestic front. The town of Nardaran was the exception to the rule. This bastion of radical Shi'a Muslims was rocked in 2015 by a series of riots. It began in January 2015 when young Shi'a clerics such as Taleh Bagirzade and Elcin Gassymly founded the Muslim Unity Movement (MUM). The clerics had lived in Iran and were supporters of Khomeinism—the idea that a radical

[62] de Waal, ibid., 238.

[63] de Waal, ibid., 262–263.

revolutionary ideology based on Islam should be directed toward social and governmental change rather than individual spiritual fulfillment. By November 2015, the MUM had armed itself with illegal weapons and led violent demonstrations in the town. Officials at the scene claimed someone inside a house opened fire on police. At some point, a grenade was thrown. In the end, six people were dead, two of them police officers, and 15 men were in custody.[64] Security forces sealed off the town until order could be restored.[65]

Bagirzade was arrested at the time of the demonstrations, but the story did not end there. Authorities in Baku claimed that the town's residents planned an armed coup and were working with a foreign power (probably Iran but unnamed for diplomatic reasons) against Azerbaijan's national security interests. In early January 2016, the head of the town's council of elders, Natig Karimov, was arrested on charges of treason and espionage. The following week, authorities arrested over 60 individuals.[66]

Voters approved a package of 29 constitutional amendments by 86.6% in September 2016. They included an extension of the president's term in office from 5 to 7 years, granted the president the power to dissolve parliament, and eliminated the requirement that a citizen must be at least 35 years old to run for president. They also created vice presidential posts, to be appointed and dismissed by the president, with the first vice-president authorized to assume presidential powers in the event the president is absent or incapable of discharging his duties. President Aliyev then appointed the person he trusted the most to the position of first vice president, his wife Mehriban Aliyeva.[67] The UNESCO and ISESCO Goodwill Ambassador Aliyeva was already deputy chairwoman of the ruling New Azerbaijan Party, and head of the country's largest NGO—the Heydar Aliyev Foundation. "Aliyeva has been playing an

[64] Runey, Mike. "Azerbaijan's Nardaran Affair," Open Democracy, 24 August 2016. Web. Retrieved 30 July 2019. https://www.opendemocracy.net/en/odr/nardaran-affair/.

[65] Mamedov, Eldar. "Azerbaijan: Examining the Source of Discontent in Nardaran," Eurasianet, 8 December 2015. Web. Retrieved 30 July 2019. https://eurasianet.org/azerbaijan-examining-the-source-of-discontent-in-nardaran.

[66] Lomsadze, Giorgi. "Azerbaijan: More Trouble in Nardaran," Eurasianet, 11 January 2016. Web. Retrieved 30 July 2019. https://eurasianet.org/azerbaijan-more-trouble-in-nardaran.

[67] "Azeri President Appoints Wife as First-Vice President," *Hurriyet Daily News*, 21 February 2017. Web. Retrieved 31 July 2019. http://www.hurriyetdailynews.com/azeri-president-appoints-wife-as-first-vice-president-109997.

important role in social, political, cultural and international activities for many years," the president said. "In general, her multifaceted activities have been successful. I have taken into account exactly these factors when making the decision to appoint her to the post of the first vice president of Azerbaijan."[68]

In the 2018 presidential election, the opposition coalition National Council of Democratic forces announced they would boycott the election,[69] most likely because they did not want their electoral weakness exposed to the public. Despite President Aliyev's occasional amnesties, international human rights groups pressed the government for more meaningful, consistent, and substantive political reforms.

Even though there were seven other candidates in the race, Human Rights Watch complained that the voters had not been offered a viable choice.[70] The election commission certified the turnout at 75%, with Aliyev receiving 86.09% of the vote. The president was reelected in a landslide.[71]

Nagorno Karabakh

Little is known in the West about political developments inside Nagorno-Karabakh since it is not recognized as an independent state, is totally dependent on Armenia for its existence, and is not a party to peace negotiations. In 1992, the "parliament" gave Robert Kocharyan, as leader of the State Committee for Defense, plenipotentiary powers. Kocharyan ruled with the support of the ANM. He soon sidelined his main opposition, the Dashnaks. The "parliament" then elected Kocharyan de facto president of Nagorno-Karabakh on 22 December 1994. This was later confirmed in

[68] "Aliyev Appoints Wife as First-Vice President of Azerbaijan," Radio Free Europe/Radio Liberty, 21 February 2017. Web. Retrieved 31 July 2019. https://www.rferl.org/a/azerbaijan-aliyev-names-wife-aliyeva-vice-president/28322210.html.

[69] "Azerbaijani Opposition Coalition to Boycott Early Presidential Election," Radio Free Europe/Radio Liberty, 6 February 2018. Web. Retrieved 30 July 2019. https://www.rferl.org/a/azerbaijan-opposition-boycott-early-presidential-election/29021979.html.

[70] "Azerbaijan's President Aliyev Set to Win Fourth Term As Polls Close," Radio Free Europe/Radio Liberty, 11 April 2018. Web. Retrieved 31 July 2019. https://www.rferl.org/a/azerbaijan-aliyev-expected-win-reelection-april-11-vote/29158177.html.

[71] Bagirova, Naila. "Azerbaijan's Aliyev Wins Fourth Term as President," Reuters, 11 April 2018. Web. Retrieved 31 July 2018. https://www.reuters.com/article/us-azerbaijan-election/azerbaijans-aliyev-wins-fourth-term-as-president-idUSKBN1HH3CJ.

November 1996 by a popular vote of those residents who remained in Karabakh.

He did not remain long in the position. Seeking to broaden his political base, Armenian president Levon Ter-Petrosyan reached into Karabakh in March 1997 and appointed Kocharyan prime minister of Armenia. In Karabakh, the people felt abandoned. Kocharyan's post was filled in September with the election of Arkady Ghukasian who received 85% of the vote. Condemnation of an illegal election was expected from Azerbaijan; more surprising was Russia's condemnation.

Wartime commander Samvel Babayan had become rather wealthy. He controlled companies that had become leading importers of gasoline and tobacco products in Armenia and Babayan had used Karabakh Army military trucks to transport the cargo. In addition, Babayan meddled in the government affairs in Karabakh, forcing then-Prime Minister Leonard Petrossian to resign in June 1998. He was succeeded by a Babayan ally, Zhirayr Pogossian, who was forced out of office after bugging devices were found in Ghukasian's office.

Babayan also involved himself in Armenian politics, funding the parliamentary campaigns of two political parties in May 1999. Ghukasian and his allies were displeased, and in June 1999, Ghukasian removed him from his position of "defense minister" and later commander of the army.[72]

In March 2000, Babayan was involved in the attempted assassination of Ghukasian who was seriously wounded in the attack. The authorities arrested Babayan in the aftermath and sentenced to 14 years in prison. Babayan was released from prison in September 2004 for health reasons, after which he entered politics in Karabakh and later Armenia.

In June 2000, Karabakh held unrecognized parliamentary elections. According to the Central Election Commission, there was a 60% turnout in the election. The Artsakh Union movement (supporters of Ghukasian) won 13 seats, ARF (Dashnaks) 9, independents 10, and the Armenicam Party 1. No serious problems were reported. It was the first election in which the Dashnaks had participated, as they had been outlawed in

[72] "The Rise and Fall of Samvel Babayan," Armenian News Network, 6 October 2004. Web. Retrieved 2 August 2019. http://groong.usc.edu/ro/ro-20041006.html.

the 1995 elections. With Babayan temporarily out of the picture, the Dashnaks became the leading opposition party.[73]

Ghukasian was reelected on 12 August 2002 with 89% of the vote. His closest competitor, Artur Tovmasian, received just 8%. Voter turnout was 75%.[74] According to the Nagorno-Karabakh "constitution," Ghukasian could only serve two terms so this would be his last election.

In August 2004, the opposition Movement-88 candidate Eduard Aghabekian scored a major success by winning the Stepanakert mayoralty. They were unable to capitalize on the momentum, however. In the fourth "parliamentary" elections held in June 2005, the main opposition bloc uniting the Karabakh branch of the ARF and the Movement-88 party won only three seats. Political parties loyal to "president" Ghukasian won a surprise landslide victory, winning nearly two-thirds of the vote. Preliminary results released by Karabakh's Central Election Commission (CEC) on Monday showed Ghukasian's Democratic Party of Artsakh winning 12 out of the 33 seats in the unrecognized republic's legislature. The Free Fatherland party, an obscure pro-establishment group, finished second with 10 seats. Eight other seats were won by individual candidates not affiliated with any party. Most of them were also thought to be loyal to Ghukasian. The CEC put the voter turnout at 78%.[75]

Ghukasian chose as his successor former National Security Service chief Bako Sahakyan who was elected in 2007 with 85% of the vote. Supposedly Bako also had the support of both the Russian and Armenian governments. He was reelected in 2012 on a platform of continuity in pursuing independence and development.[76] He extended his rule in 2017 when Karabakh adopted a new "constitution." "Parliament" extended his term of office for a three-year transition period as the enclave moves to a strong

[73] "Nagorno Karabakh Parliamentary Election, 18 June 2000," BHHRG, date unknown. Web. Retrieved 2 August 2019. http://www.bhhrgarchive.org/Countries/Nagorno%20Karabakh/Nagorno%20Karabakh%20parliamentary%20election%202000.pdf.

[74] "Nagorno Karabakh," Freedom House, 2007. Web. Retrieved 2 August 2019. https://freedomhouse.org/report/freedom-world/2007/nagorno-karabakh.

[75] "Ruling Party Wins Karabakh Vote Amid Opposition Outcry." Azatutyun, 20 June 2005. Web. Retrieved 2 August 2019. https://www.azatutyun.am/a/1577392.html.

[76] Hale, Henry E. *Patronal Politics* (Cambridge University Press, 2015), 302–304.

presidential system. He has declared he will not run for reelection in 2020.[77]

Voters in Karabakh went to the polls on 23 May 2010 to elect their fifth "parliament" since the early 1990s. Results published by the Karabakh "Central Election Commission" (CEC) on May 24 showed Karabakh "Prime Minister" Ara Harutiunian's Free Fatherland party leading the vote with some 47%. "Parliament speaker" Ashot Ghulian's Democratic Party of Artsakh and the Armenian Revolutionary Federation (Dashnaktsutyun) garnered some 32 and 24% of the vote, respectively. The Communist Party reportedly failed to clear the 6% hurdle, which is required under Karabakh's election laws to enter the legislature. More than 70% of some 95,000 eligible voters turned out to vote in the elections, according to the CEC. Four political parties with a total of 82 candidates were vying for 17 parliamentary seats. The remaining seats in the 33-seat body were contested by 44 candidates in single-mandate constituencies.[78]

The sixth "parliamentary" election was held on 3 May 2015. Seven parties participated in the vote, and five passed the threshold to gain seats. Results were similar to the 2010 elections, but not identical. Prime Minister Arayik Harutyunyan's Free Motherland party maintained its dominant position in the legislature, winning 15 seats. Fellow coalition partners ARF and the Democratic Party of Artsakh gained seven and six seats, respectively. The big difference from the previous election was that two opposition parties gained representation—Movement 88 gained three seats, while National Revival captured one. An independent candidate won the remaining seat.[79]

Elections in Nagorno-Karabakh have never been recognized internationally. Azerbaijan and the European Court of Human Rights believe

[77] "Artsakh President Bako Sahakyan Not to Seek Reelection in 2020," *Armenian Weekly*, 12 June 2018. Web. Retrieved 2 August 2019. https://armenianweekly.com/2018/06/12/artsakh-president-bako-sahakyan-not-to-seek-reelection-in-2020/.

[78] "Armenia Praises Karabakh Parliamentary Elections," Radio Free Europe/Radio Liberty, 25 May 2010. Web. Retrieved 2 August 2019. https://www.rferl.org/a/Armenia_Praises_Karabakh_Parliamentary_Elections/2052293.html.

[79] "Freedom in the World 2016-Nagorno Karabakh," Freedom House, 18 August 2016. Web. Retrieved 2 August 2019. https://www.refworld.org/docid/57bc4f2fe.html.

that Armenia effectively controls the occupied territories.[80] Despite some disagreements between Stepanakert and Yerevan, the governments are strategically united in a quest for unification. In August 2019 Armenian President Pashinyan visited Stepanakert and stated "Artsakh is Armenia, and that's it." In doing so, Pashyinyan confirmed his commitment to "miatsum" (unification in Armenian), the goal of Armenian nationalists since it was first voiced in February 1988.[81]

Conclusion

Neither Armenia nor Azerbaijan meet Western standards as democracies. This should surprise no one, since both remain on a war footing. When a people feel threatened by an outside enemy, they seek a leader who exhibits strength and who promises them security. Since 1991, that has meant rule in Armenia by the leaders of the Karabakh military, in Azerbaijan by Aliyevs, and in Karabakh by individuals supported by the government of Armenia.

In the two internationally recognized countries, the war has functioned as a legitimating force. Armenia consciously used the cause of Nagorno-Karabakh to build its sense of identity. Azerbaijan had the war foisted upon it by its neighbor, and its political identity has been formed in opposition to the invaders. As a result, both sides tend to take maximalist positions on what is required to end the war. This makes compromise difficult and the continuation of the status quo more palatable.

[80] Chiragov and Others v. Armenia, European Court of Human Rights, 16 June 2015. Web. Retrieved 3 June 2020. https://hudoc.echr.coe.int/eng#{%22itemid%22:[%22001-155353%22]}.

[81] Kucera, Joshua. "Pashinyan Calls for Unification Between Armenia and Karabakh," Eurasianet, 6 August 2019. Web. Retrieved 4 December 2019. https://eurasianet.org/pashinyan-calls-for-unification-between-armenia-and-karabakh.

CHAPTER 4

The Economics of Frozen Conflict

Introduction

There are only two economic stories in this conflict, that of the Republics of Armenia and Azerbaijan. The separatist enclave of Nagorno-Karabakh is cut off from the international economy, and totally dependent on subsidies from the Republic of Armenia and from the Armenian diaspora. It has no real, independent economic life.

As for the two republics, their economic stories are polar opposites. The history of the Armenian economy is the story of an agrarian country trying to survive in a hostile environment. Cut off in the west by Turkey and in the east by Azerbaijan, it must rely on economic ties with Georgia, Iran, and Russia. Georgia is almost as impoverished as Armenia and provides little help to the economy (other than as a window to the West). Iran has supported Armenia in its struggle with Azerbaijan and, as an oil-producing country, could provide investments in the country—but they do not. The major investor is Russia. Over time, Russia has purchased all of Armenia's major assets. The interconnection between Armenia and Russia is so complete that it is almost impossible to separate the economic parts of the alliance from the diplomatic or the military.

Azerbaijan, by contrast, became a regional economic powerhouse commencing in 2006 when it began marketing its offshore oil to the West. Balancing this Western economic orientation with an eastern-leaning diplomatic/military perspective, the Baku-Ceyhan pipeline has

J. J. Coyle, *Russia's Interventions in Ethnic Conflicts*,
https://doi.org/10.1007/978-3-030-59573-9_4

given the country the economic power to avoid falling totally into the Russian or Iranian orbit. As its oil production begins to decline, Azerbaijan is devoting itself to developing a post-petroleum economy by producing natural gas and by becoming a transportation hub. The economic costs of the conflict with Armenia are the massive weapons purchases from Russia and other countries, and the cost of housing almost a million internally displaced people or refugees who fled either Nagorno-Karabakh or Armenia.

Armenia

The story of the Armenian economy has been one of slow growth. GDP has risen from \$2.26 billion in 1990 to \$11.54 billion in 2017, one-seventh that of neighboring Azerbaijan. Life expectancy has increased from 68 to 75 in the same period.[1] GDP per capita has risen from \$195.88 in 1994 to \$3872 in 2017. The rate has gone from almost double Azerbaijan at the time of independence to approximately 25% less. Unemployment rates tell a similar story: rising from 14.7% in 2008 to 16.9% in December 2018. Unemployment peaked in 2011 at 20.7%.[2] Human Rights Watch reported that the most telling indicator of the toll the war and embargo had on life in Armenia was the willingness of people to leave it. They estimated 20% of Armenia's population of three million had deserted the country in the twelve months before the end of the war in May 1994.[3]

The country was so poor that the major economic moves that began in 1994 were a fire sale of Armenian assets. In February, it signed a bilateral barter deal with the Russians for vital resources.[4] The Metsamor nuclear power plant, closed since the 1988 earthquake since it is located on an earthquake fault, was reopened in 1995 because of Armenia's need for an energy supply. To achieve this goal, Russia and Armenia agreed in March 1994 that the plant would be jointly operated. Four months later,

[1] "Country Profile, Armenia," The World Bank. Web. Retrieved 26 June 2019. https://databank.worldbank.org/views/reports/reportwidget.aspx?Report_Name=CountryProfile&Id=b450fd57&tbar=y&dd=y&inf=n&zm=n&country=ARM.

[2] "Armenia," CEIC. Web. Retrieved 26 June 2019. https://www.ceicdata.com/en/country/armenia.

[3] Human Rights Watch, ibid., 130.

[4] "Armenia Relations with Russia," GlobalSecurity.org, ibid.

Russia lent Armenia 100 billion rubles, approximately $35 million, to reactivate the station. Russia then provided on credit to the facility the nuclear fuel it needed. When the country proved unable to pay back the money, in 2003 the Russian energy company RAO United Energy Systems took over Metsamor's finances, as well as the ownership of Armenia's five hydroelectric plants.[5] In March 2014, Russia gave Armenia a loan of $270 million and a grant of $30 million to upgrade part of the plant and extend its life.[6]

Other parts of the energy grid fell into the hands of Russia throughout 2003–2006 in a series of asset for debt agreements, including the Armenian electrical and gas grids. Gazprom gained 100% ownership of the natural gas pipelines by 2014.[7] Russian giant Vympelcom purchased the Armentel telecommunications company from its Greek owner Hellenic Telecommunications in 2006. It thus gained control of Armenia's fixed-line telephony network, as well as 40–50% of the mobile phone network. Russia's Comstar Telesystems acquired Armenia's telecommunications company CallNet and its subsidiary, the Internet service provider Cornet, the second-largest telecommunications group in Armenia. Russia's state-owned Foreign Trade Bank (Vneshtorgbank) acquired 70% of the shares of Armenia's Saving Bank, which became Vneshtorgbank Armenia. The Yerevan-based ArmenAl, a major producer of aluminum foil, idled in the 1990s, was acquired in 2002 by RusAl.[8]

During his last press conference before the end of his posting in April 2005, Russian Ambassador to Armenia Anatoliy Dryukov cited the large

[5] "Russian Utility Wants to Stop Managing Armenian Nuclear Plant," Radio Free Europe/Radio Liberty, 25 November 2011. Web. Retrieved 8 July 2019. https://www.rferl.org/a/russian_utility_wants_to_stop_managing_armenian_nuclear_plant/24402275.html.

[6] "Armenia and Russia Discussed Modernization of Metsamor Nuclear Power Plant," ARKA News Agency, 12 March 2019. Web. Retrieved 8 July 2019. http://arka.am/en/news/technology/armenia_and_russia_discussed_modernization_of_metsamor_nuclear_power_plant/.

[7] "Gazprom Increasing Its Stake in ArmRosgazprom to 100 Per cent," Gazprom Press Release, 20 January 2014. Net. Retrieved 8 July 2019. http://www.gazprom.com/press/news/2014/january/article182633/.

[8] Socor, Vladimir. "Armenia Selling More Infrastructure, Industry to Russia," *Jamestown Foundation Eurasia Daily Monitor* 3/206, 7 November 2006. Web. Retrieved 8 July 2019. https://jamestown.org/program/armenia-selling-more-infrastructure-industry-to-russia/#.VWWqxc-qqkp.

influx of Russian capital to Armenia, saying that Russia had invested more than USD 300 million in Armenia since independence. Dryukov explained that Russian capital was behind nine of Armenia's 20 banks and made up one-third of the total authorized capital stock of Armenia's banking system. A significant proportion of the investments that Dryukov mentioned were made by Russian firms that were largely state-owned and have Russian government seats on the board.[9]

After a decade of ownership, however, some Russian companies decided to monetize their holdings. Inter RAO, a subsidiary of RAO United Energy Systems, pulled out in 2015, selling Armenia's electrical distribution network to the Tashir Group. This is a group of companies controlled by an Armenian billionaire, Samvel Karapetian. An American corporation, Contour Global, took over the country's largest hydroelectric complex from RusHydro.[10] Even with the changes in ownership in these companies, however, Russia continued to be the source of 80% of the nation's energy supply.

Russia provided Armenia another loan in 2009 to help weather the global recession. Experts debated whether Russia would demand an asset swap for repayment but, as one Armenian government official said, there was nothing left to sell.[11] The government found something in 2015, however, when it sold to Gazprom its section (41 kilometers) of an Iranian gas export pipeline. The decision left Moscow in full control of natural gas supply routes to Armenia.[12]

The final indicator of Armenia's total economic subservience to the Kremlin is the story of how Armenia joined the Eurasian Economic Union (EEU). In July 2013, Yerevan completed technical talks on a "deep and comprehensive free-trade agreement" (DCFTA) with the European Union (EU). In addition to the free trade deal, Armenia was working toward the signing of an association agreement, a framework agreement on cooperation that was seen as a first step toward political integration

[9] GlobalSecurity, ibid.

[10] Danielyan, Emil. "U.S. Takeover of Armenian Power Plants Completed," Radio Free Europe/Radio Liberty, 8 May 2015. Web. Retrieved 8 July 2019. https://www.azatutyun.am/a/27002502.html.

[11] GlobalSecurity, ibid.

[12] "Armenia to Sell Iran Gas Pipeline to Gazprom," Press TV, 5 June 2015. Web. Retrieved 22 July 2019. https://www.presstv.com/Detail/2015/06/05/414428/Iran-gas-armenia-pipeline-ga.

with the EU. Ukraine was also working on the association agreement and the DCFTA. On 14 August, however, Russian officials announced custom checks on Ukrainian goods. They added such restrictions could become permanent if Ukraine signed the agreements with the EU.[13] While the direct threat was to Ukraine, Armenia could also see the possible Russian retaliation for too close a relationship with the Europeans. Two weeks later, Putin asked for a meeting with President Sargsyan in Moscow. What exactly was said at the meeting remains unknown, but immediately afterward Sargsyan announced that Armenia was joining the EEU. To avoid the immediate impact of accompanying price increases, the government negotiated with the EEU an initial grace period, which began in 2015 and will end in 2022.[14] Even more difficult for Yerevan than increased prices, Nagorno-Karabakh could not follow them into the Union because neither Armenia nor member states recognized Nagorno-Karabakh as a state.

Over the previous three years all statements by Armenian government officials, from President Sargsyan to Prime Minister Tigran Sargsyan, as well as numerous statements by the Foreign Ministry, pointed toward Armenia's initialing of the EU Association Agreement. Moreover, throughout this period Armenian legislators had drafted and passed European financed reforms aimed at increasing compliance with the EU's Association Agreement requirements—reforms that were already being undertaken. The decision to abandon the ties with Europe after a single hour meeting with President Putin thus came as a surprise to all, even Sargsyan's innermost circle.[15] According to the Economist, the decision

[13] Gardner, Andrew. "Armenia Chooses Russia over EU," *Politico*, 3 September 2013. Web. Retrieved 9 July 2019. https://www.politico.eu/article/armenia-chooses-russia-over-eu/.

[14] Chilingaryan, Aharon and Anahit Simonyan. "Armenia-Changes in the Customs Duty Rates for Armenia within the EEU," BDO, March 2019. Web. Retrieved 9 July 2019. https://www.bdo.global/en-gb/microsites/tax-newsletters/indirect-tax-news/issue-1-2019/armenia-changes-in-the-customs-duty-rates-for-armenia-within-the-eeu.

[15] Dergrigorian, Babken. "Armenia's Membership in the EEU Raises More Questions than it Answers," Asbarez, 17 October 2014. Web. Retrieved 9 July 2019. http://asbarez.com/127993/armenias-membership-in-the-eeu-raises-more-questions-than-it-answers/.

to join the EEU was taken under duress, as Russia threatened to reconsider its alliance if Armenia signed an association agreement with the European Union.[16]

To some, the choice of Russia over Brussels was logical. Economist Hamlet Tadevosyan pointed out that 90% of Armenian companies did not meet European standards.[17] While it is impossible to predict how little or how much the Armenian economy would have grown with an association with the EU, the economy has improved since it joined the EEU. Ashot Tavadyan, the head of the Department of Economic and Mathematical Methods at the State Economic University of Armenia, said that exports grew by 50% in 2016 and 2017. He attributed the growth to preferential prices for energy resources Armenia receives from Russia and deepening economic integration within EEU. In 2017 alone, Armenia managed to save $60 million on exports to EEU member countries.[18] President Sargsyan supported the idea. "One-third of Armenia's exports go to Russia and its partners, including agricultural products on which thousands of jobs depend," he said. "In addition, Russia sells natural gas to landlocked, energy-poor Armenia at quite a good price."

Others, however, disagreed that growth in the Armenian economy is the result of EEU membership. There is no common land border between Armenia and the other members of the EEU, and free trade within the CIS was already in force before creation of the economic zone.[19] According to Armenia's official statistics bureau, exports to the EU in 2014 surpassed those to Russia and fellow EEU members Belarus and Kazakhstan (28.8–21.4%).[20] By January 2018, after three years in the

[16] "Stuck with Each Other," *Economist*, 20 May 2015. Web. Retrieved 9 July 2019. https://www.economist.com/europe/2015/03/20/stuck-with-each-other.

[17] "Expert: Armenia EEU Accession Did Not Create Economic Problems for Country," News.am, unknown date. Web. Retrieved 9 July 2019. https://news.am/eng/news/266563.html.

[18] "Armenia saved $60 Million Due to Membership in EEU," ARKA News Agency, 26 February 2018. Web. Retrieved 9 July 2019. http://arka.am/en/news/economy/armenia_saved_60_million_due_to_membership_in_eeu/.

[19] "Armenia and EEU: Yerevan Approves Draft Treaty Ahead of Signing Slated for Next Week," Armenia Now, unknown date. Web. Retrieved 9 July 2019. https://www.armenianow.com/commentary/analysis/57324/armenia_eurasian_union_government_treaty.

[20] "Armenia: Trying to Break Free of Economic Dependence on Russia?" EurasiaNet, 19 May 2015. Web. Retrieved 22 July 2019. https://eurasianet.org/armenia-trying-to-break-free-of-economic-dependence-on-russia.

union, exports to Russia had not increased and investments in Armenia dropped by around 60%. In addition, to protect their own labor force, Russia closed itself off to Armenian products and workers in many parts of the economy. Russia increased excise duties on alcohol, and even revoked the validity of Armenian drivers licenses in Russia. Gazprom's monopoly on gas supplies and pricing meant that Armenia was paying twice as much as Ukraine for natural gas.[21]

The decision to abandon Europe in favor of the EEU was not a popular one. In 2018, the Analytical Center on Globalization and Regional Cooperation, in combination with the National Endowment for Democracy, published a poll of the Armenian people. It found 57.67% of Armenian citizens believed membership in the EEU had a negative impact on the country, and 78.67% disagreed with Armenia's refusal to sign an Association Agreement with the European Union. Most citizens (58.89%) believed that the future of Armenia was linked to Europe, and 88.67% felt positively toward active Armenian-EU relations. Only 34.3% responded positively that Russia was an ally of Armenia, and 56.33% said Russia had a negative impact on the settlement of the conflict in Nagorno-Karabakh. In case of war with Azerbaijan, only 31.22% of respondents believed that the CSTO would support Armenia, while a full 63.4% believed the CSTO would not.[22]

Armenian NGOs and opposition parties were not happy with the decision to join the Eurasian Economic Union. "At a time when our partner Russia is isolated and there's no hope that it will enter into constructive dialogue with the West, we are planning to join a union that is under sanctions," said former foreign minister Alexander Arzumanyan. The Association of Informed Citizens' Daniel Ionesyan said the agreement violated the Armenian constitution, because it meant Yerevan was entrusting its entire taxation and trade policy to Moscow. "We will cease to be an independent state with regard to our foreign trade policy," he

[21] Grigoryan, Stepan. "Opinion: Armenia's U-turn Back to 'Multi-vector Foreign Policy,'" OC Media, 12 January 2018. Web. Retrieved 28 July 2019. http://oc-media.org/armenias-u-turn-back-to-multi-vector-foreign-policy/.

[22] "Analysis of Policies of Political Parties and Public Sector in Armenia Regarding the EU, NATO, CSTO as well as EEU and Results of the Public Opinion Poll," Analytical Center on Globalization and Regional Cooperation, February 2018, 34–35. Web. Retrieved 22 July 2019. http://www.encouncil.org/wp-content/uploads/2018/02/Analysis-of-Political-Parties%E2%80%99-Policies-and-Public-Sector-Opinions-in-Armenia-regarding-the-EU-NATO-CSTO-and-the-EEU.pdf.

said. "For instance, we will have to obtain Moscow's approval before starting negotiations with the World Trade Organization or with other countries." The director of the Centre for National and International Studies in Yerevan, Manvel Sargsyan, saw the process as a gradual ceding of sovereignty to Russia. "The Eurasian Economic Union is a wholly political process," he said, "a Russian geopolitical mechanism for the post-Soviet region."[23]

Armenian Prime Minister Nikol Pashinyan's position on EEU membership changed over the years. When he was a member of the opposition, he repeatedly spoke out against the country's membership in the EEU, claiming Armenia had been forced to join it. In September 2017, his party Yelk submitted a motion asking the National Assembly to terminate Armenia's membership in the EEU. Once elected Pashinyan's position began to transform. On 24 April 2018, he stated the issue of Armenia's withdrawal from the EEU could be decided only by referendum. The following month at a meeting of the Supreme Eurasian Council, Pashinyan said Armenia was interested in the expansion of trade and economic cooperation within EEU. Finally, at a meeting with Russian President Putin on 27 December Pashinyan said that Armenia was committed to further integration within the framework of the Eurasian Economic Union.[24]

In January 2015, the credit agency Moody's downgraded Armenia's issuer and government bond rating to Ba3 from Ba2 and changed the outlook to negative from stable. Moody's also lowered the local-currency bond and deposit ceilings to Ba1 from Baa3, the foreign currency bond ceiling to Ba2 from Ba1, as well as the foreign currency deposit ceiling to B1 from Ba3. The short-term foreign currency bond ceiling and the foreign currency deposit ceiling remained at NP. Moody's reasoned that remittances represented about 15% of Armenia's GDP, with over 90% of total remittances coming from Russia. Moody's was predicting a sharp recession in Russia, with a falloff in this level of remittances.

[23] "Armenia's Eurasian Deal: Sell-out or Fair Trade?" Eurasia Review, 27 October 2014. IWPR. Web. Retrieved 28 July 2019. https://iwpr.net/global-voices/armenias-eurasian-deal-sell-out-or-fair-trade.

[24] "Armenian Parliament Creates Standing Committee to Address Issues Stemming from Armenia's Membership in EEU," ARKA News Agency, 16 January 2019. Web. Retrieved 9 July 2019. https://arka.am/en/news/economy/armenian_parliament_creates_standing_committee_to_address_issues_stemming_from_armenia_s_membership_/.

This would put pressure on the country's balance of payments which would then negatively impact Armenia's foreign currency reserves, and 83% of Armenia's government debt was denominated in foreign currency. With Armenia depreciating its currency over 15% in the previous two months, there would be a great deal more pressure put on the foreign currency reserves. Moody's was also influenced by the country's impaired growth outlook, compounded by negative growth spillovers from Russia, weak investment activity, and constraints on trade with countries outside the Eurasian Economic Union (EEU). Further exacerbating the slowing dynamics for potential growth—excepting some more active sectors such as the information technology industry—were Armenia's weak investment activity, its slow productivity growth since the global financial crisis, and its adverse net migration dynamics.[25]

As the economy continued to deteriorate, a number of other companies decided to close their business operations. These non-European companies included the UAE's Etihad Airways, South Korea's Samsung, and the EU's Orange telecom company (France). Armenia pretended it didn't matter. "Companies come and go every day," said Minister of Economy Karen Chshmaritian.[26]

To try to maintain a balance between East and West, Armenia and the European Union finally signed a Comprehensive and Enhanced Partnership Agreement (CEPA) at the fifth Eastern Partnership summit in Brussels, on 24 November 2017. It took nearly two years of consultations and negotiations to conclude the agreement, but it lacked the free trade zone that the EU had offered in 2013.[27] As a result, membership in CEPA provides no economic benefit to the country.

Moscow's favored position had begun to change with the 2018 Velvet Revolution. Russia looked askance at all color revolutions, perceiving them to be part of a Western plot against the Kremlin. In this case,

[25] "Rating Action: Moody's Downgrades Armenian Government Bond Rating to Ba3 from Ba2, and Changes Outlook to Negative from Stable," Moody's, 15 January 2015. Web. Retrieved 8 July 2019. https://www.moodys.com/research/Moodys-downgrades-Armenias-government-bond-rating-to-Ba3-from-Ba2--PR_316326.

[26] Harutyunan, Sargis. "Armenia Plays Down Departure of International Businesses," Radio Free Europe/Radio Liberty, 30 July 2015. Web. Retrieved 22 July 2019. https://www.refworld.org/docid/55ee963713.html.

[27] Grigoryan, Armen. "Armenia and EU Sign New Partnership Agreement," *Jamestown Foundation Eurasia Daily Monitor* 14/156, 4 December 2017. Web. Retrieved 9 July 2019. https://jamestown.org/program/armenia-eu-sign-new-partnership-agreement/.

however, even though it remained silent on the outcome, Moscow was more unhappy than usual. Their staunch ally Serzh Sargsyan was forced to resign. Then, under the guise of fighting corruption, Prime Minister Pashinyan prosecuted other Kremlin allies such as former President Robert Kocharyan and former army chief and later commander in chief of the CSTO Yuri Khachaturov. There were other problems in the relationship, such as snap Russian military drills near the Armenian village of Panik, as well as the December 2018 murder of an Armenian woman in Gyumri by a Russian soldier.

All this led to disagreements in other traditionally strong areas of Russian-Armenian cooperation, including the energy sector. In the anti-corruption campaign launched by Prime Minister Pashinyan, the Armenian State Revenue Committee audited Gazprom Armenia, a subsidiary of Russia's Gazprom. The inspection revealed numerous violations, ultimately prompting prosecutors to press charges of tax evasion against the Russian gas giant. Russia then increased the price of natural gas from $150 per thousand cubic meters (tcm) in 2018 to $165 per tcm in 2019, disappointing Armenian officials who had previously expressed hope that Russia would actually lower the cost of natural gas.[28]

Pashinyan tried to smooth things over with multiple visits to the Kremlin. His relationship with Putin seemed proper; he had less luck with many in Putin's orbit. During a visit to Moscow in September 2018, he met with Ruben Vardanyan, a Russian-Armenian billionaire businessman-philanthropist. Vardanyan called Pashinyan "disrespectful" for closing down the Center for Strategic Initiatives, a government-run effort to attract foreign investment with which Vardanyan has worked. Vardanyan had termed the success of the Center to be vital to Armenia and to Nagorno-Karabakh. "You have the right to do whatever you want with your organization," he told Pashinyan, "but if it's created jointly with the private sector, and you do not even ask before closing it, but you (should) notify us. To say the least this is disrespectful." An unspoken issue was probably Vardanyan's relationship with former president Sargsyan whose allies had been defeated in the election that brought Pashinyan to power.[29]

[28] "What the Chill in Russian-Armenian Relations Means," STRATFOR, 21 January 2019. Ibid.

[29] Mejluman, Ani. "In Moscow Pashinyan Gets Along with Putin, Clashes with Russian-Armenian Philanthropist," Eurasianet, 10 September 2018. Web. Retrieved

Economic Ties Between Armenia and Iran

From the beginning of Armenia and Azerbaijan's independence, Iran wanted an economic partner on its northern border. When the West squeezed it out of participation in the Baku-Ceyhan pipeline consortium, it had few options. It followed balance of power tactics and aligned with the weaker side in the conflict between the two Caucasus states. While it did not usually engage militarily with either side, it became an indispensable economic partner for Armenia. Prime Minister Hrant Bagratyan signed a number of economic cooperation agreements with Tehran in May 1995, including deals to provide energy-starved Armenia with natural gas and electricity for 20 years. Three weeks later, it temporarily cut energy supplies to Nakhichevan—the Azerbaijani exclave surrounded on three sides by Armenia.[30]

Armenia looked to Iran as one of two windows to the outside world (since the Turkish and Azerbaijani borders were closed). Armenian Prime Minister Nikol Pashinyan told US national security advisor John Bolton that special relations with Iran were in Armenia's national interest because, along with Georgia, it was one of Armenia's only gateways to the outside world.[31]

Russia opposed closer relations between Iran and Armenia. In 2005, there was a proposal to use Armenia as a transit country, to carry Iranian natural gas to Europe via Georgia and Ukraine. Under heavy Kremlin pressure, the Armenian government rejected the proposal. Prime Minister Andranik Margaryan openly admitted that the government could not neglect Russia's interests. To make certain that the Iran-Armenia pipeline could not be used for transit gas, the diameter was reduced from the initially planned 56 to 28 inches. As construction was completed in 2007, Armenia sold its share to Russia, causing further Iranian disappointment. As a result, only about 35% of the pipeline capacity was used for supplying limited quantities of gas from Iran in exchange for electricity. In 2013, the Armenian government again rejected an Iranian offer to supply

15 July 2019. https://eurasianet.org/in-moscow-pashinyan-gets-along-with-putin-clashes-with-russian-armenian-philanthropist.

[30] Cornell, ibid., 95.

[31] "Pashinian Says He Made 'Clear' to US That Armenia Will Maintain Ties with Iran," Radio Free Europe/Radio Liberty, 2 November 2018. Web. Retrieved 28 July 2019. https://www.rferl.org/a/pashinian-says-made-clear-to-us-bolton-armenia-will-maintain-ties-with-iran/29578365.html.

cheaper gas than Russia, and signed another agreement that guaranteed Gazprom's monopoly position on the Armenian market for 30 years. In January 2015, Iranian Minister of Foreign Affairs Mohammad Javad Zarif stated that Iran would be ready to invest in the construction of a new gas pipeline with a larger diameter but the Armenians failed to provide a clear reply.

Another proposed connection to Iran was the proposed railway link through Armenia connecting Russia and Iran. This would require the line to transit Georgia and enter Russia via Abkhazia, something the Georgian government had firmly rejected. Georgia's position was firm: railway traffic via breakaway Abkhazia would not be resumed as long as the region remained under Russian occupation.[32] Russia lost interest in the project, claiming it was not economically viable. Vladimir Yakunin, President of Russian Railways (and therefore the manager of the Armenian National Railway as well), compared the $3 billion project to "cutting a window into the wall to nowhere: into the wall of a neighboring house." He noted the project had no prospects.[33]

From Iran's viewpoint, Armenia was a possible mechanism to skirt US, European, and UN sanctions. As examples, in May 2007 the US embassy in Yerevan complained that the Armenian government was slow to implement an asset freeze on Bank Sepah. This bank was under UN sanctions, and maintained correspondent account with the Armenian branch of Iran's Bank Mellat in breach of UN restrictions. In 2010, the UN Security Council noted the Armenian branch of Iran's Bank Mellat as funding Iran's nuclear work. "Over the last seven years, Bank Mellat has facilitated hundreds of millions of dollars in transactions for Iranian nuclear, missile, and defense entities," it said. Reuters reported that in May 2012 a Western intelligence service said Iran was searching for "convenient locations to develop alternative banking relationships away from spy agencies and other international monitoring bodies. It said an expanded presence in Armenia was one of Iran's goals. "Increasing pressure…has forced the Central Bank of Iran economists to seek financial alternatives in countries that do not work according to the dictates of the West," it said, referring

[32] Abrahamyan, Eduard. "The Potential and Obstacles to Armenia-Iran Strategic Relations," The Central Asia-Caucasus Analyst, 16 March 2016. Web. Retrieved 23 July 2019. https://www.cacianalyst.org/publications/analytical-articles/item/13343-the-potential-and-obstacles-to-armenia-iran-strategic-relations.html.

[33] "Russian Official Speaks against Building Iran-Armenia Railway," Azatutyun, 9 June 2015. Web. Retrieved 29 July 2019. https://rus.azatutyun.am/a/27062919.html.

to Armenia.[34] US officials have stated Iran has easy access to Armenian banks operating in Nagorno-Karabakh, and Iran is able to withdraw funds from them.[35]

In December 2015 Armenia, Iran, Georgia, and Russia held talks to establish a coordinating group establishing an energy corridor among the four countries. There was concern that Russia might oppose any move to bring Iranian gas into Georgia via Armenia but, since Gazprom owned the pipelines that would be used, experts predicted little Kremlin opposition.[36] The four countries launched the "North-South electric energy corridor" linking the energy transmission lines among the countries.[37]

Armenia continued to deepen its economic ties with Iran by opening in December 2017 a free economic zone at Meghri, on the Iranian border. Entrepreneurs, including Iranian investors, in the zone were free of income tax, value-added tax, and customs fees.[38] The economic zone was opened with the approval of Armenia's patron, Russia. Two months previously, Russian Prime Minister Dmitri Medvedev had said Russia wanted to take part in the free trade zone. "We have good relations with Iran," he said. "Therefore, we are ready to get involved if our EAEU friends and partners set up a free economic zone with Iran, including by inviting Russian businesses there."[39]

[34] Charbonneau, Louis. "Exclusive: Iran Looks to Armenia to Skirt Bank Sanctions," Reuters, 21 August 2012. Web. Retrieved 15 July 2019. https://www.reuters.com/article/us-iran-sanctions-armenia/exclusive-iran-looks-to-armenia-to-skirt-bank-sanctions-idUSBRE87K05420120821.

[35] Burton, Dan. "Is Armenia America's Ally or Iran's?" *The Daily Caller*, 12 March 2015. Web. Retrieved 23 July 2019. https://dailycaller.com/2015/03/12/is-armenia-americas-ally-or-irans/.

[36] Abrahamyan, Gayane. "Armenia: Looking to Receive an Economic Boost from Iran," Eurasianet, 10 February 2016. Web. Retrieved 8 July 2019. https://eurasianet.org/armenia-looking-to-receive-an-economic-boost-from-iran.

[37] Davtyan, Erik. "Armenia's Regional Policy: New Cooperation with Georgia, Iran and Turkmenistan?" Foreign Policy Research Institute, 8 August 2017. Web. Retrieved 23 July 2019. https://www.fpri.org/article/2017/08/armenias-regional-policy-new-cooperation-georgia-iran-turkmenistan/.

[38] "Free Economic Zone Opens on Armenian-Iranian Border," *JAM News*, 18 December 2017. Web. Retrieved 22 July 2019. http://jam-news.net/?p=76455.

[39] "Russia Offers to Join Development of Iran-Armenia Free Trade Zone," *Financial Tribune*, 26 October 2017. Web. Retrieved 22 July 2019. https://financialtribune.com/articles/economy-business-and-markets/74950/russia-offers-to-join-development-of-iran-armenia-free.

Armenia-China

In 2000, the total amount of bilateral trade between Armenia and the Peoples' Republic of China reached $5.98 million, mainly in exports. China occupied 22nd place in Armenia's export balance. By 2009, the trade volume between the two countries reached almost $302.5 million, exceeding the 2000 index more than 50-fold. In 2013, the volume of bilateral trade constituted almost $430 million and China, with 7.6% of Armenian foreign trade by volume, maintained its position as Armenia's second-largest trading partner for four consecutive years, lagging only behind Russia.

China also made foreign direct investment (FDI) in Armenia, including the Shanxi-Nairit joint venture factory. China participated in a number of different energy projects in Armenia, such as the reconstruction and repair of thermoelectric power plants. Private Chinese businesses were also gaining a foothold in the Armenian economy. The main spheres of cooperation were construction, stone processing, and hydro energy.

Prior to 2005, there was no bilateral trade between China and the Nagorno-Karabakh Republic. That year, the volume of the first bilateral trade constituted $41,100. In 2008, bilateral trade grew to $164,000, and by 2011 it had reached $1.28 million. Still, the amounts remained miniscule. In 2010, the Chinese share in Karabakh's exports was only 0.4%, and in imports, 3.6%.[40] The Karabakh side also purchased Chinese turbines for several hydroelectric plants.

Armenian National Congress lawmaker Aram Manukyan summed up Armenia's economic situation in a press interview. "We are bypassed by all regional and international routes—transport, railway, oil, gas and other-s...we simply do not exist in the Caucasus, and this situation has not changed in the last 20 years...Over the years, we have been bypassed by a lot of projects, including the Baku-Tbilisi-Ceyhan pipeline and the Baku-Tbilisi road, which were built through Georgia instead of Armenia, and now these are the North-South International Transport Corridor and China's Silk Road. We seem to be out of the region." Manukyan admitted, "Armenia's very first problem and the biggest challenge is the

[40] Babayan, David. "New Silk Roads in the Southern Caucasus: Chinese Geopolitics in a Strategic Reason," *Yale Journal of International Affairs*, 6 October 2014. Web. Retrieved 8 July 2019. http://yalejournal.org/article_post/new-silk-roads-in-the-southern-caucasus-chinese-geopolitics-in-a-strategic-region/.

settlement of the Karabakh conflict…We can't go on like this…We must get out of this hole, this situation…If we could resolve the Karabakh conflict, then the issue of unblocking of our borders with Azerbaijan and Turkey will be resolved."[41]

Because Karabakh is totally dependent on Armenia for its economic well-being, it shares in its larger neighbor's slow growth. Azerbaijan in July 2019 found a new way to put economic pressure on the separatists in Nagorno-Karabakh. The Financial Market Supervisory Authority of Azerbaijan met with representatives of Visa and Mastercard. The Azerbaijanis took the position that the card companies were providing financial services within internationally recognized Azerbaijan without the approval of the authorities in Baku. This violated the sovereignty and territorial integrity of Azerbaijan and the norms of international law. It created favorable conditions for money laundering and financing of terrorism, and was in non-compliance with the requirements of international payment systems. As a result of this meeting and Azerbaijani complaints, acceptance of the payment cards was halted at the ATM networks of some banks in Karabakh, as well as payments via the website of the Nagorno-Karabakh "ministry of finance."[42]

Azerbaijan

If the twentieth century was the age of hydrocarbons, that age began in 1848 in Baku where the first commercial quantities of oil were produced. The Rothschilds, Nobel brothers, and other European oil companies profited from Baku oil until the time of the Russian Revolution. After that, the bounteous fields of the Absheron Peninsula were in the service of the Soviet Union. During the Second World War, 90% of the fuel used by the Red Army to defeat the Nazis was produced by Azerbaijan.

Soviet production tactics, however, were exploitative. Little attention was given to maintenance, or the replenishment of the pressure in the fields to bring up more oil. As a result, by the time of the collapse of the

[41] Kamaras, Jacob. "Armenia Is an Isolated Backwater Dump Because It Hitched Its Wagon to Moscow," *The Daily Caller*, 9 April 2018. Web. Retrieved 22 July 2019. https://dailycaller.com/2018/04/09/armenia-isolated-backwater-dump-because-of-russia/.

[42] "Azerbaijan Stops Illegal Fundraising in Occupied Territories," *Trend*, 6 July 2019. Web. Retrieved 31 July 2019. https://www.azernews.az/karabakh/153188.html.

Soviet Union the Azerbaijani oil fields were played out—even though an ocean of oil remained underground. Between 1975 and 1995, production dropped by almost half, from 17 to 9 million tons per year.[43] Azerbaijan faced the same bleak economic fate of the rest of the Caucasus, as there was no engine of economic growth.

Although the onshore oil fields were done, geologists reported unexplored offshore oil and gas deposits in the Caspian Sea. As Azerbaijan lacked the capital to develop these resources by itself, President Heydar Aliyev negotiated for two things: Western oil companies to come and develop the new fields; and, a pipeline to take the oil to world markets. These efforts came to fruition on 20 September 1994, when he signed the "Contract of the Century." Thirteen companies from eight countries signed a production sharing agreement that allowed the development of deposits in three fields: Azeri, Chiraq, and Guneshli (ACG). Nearly $36 billion were invested in the development of offshore oil reserves and, as of 2017, 3.5 billion barrels of oil were produced from the ACG fields. In addition, a total of 30 billion cubic meters of associated gas were produced from the ACG oil field and given to the Azerbaijani government.[44]

The 1994 agreement was extended from 2017 to 2050. Under the new agreement, the State Oil Company of Azerbaijan increased its share to 25% of the consortium while British Petroleum's stake declined to from 35.8 to 30.37%. BP remained the operator, and the consortium agreed to pay the government an additional $3.6 billion in eight tranches over the following eight years.[45]

To get the petroleum to market, Aliyev picked British Petroleum to head an 11-company consortium to build a pipeline, the Azerbaijan International Operating Company (AIOC). The quickest way to get started was to use existing Soviet pipeline structure. This would allow the fuel to be fed into the Russian oil flow. What that meant, however, was that

[43] Kaldor, Mary. "Oil and Conflict: The Case of Nagorno-Karabakh," in Mary Kaldor, Terry Karl and Yahia Said, Oil *Wars* (London: Pluto Press, 2007), 67.

[44] Aliyev, Ilham. "Oil Sector." Web. Retrieved 25 June 2019. http://en.president/az/azerbaijan/contract.

[45] Bagirova, Naila. "BP-led Group Extends Azeri Oil 'Contract of the Century,'" *Reuters*, 14 September 2017. Web. Acquired 30 July 2019. https://www.reuters.com/article/us-bp-azerbaijan-agreement/bp-led-group-extends-azeri-oil-contract-of-the-century-idUSKCN1BP11O.

Azerbaijan would be an economic vassal state of Russia. Moscow could decide how much energy to purchase or not purchase, and the price that the oil would receive.

The most direct route to the sea would have been straight south, through Iran. This was another precarious route, however, given Iran's rocky relationship with the West. Aliyev opted for a third route, through Georgia and into Turkey. Once on the Anatolian peninsula, the pipeline would turn south to the Mediterranean, at the Turkish oil port of Ceyhan. The route was longer, but it bypassed the twin dangers presented by using either Russian or Iranian territory. It also bypassed another potential shortcut to Turkey, across Armenia.

Moscow threatened to block the project. Using legal arguments about the status of the Caspian Sea, it claimed that ACG belonged to all the littoral states. Since under this interpretation one-fifth of the production was its own, Russia would not allow the project to proceed unless the product was shipped north through the old Soviet network.

The lead negotiator was then-first vice president of the State Oil Corporation of Azerbaijan (SOCAR), Ilham Aliyev. To break the Kremlin's opposition, Aliyev took two steps. The first step was to grant a 10% share of the production rights to Lukoil, an independent Russian oil company controlled by Azerbaijani oligarch Vagit Alekperov. If the Kremlin continued to oppose the project, it would also oppose a major Russian economic interest. Aliyev's second step was to direct the first ACG production through the old pipes into Russia. The first ACG oil was not shipped from Ceyhan, Turkey but from the Russian port of Novorossiysk in December 1999. The early oil project also included construction between 1997 and 1999 of a new 830-km export pipeline from Baku to Supsa on Georgia's Black Sea coast, at a cost of $560 million.[46]

The Baku to Novorossiysk pipeline was used to ship the first oil but, over time, whenever the later-developed main Baku-Tbilisi-Ceyhan pipeline needed an increase in volume it came from the Russian flow. Russian pipeline operator Transneft began to incur losses so, in December

[46] Shaban, Ilham. "Contract of the Century What Has It Done for Azerbaijan?" *Visions of Azerbaijan*, July–October 2014. Web. Retrieved 25 June 2019. http://www.visions.az/en/news/589/069c9584/.

2013 it announced it would close the pipeline.[47] The official reason given was not loss of profits but that Baku had not signed a necessary new commercial agreement.[48] When the contract finally expired on 14 February 2014, however, Transneft announced it was extending the existing contract while negotiations on a new contract continued.[49] The new agreement was signed four days later, reducing the targeted oil flow from five million tons per year to two million.[50] As volumes continued to fall, a third contract was required in 2016.[51]

The question of the legal status of the Caspian remained unanswered. In 2003, Kazakhstan, Azerbaijan, and Russia divided the northern portion of the sea among themselves; Kazakhstan and Turkmenistan delineated their border in 2015. But whenever Azerbaijan tried to make its legal claims, or to negotiate a bilateral agreement with Turkmenistan to build a Trans-Caspian pipeline, Moscow and Tehran would oppose the deal. In 2001 Iran sent gunboats to chase BP survey vessels away from a disputed Azerbaijani field in the south. Azerbaijan did the same to Turkmenistan in 2008. In 2009, Iran moved a drilling rig into the 2001 disputed waters. Azerbaijan fretted that it did not have the military power to take on the Iranians.[52] Finally, in August 2018, the littoral states announced an agreement had been made. Fifteen-mile naval territorial borders were assigned, fishing rights negotiated, and an agreement made that only naval forces

[47] Elliott, Stuart. "Russia-Azerbaijan Tension Closes off an Oil Pipeline Route," *Platts* (blog), 12 December 2013. Web. Retrieved 30 July 2019. https://blogs.platts.com/2013/12/12/baku-russia/.

[48] "Russia to Suspend Work Through Azeri Oil Pipeline," UPI, 10 January 2014. Web. Retrieved 30 July 2019. http://caspianbarrel.org/az/2014/01/russia-to-suspend-work-through-azeri-oil-pipeline/.

[49] "Igor Dyomin: 'Transneft Will Not Shut Down Baku-Novorossiysk Pipeline For Now,'" Azeri Press Agency, 14 February 2014. Web. Retrieved 14 February 2014. http://en.apa.az/207109.

[50] "SOCAR, Transneft Sign New Agreement on Baku-Novorossiysk Pipeline," Trend, 18 February 2014. Web. Retrieved 30 July 2019. https://en.trend.az/business/energy/2243511.html.

[51] "SOCAR, Transneft Ink New Deal on Oil Supply," Azernews, 23 February 2016. Net. Retrieved 30 July 2019. https://www.azernews.az/oil_and_gas/93364.html.

[52] Kucera, Joshua. "Iran, Azerbaijan in Tense Caspian Standoff, Cables Show," Eurasianet, 4 October 2011. Web. Retrieved 15 July 2019. https://eurasianet.org/iran-azerbaijan-in-tense-caspian-standoff-cables-show.

from the littoral states would sail in the Caspian. Most importantly, the various oil and gas fields were parceled out. The agreement failed to delineate the seabed.[53]

The pipeline took on its first oil in May 2005 and the first tanker departed Ceyhan 13 months later, in June 2006. The government used the influx in petrodollars to invest in infrastructure and to create jobs. As a result Azerbaijan led the South Caucasus in all indicators of economic wellbeing. GDP rose from $9 billion in 1990 to $75 billion in 2014. Life expectancy in the same period rose from 65 years to almost 72 years.[54] GDP per capita went from $98.30 in 1991 to $4780 in 2018. The unemployment rate in March 2019 was less than 5%.[55] The economy was heavily dependent on oil exports, accounting in 2016 for over half its GDP.[56]

By 2012, Azerbaijan exported 24 million tons of oil and 7 billion cubic meters of natural gas.[57] The gas was originally a by-product of the oil production but, with the discovery of the Shah Deniz II natural gas fields, authorities decided to turn this into another revenue stream. On 25 January 2018 British Petroleum's Azerbaijan affiliate announced that 16 of the 26 wells in the Shah Deniz 2 gas field had been drilled and 99% of the gas pipeline constructed. The effect was instantaneous in Georgia, Azerbaijan's neighbor with large swaths of its territory under Russian control. It announced it would no longer purchase natural gas from Russia, but instead would purchase 2.680 billion cubic meters of gas from Azerbaijan.[58]

[53] Auyezov, Olzhas. "Russia, Iran and Three Others Agree Caspian Status, but Not Borders," Reuters, 12 August 2018. Web. Retrieved 15 July 2019. https://www.reuters.com/article/us-kazakhstan-caspian-borders/russia-iran-and-three-others-agree-caspian-status-but-not-borders-idUSKBN1KX0CI.

[54] "Azerbaijan: Data." The World Bank. Web. Retrieved 26 June 2019. https://data.worldbank.org/country/azerbaijan.

[55] "Azerbaijan." CEIC. Web. Retrieved 26 June 2019. https://www.ceicdata.com/en/country/azerbaijan.

[56] "Falling Oil Prices: How are Countries Being Affected?" BBC News, 18 January 2016. Web. Retrieved 26 June 2019. https://www.bbc.com/news/world-35345874.

[57] Chausovsky, Eugene. "The Crimean Crisis and the Energy Ramifications for Azerbaijan," Eurasianet, 26 March 2014. Web. Retrieved 30 July 2019. https://eurasianet.org/the-crimean-crisis-and-the-energy-ramifications-for-azerbaijan.

[58] Kamaras, Jacob. "The United States Can Counter Russia by Putting More Energy Into Its Relationship With Azerbaijan," *The Daily Caller*, 6 March 2018. Web. Retrieved

The gas was transported to the Turkish market via the Baku-Tbilisi-Erzurum natural gas pipeline. The line was constructed between 2002 and 2006 and was underutilized. It became the middle section of the Trans Anatolian Pipeline (TANAP), completed in 2019. This 1850-kilometer pipeline was built to carry 16 billion cubic meters of gas per year, from the Turkish-Georgia border to the Turkish-Greek border. Along the way 6 billion cubic meters would be offloaded for Turkish consumption, leaving 10 billion for the European market. TANAP was scheduled to connect with the Trans Adriatic Pipeline (TAP) that could distribute the oil to markets in Greece, Albania, and Italy.[59] Additional plans called for the doubling of the pipeline's capacity, but no source for the additional gas to fill the larger pipeline had been identified.[60]

The price of oil plummeted from over $113 per barrel in June 2014 (highest price was over $153 per barrel in 2011) to just over $41 a barrel in June 2016.[61] As the price of oil production in Azerbaijan is roughly $11 per barrel,[62] the country still had a surplus, but it was significantly less than that to which the government and people were accustomed. The Central Bank announced it would no longer prop up the value of the Azerbaijani currency, the manat. As the currency floated against other currencies, it dropped a third in value. The Foreign Ministry announced it was looking for staff cuts and ways to reduce the cost of embassies abroad.[63]

28 July 2019. https://dailycaller.com/2018/03/06/the-united-states-can-counter-russia-by-putting-more-energy-into-its-relationship-with-azerbaijan/.

[59] "TANAP Now Fully Ready to Deliver Natural Gas to Europe," *Daily Sabah*, 2 July 2019. Web. Retrieved 30 July 2019. https://www.dailysabah.com/energy/2019/07/02/tanap-now-fully-ready-to-deliver-natural-gas-to-europe.

[60] O'Byrne, David. "Azeri-Turkish TANAP Gas Pipeline Finished and Ready to Export," Platts, 1 July 2019. Web. Retrieved 30 July 2019. https://www.spglobal.com/platts/en/market-insights/latest-news/natural-gas/070119-azeri-turkish-tanap-gas-pipeline-finished-and-ready-to-export.

[61] "Crude Oil Prices—70 Year Historical Chart," Macrotrends. Web. Retrieved 26 June 2019. https://www.macrotrends.net/1369/crude-oil-price-history-chart.

[62] Salimova, Gulnar. "Oil Price Drop Sinks Azerbaijan's Economy," *Kyiv Post*, 12 January 2016. Web. http://www.kyivpost.com/article/content/world/oil-price-drop-sinks-azerbaijans-economy-405747.html.

[63] Geybullayeva, Arzu and Tony Wesolowsky. "Azerbaijan Hit by Currency Crash, Low Oil Prices," Radio Free Europe/Radio Liberty, 12 January 2016. https://www.rferl.org/a/azerbaijan-suffers-currency-crash-oil-prices/27479606.html.

The hydrocarbon wealth had allowed President Aliyev to turn his capital into a model city. It also allowed him to expand his defense budget. Military spending went from $175 million in 2004 to an estimated $3.1 billion in 2011, exceeding Armenia's entire national budget.[64] Even with the decrease in oil revenues, the defense budget for 2019 was still almost $2 billion, representing 13.4% of all state budgetary expenditures.[65]

Since the military expenditures were paid by the money earned from energy exports, the Baku-Ceyhan pipeline became an Armenian strategic target. Nagorno-Karabakh's "minister" of war, Levon Mnatsakanyan, said that in a new war the pipeline would be one of the first targets. "This is a very serious financial resource for Azerbaijan and we need to deprive them of these means," he said. "If we'd known the situation would be like this today, we'd never have signed that truce 20 years ago."[66] During the 2020 6 week war, the pipeline came under Armenian fire.

Post-petroleum Azerbaijan

The drop in the world's oil prices, and the subsequent drop in its GDP, was a wake-up call to Azerbaijan. The government realized it needed to begin planning for a post-petroleum economy. Baku began to look for other projects, and to capitalize on its location in the middle of the Eurasian continent. They decided to develop the country into a transportation hub. Some of the projects had been on the board since the early days of independence; economics now dictated they be implemented.

While pipeline politics in Azerbaijan was focused on the west (Turkey and Europe) or north (Russia), there was still another major player in the South Caucasus, China. Beijing carved a niche for itself in Azerbaijan's oil

[64] German, Tracey. "The Nagorno-Karabakh Conflict between Azerbaijan and Armenia: Security Issues in the Caucasus," *Journal of Muslim Minority Affairs* 32/2, June 2012, 218.

[65] Mendiyev, Mushwig. "Azerbaijan Announces All Time High Defense Budget for 2019," Caspian News, 22 January 2019. Web. Retrieved 26 June 2019. https://caspiannews.com/news-detail/azerbaijan-announces-all-time-high-defense-budget-for-2019-2019-1-22-18/.

[66] Khojoyan, Sara and Anthony Halpin. "Frozen War Thaws in Russian Backyard as Karabakh Flares," Bloomberg, 22 October 2015. Web. Retrieved 26 June 2019. https://www.bloomberg.com/news/articles/2015-10-22/frozen-war-thaws-in-russian-backyard-as-nagorno-karabakh-flares.

sector. China's energy giant, Sinopec, had a stake in two projects—K&K and Gobustan—with investment of more than $250 million.

China was building infrastructure in Azerbaijan and was actively helping Azerbaijan reconstruct and repair thermoelectric and hydropower plants. The China National Electric Equipment Corporation, or CNEEC, is the top performer in this area. In 2007, this corporation won a tender to rebuild the Azerbaijani Thermoelectric Power Station and modernize its seven power-generating units. This thermoelectric power station accounts for 45% of all the electric power generated in the country. In 2013, the Azerbaijani Thermoelectric Power Station generated 7.63 billion kilowatt-hours of electricity. In 2010, CNEEC also acquired the right to repair the Mingechevir cascade of a hydropower plant comprised of the Mingechevir and Varvara hydropower stations.[67]

In 2013, Azerbaijani Deputy Prime Minister Abid Sharifov and Chinese ambassador to Azerbaijan Hong Jiuyin signed an agreement on economic and technological cooperation. Under the agreement, China agreed to provide Azerbaijan with grant aid worth $4.89 million to promote bilateral economic and technological cooperation. In return, Azerbaijan agreed to import various Chinese products.[68] By 2018, officials from the two countries were discussing the creation of the Trans-Caspian International Transport Route (TCITR), a corridor of 6500 kilometers linking Asia with Europe. A major link in this transportation corridor was the Baku-Tbilisi-Kars Railway. This rail line was originally proposed in 1993, after Turkey closed its border to a railroad that traversed Armenia. In 2007, leaders of Azerbaijan, Georgia, and Turkey agreed to construct the line. The planning was stimulated when the US and EU sanctioned Russia over its occupation of Crimea and the Kremlin responded by banning the shipment of EU-origin foodstuffs through Russia. This new, southern rail route would not cross Russian territory. Under pressure from Armenian diaspora groups, Western powers refused to provide financing. They hoped to force the planners to incorporate the older, Armenian line into the new route. (This

[67] Babayan, David, ibid.

[68] "China, Azerbaijan Sign Deal on Economic Co-Op," China Invests Overseas, 2013-12-09. Web. Internet. Retrieved 26 June 2019. http://www.china-invests.net/20131209/32048.aspx.

would have reopened a portion of the Turkish border with Armenia.) Instead, Azerbaijan and Turkey quickly agreed to finance their portions of the project, but impoverished Georgia was unable to do so. The State Oil Fund of Azerbaijan agreed to lend Georgia the money needed to construct its portion of the line.[69] As of July 2019, the Azerbaijan Railways CJSC was ready to begin passenger transportation once customs issues were resolved.[70] The first cargo was delivered from Turkey to Georgia on 23 July 2019.[71]

Once completed, the TCITR would cut the transportation time of freight from Urumqi in China to Europe from about 60 days by sea to 14 days by train, and at one-fourth the cost of air freight. "Cooperation with China in the transit sector is one of our priority areas," said Azerbaijan's Minister of the Economy Shahin Mustafayev. "In 2017, the trade turnover between Azerbaijan and China increased by 43%, amounting to $1.2 billion. Exports to this country grew 2.1 times."[72]

The International North-South Transit Corridor is another transportation project. Once completed, it has the possibility of bringing Armenian allies Iran and Russia closer to Azerbaijan. A few days after the April 2016 "Four Day War" in Karabakh, Russian Foreign Minister Sergey Lavrov met with his Iranian and Azerbaijani counterparts in Baku. The three agreed to integrate their transportation infrastructure to create a land corridor uniting India with the European Union.[73] The first step in

[69] Shepard, Wade. "Reconnecting Asia: The Story Behind the Emerging Baku-Tbilisi-Kars Rail Line," Forbes, 15 December 2016. Web. Retrieved 30 July 2019. https://www.forbes.com/sites/wadeshepard/2016/12/15/reconnecting-asia-the-story-behind-the-emerging-baku-tbilisi-kars-rail-line/#d9c60b239785.

[70] Mammadli, Kamala. "Azerbaijan Ready to Launch Passenger Transportation via Baku-Tbilisi-Kars Route," Trend, 29 July 2019. https://menafn.com/1098816871/Azerbaijan-ready-to-launch-passenger-transportation-via-BakuTbilisiKars-route.

[71] Mammadova, Tamilla. "First Cargo Delivered via Baku-Tbilisi-Kars Railway from Turkey to Georgia," Trend, 24 July 2019. Web. Retrieved 31 July 2019. https://www.azernews.az/business/154002.html.

[72] Shahbazov, Fuad. "China to Europe by Way of Azerbaijan's Trans-Caspian Gateway," *The Diplomat*, 16 February 2018. Web. Retrieved 29 July 2019. https://thediplomat.com/2018/02/china-to-europe-by-way-of-azerbaijans-trans-caspian-gateway/.

[73] Korybko, Andrew. "Russia's New Thinking Towards Armenia and Azerbaijan: An 'Obstructionist' vs. an 'Integrationist,'" Global Research, 16 September 2017. Web. Retrieved 23 July 2019. http://www.globalresearch.ca/russias-new-thinking-towards-armenia-and-azerbaijan-an-obstructionist-vs-an-integrationist/5609262.

seeing this achieved would be the creation of a 7200-kilometer road and rail network from Russia to Azerbaijan to Iran. The connection to India would then be a maritime route. Experts planned the route to transport 6 million tons of cargo in its first year, with a later expansion to 10 million tons.[74] Originally planned to open in 2018, the INSTC remains mired in political controversy and insufficient infrastructure.

Conclusion

Armenia's growth was steady but slow. Because of its choice to remain mired in a conflict with its neighbor, Armenia cut itself off from benefiting from trade with Azerbaijan and Turkey. As a result, it remained primarily a rural economy. It survived by placing itself in subservience to the Kremlin, and selling off all its economic assets.

By contrast, Azerbaijan's economy prospered by exploiting its offshore oil and gas deposits. As the price of fossil fuel dropped on the world market, the Baku government took steps to reinvent itself as a transportation hub. The cost of the war impacted Armenia directly through lost opportunities. It impacted Azerbaijan, as well, in that its meteoric growth was held back by the need to pay for the resettlement and housing of almost a million internally displaced people. A resolution of the conflict would benefit the economies of both countries.

[74] "In the Caucasus, Competition Will Limit Cooperation," Assessment. Stratfor, 7 February 2018. Web. Retrieved 29 July 2019. https://worldview.stratfor.com/article/caucasus-competition-will-limit-cooperation.

CHAPTER 5

Diplomacy Surrounding Frozen Conflict

Diplomatic Maneuvers

The Armenia-Azerbaijan conflict over Nagorno-Karabakh is of considerable interest to the countries surrounding the two countries: Russia, Turkey, and Iran. Europe and the United States have also played a diplomatic role. Except for votes at the United Nations, however, the rest of the world ignores the conflict.

To Russia, the Caucasus and all the countries of the former Soviet Union still belong to them. A country that "defects" to the West by looking for support from a country other than the Kremlin is perceived as a traitor. The Kremlin does not concede there is room for any other power in what they consider to be their sphere of influence. "Russia continues to have a vital interest in the cessation of all armed conflicts on the territory of the former USSR," said the country's first president, Boris Yeltsin. "The world community is increasingly coming to realize our country's special responsibility in this difficult matter. I believe the time has come for the authoritative international organizations, including the United Nations to grant Russia special powers as the guarantor of peace and stability in the region."[1]

[1] Yeltsin, Boris in Pavel Baev. *The Russian Army in a Time of Troubles* (Washington, DC: Sage, 1996), 151. Bolukbasi, Suha. Ibid., 181.

J. J. Coyle, *Russia's Interventions in Ethnic Conflicts*,
https://doi.org/10.1007/978-3-030-59573-9_5

Twenty years later, then-President Dmitri Medvedev repeated the same message. "Russia, like other countries in the world, has regions where it has privileged interests. These are regions where countries with which we have friendly relations are located…It is the border region, but not only."[2]

This attitude is shared by Russia's current president, Vladimir Putin, who has an active program of offering Russian passports to people in Ukraine, Georgia, and Moldova. The "passportization" process delivers the message that the new republics are not real states, and that the inhabitants remain citizens of the only legitimate state in the region, the Russian Federation.

During and immediately after the fall of the Soviet Union, however, Russia's power and influence was limited. When that occurred, it was willing to seek tactical allies to fulfill its policy goals. Seeking peace on its southern border, Russian SSR President Yeltsin joined with the president of the Kazakh SSR Nursultan Nazarbayev to mediate the Armenian-Azerbaijan disputes. They met with the various leaders (including Robert Kocharyan from Karabakh) in Zheleznovodsk, Russia. They negotiated an agreement for cancellation of various measures, the removal of Soviet troops from the "conflict zone," a release of hostages, and bilateral negotiations between Armenia and Azerbaijan. President Ter-Petrosyan announced that Armenia was not interested in unifying Karabakh with the Republic of Armenia, a major compromise from previously held positions of various Armenian separatist groups.[3]

The peacemaking efforts came to an end in November 1991, when an Armenian rocket shot down an Azerbaijani helicopter carrying a peace mission. All 22 people aboard were killed, including thirteen Azerbaijani government officials (two deputy prime ministers, the Secretary of State, the Prosecutor General, the Minister of Internal Affairs, members of parliament, etc.), the Kazakhstan Deputy Minister of Internal Affairs, a Russian MVD major general, a second Russian officer, and the crew.[4]

[2] Kramer, Andrew E. "Russia Claims Its Sphere of Influence in the World," *New York Times*, 31 August 2008. Web. Retrieved 29 July 2019. https://www.nytimes.com/2008/09/01/world/europe/01russia.html.

[3] Remler, ibid., 37–38.

[4] "Commemoration of the 27th Anniversary of the Tragedy Karakend," 20 November 2018. Internet. Retrieved 24 May 2019. https://en.axar.az/news/society/325705.html.

Two months later, the Conference on Security and Cooperation in Europe (CSCE) decided at a January 1992 meeting in Prague that it should involve itself in the search for peace. A British delegate noted that the organization had just admitted two new members (Armenia and Azerbaijan) between which there was a conflict. He suggested sending a fact-finding mission to the area.[5]

Armenia, Azerbaijan, and Russia asked the United Nations for help in resolving the conflict. The secretary-general sent a fact finder, special representative Cyrus Vance. The former US Secretary of State previously had some success in creating a UN-sponsored cease-fire in Yugoslavia. The secretary-general's decision to send Mr. Vance to Armenia and Azerbaijan coincided with a decision by the President of the CSCE, Foreign Minister Jiri Dienstbier of Czechoslovakia, to make a similar mediation visit to the area.[6] A delegation of six Iranian officials also came to the area in an attempt to impose a seven-day cease-fire to correspond with Vance's visit. Within minutes of the Iranians' departure, however, the fighting resumed.[7]

Russia's Foreign Minister Andrei Kozyrev sponsored talks in Moscow with foreign ministers Raffi Hovannisyan of Armenia and Hussain Sadikhov of Azerbaijan. The two agreed to recommend to their presidents to accept a cease-fire.[8]

Iranian President Ali Akbar Hashemi-Rafsanjani tried his hand at negotiations, inviting the presidents for discussions in Tehran. While the Iranians no doubt wanted to eliminate tensions on their northern border, their main interest was in reducing Turkey's influence. Western analysts frequently view Iranian moves through a sectarian lens, i.e., Sunni v.

[5] Maresca, John. "Lost Opportunities in Negotiating the Nagorno Karabakh Conflict," International Negotiation 1/3 (1996) 475.

[6] Lewis, Paul. "U.N. Giving Vance a New Peace Mission in Caucasus Dispute," *The New York Times*, 14 March 1002. Web. Retrieved 23 May 2019. *AcademicOneFile*. http://link.galegroup.com/apps/doc/A174800604/AONE?u=chap_main&sid=AONE&xid=3ee9ce88.

[7] "Caucasus Shooting Resumes After Vance and Iran Efforts," *The New York Times*, 21 March 1992. Web. Retrieved 23 May 2019. *AcademicOneFile*, http://link.galegroup.com/apps/doc/A174797920/AONE?u=chap_main&sid=AONE&xid=6e67be29.

[8] "Cease Fire Is Sought in Nagorno Karabakh," *The New York Times*, 21 February 1998. Web. Retrieved 23 May 2019. http://link.galegroup.com/apps/doc/A174789439/AONE?u=chap_main&sid=AONE&xid=90c7e8e5.

Shia, Islam v. the West. The rulers of Iran do not share this viewpoint, however; they view things through a geopolitical lens. Thus, in the North, Iran supported Christian Armenia against Turkey's ally, the Muslim, Shia country of Azerbaijan. In this case, however, Iran tried to be an unbiased mediator. In May 1992, Iran sponsored peace talks between Armenian president Ter-Petrosyan and Azerbaijani acting president Yakub Mammadov. The two leaders signed the Tehran Communique on 9 May outlining the general principles of a peace agreement. It mandated a cease-fire and reopening of communications and transportation links within a week of the arrival in the region of Mahmud Vaezi, Rafsanjani's special representative. The agreement never really had a chance, since Armenia had conquered Shusha two days earlier against the wishes of Ter-Petrosyan. Armenian foreign policy advisor Ashot Manucharyan said the timing of the capture of Shusha was intentional, in order to derail a settlement that Karabakh leaders found less than desirable.[9] Nine days later, Armenian forces captured Lachin. The proposed Iranian cease-fire never went into effect, and Iran has been absent from subsequent mediation, as the Azerbaijan side lost all confidence in Iran's peacemaking abilities. The Armenians may have been willing to pursue further discussions, however, since they were using Iranian-brokered cease-fires to rearm their troops.[10]

A decision was made to convene a conference on the issue. Following the February 1992 Khojaly massacre, the CSCE held preliminary discussions in Minsk on 24 March 1992 to prepare for a June conference in Rome of the full CSCE. While the actual conference never took place, the preliminary talks highlighted the positions of the two sides. Azerbaijan welcomed the CSCE's involvement since the CSCE principles guaranteed Azerbaijani sovereign rights. The Armenians were less happy, since the CSCE supported the principle of inviolability of borders and excluded Armenia's territorial claims in any form.[11]

The CSCE created the Minsk group, with the chairmanship rotating among eleven members. Two major sticking points were Armenia's claim that it was not a party to the dispute, and Azerbaijan's unwillingness to negotiate with anyone from Karabakh for fear of giving the former

[9] Bolukbasi, ibid., 191.

[10] Cornell, ibid., 93.

[11] Mehtiyev, Elkhan. *Armenia-Azerbaijan Prague Process: Road Map to Peace or Stalemate for Uncertainty?* Oxford: Conflict Studies Research Centre (May 2005) 2. Web. Retrieved 1 June 2019. https://www.files.ethz.ch/isn/87489/05_may.pdf.

oblast de facto recognition as an independent entity.[12] The Republic of Armenia suspended its participation in the preparatory talks when Azerbaijan launched a June 1992 offensive to reclaim the northern part of the enclave.[13]

Faced with Armenian and Azerbaijani intransience in Minsk, Russia announced unilaterally its terms for a cease-fire that was ignored by all sides. Then, in September Russian Minister of Defense, General Pavel Grachev, held a meeting with the region's defense ministers in Sochi. Supposedly, they signed an agreement that would give Russia access to the Lachin corridor as peacekeepers, and a cease-fire. Grachev sent 56 peacekeepers to keep his end of the bargain but had to withdraw them because of active fighting in the area. In addition, neither the Azerbaijanis nor the Russians (and probably the Armenians) had the approval of their political leaders to sign such a deal.[14] It was one of many Russian attempts over the years to push the international community aside and proceed unilaterally.

The Minsk Group met 25 February to 2 March 1993. They agreed to send a group to the area to assess the situation. On 8 April Finnish Colonel Heiki Heppponen lead a CSCE cease-fire monitoring mission to Baku.[15] In late March, the CSCE convened talks in Rome. These talks were called "5+1" discussions. The five powers were Armenia, Azerbaijan, Russia, Turkey, and the United States. The CSCE itself was the "1." Talks appeared to be making progress, and so the negotiators decided they needed to consult with their capitals to make sure they were on the right track. They took a recess from the discussions. During the recess, however, Armenia seized Kelbajar.[16] Military action ended talks of peace. The talks reconvened in April, but to no effect.

The 27 March–3 April 1993 fighting in Kelbajar, and the spillover of the conflict into areas not traditionally considered parts of Nagorno-Karabakh, finally stirred the international community into action.

[12] Croissant, ibid., 86–87.

[13] Schmemann, Serge. "In the Caucasus, Ancient Blood Feuds Threaten to Engulf 2 Republics," *The New York Times*, 8 July 1992. Web. Retrieved 23 May 2019. http://link.galegroup.com/apps/doc/A174928554/AONE?u=chap_main&sid=AONE&xid=f62cee10.

[14] de Waal, ibid., 217.

[15] Human Rights Watch, ibid., 29.

[16] Remler, ibid., 47–48.

On 23 April 1993, the United Nations Security Council adopted Resolution 822, which demanded an immediate cease-fire, the withdrawal of "all occupying forces" from the Kelbajar region of Azerbaijan, the resumption of negotiations, and open access for humanitarian efforts. It also urged the parties to cooperate with the Minsk process to negotiate a peace agreement.[17]

The resolution mostly supported Azerbaijani diplomacy. The UN respected the sovereignty and territorial integrity of the states in the area and reaffirmed the inviolability of international borders. It reinforced the inadmissibility of the use of force for acquiring territory. Russia was able to use its position as a permanent member of the security council to gain at least one concession for its Armenian ally: the resolution stated Kelbajar had been invaded by "local Armenian forces." There was no mention of the Republic of Armenia, or any Russian support for the invading forces.

After the passage of UNSCR 822, another plan surfaced at the CSCE. This one, jointly sponsored by Russia, the United States, and Turkey called for a cease-fire, and the withdrawal of Armenian troops from all Azerbaijani territory outside of Nagorno-Karabakh. It was adopted by Azerbaijan, Armenia, and the Karabakh Armenians. Before the plan could be implemented, however, the Azerbaijan political scene was ripped apart in June 1993 when battlefield commander Surat Huseynov revolted and attempted to stage a coup d'etat. Taking advantage of Azerbaijani weakness, Armenia broke the cease-fire and seized the town of Aghdam.

Baku turned to Moscow for help in restoring the cease-fire. President Yeltsin was pleased to accept the unilateral role it was offered, but his price for cooperation was high. Yeltsin reiterated the Grachev plan of requiring the deployment of Russian peacekeepers, but he upped the ante: Russia would deploy a full paratrooper division on Azerbaijani soil, and Russian border guards would assume their old Soviet positions. President Aliyev refused to acquiesce in the Russian extortion, concerned about maintaining Azerbaijani sovereignty. In addition, Aliyev was convinced that once Russian troops were on Azerbaijani soil, Russia would allow Armenia to maintain the territory it had seized.[18]

On 16 April 1993, having regained control over Kelbajar and surrounding areas, the Armenian authorities of Karabakh announced

[17] United Nations Security Council. Security Council Resolution 822 (1993), 3205th Meeting. 30 April 1993, S/RES/822 (1993). Web. Accessed 1 June 2019. http://unscr.com/en/resolutions/doc/822.

[18] Croissant, ibid., 109.

a unilateral cease-fire. Russia, Turkey, and the United States met in Moscow and devised another peace proposal which they presented in May. It included calls for an Armenian withdrawal from Kelbajar, a two-month cease-fire, and further negotiations. The CSCE would send in 600 peacekeepers, wearing yellow berets. Azerbaijan, desperate to stop the Armenian advance, accepted the idea of the talks. Armenians dragged their feet, demanding more guarantees.[19]

When the Armenians seized Aghdam, the UN acted a second time, passing UNSC 853 on 29 July 1993. This resolution confused the situation further, in that the Republic of Armenia was specifically mentioned—not as a party to the conflict—but as a member state who might be able to use its influence on Karabakh Armenians to ensure their compliance with the UN's requests. The UN "condemns the seizure of Agdam and of all other recently occupied areas of the Azerbaijani republic; further condemns all hostile actions in the region, in particular attacks on civilians and bombardments of inhabited areas; ...welcomes the preparations for a CSCE monitoring mission...(and) urges the Government of the Republic of Armenia to continue to exert its influence to achieve compliance by the Armenians of the Nagorny-Karabakh region of the Azerbaijan Republic with its resolution 822 (1993) and the present resolution."[20] Karabakh Armenians opposed the measure, arguing that Azerbaijan was an aggressor trying to invade an independent Karabakh. "Acting chairman of the Nagorno-Karabakh parliament Karen Baburyan" exclaimed, "The Republic of Nagorno-Karabakh doesn't pretend to capture strange territories but when guns fire on Karabakh towns and villages we have to neutralize them. We have no other way out."[21]

Azerbaijan President Heydar Aliyev decided to open talks with the Armenians in Karabakh. In September 1993, he authorized a Moscow meeting between the Azerbaijani deputy speaker of the parliament and the "foreign minister" of Karabakh.[22] Aliyev knew he needed Russian support to stabilize the security and domestic situation within Azerbaijan, and to halt the fighting with Armenia. Russian Foreign Minister Kozyrev agreed

[19] Remler, ibid., 49.

[20] United Nations Security Council. Security Council Resolution 853 (1993), 3259th Meeting. 29 July 1993, S/RES/853 (1993). Web. Retrieved 1 June 2019. http://unscr.com/en/resolutions/doc/853.

[21] Yerevan Snark News Agency, 4 August 1993, in FBIS-SOV-93-151, 9 August 1993, as quoted by Human Rights Watch, ibid., 49–50.

[22] de Waal, ibid., 238.

that Russia was essential to peace in the Caucasus. "Whether we like it or not, there is no alternative to a Russian Federation peacekeeping contingent in this conflict…; immediately after a settlement mechanism is set in motion, this contingent should be given the status of a U.N. force and reinforced with U.N. units from neutral European CSCE countries. Here too, we ourselves, as well as the United Nations, must do our historic duty. It would be irresponsible to evade this."[23]

On 24 September 1993, Aliyev traveled to Moscow and joined the Confederation of Independent States (CIS), Moscow's attempt to maintain a hold on the former territories of the Soviet Union.

Almost immediately upon Azerbaijan's signing of the accession documents, Russia demanded that Armenia cease their attacks on Azerbaijani forces. They also pledged 200 military advisors to the Azerbaijani military. While Armenia may have been Russia's favorite in the conflict, Moscow was willing to throw its support to Azerbaijan to gain a stronger position with both sides.

Aliyev took advantage of the presence of himself and Karabakh Armenian leader Robert Kocharyan at the CIS signing ceremony to hold confidential talks. Nothing came of the discussions, but the two would meet again many times after Kocharyan had assumed the presidency of the Republic of Armenia.[24]

As Armenian troops approached within ten kilometers of the Azerbaijan-Iran border, Tehran became nervous. A newspaper close to the Islamic regime, Kayhan International, was the first to warn that Iran might not remain neutral in the conflict. "If our peace and border security is going to be threatened," it wrote, "our leaders cannot let the situation take care of itself."[25] Iran sent additional troops to its border.

The Security Council passed a third resolution on the conflict on 14 October 1993. It acknowledged that Moscow had provided a venue for Aliyev and Kocharyan to talk together. This time, in UNSC 874, the Council finally took note that Yerevan was a party to the conflict.

[23] Kozyrev, Andrei. Interview in *Nezavisimaia Gazeta*, 22 September 1993, as quoted in Laitin and Suny, ibid.

[24] de Waal, ibid., 238.

[25] Hockstader, Lee. "Major Offensive Laid to Armenians," *Washington Post*, 20 August 1993. Web. Retrieved 6 June 2019. https://www.washingtonpost.com/archive/politics/1993/08/20/major-offensive-laid-to-armenians/3d9baf4e-16d6-4b32-a155-c4ecfd16b09c/?utm_term=.61a538f743b5.

"Expressing its serious concern that a continuation of the conflict in and around the Nagorny Karabakh region of the Azerbaijani Republic and of the tensions between the Republic of Armenia and the Azerbaijani Republic," the resolution read, "would endanger the peace and security in the region...(and) calls upon the parties concerned to make effective and permanent the cease-fire established as a result of the direct contacts undertaken with the assistance of the Government of the Russian Federation in support of the CSCE Minsk group."[26] The resolution also called for the parties to abide by an "Adjusted Timetable," something to which Azerbaijan did not agree. The timetable linked the withdrawal of Armenian forces from Azerbaijani territory to the lifting of Azerbaijan's closure of its border with Armenia. Azerbaijan believed this made it seem that it was a defeated power.[27]

In November 1993, Armenian troops seized a bridge that crossed into Iran. Iran demanded publicly that Armenia cease its attacks on Azerbaijani towns and villages near Azerbaijan's southern border. As refugees flooded into Iranian territory, Tehran's Ministry of Foreign Affairs issued a statement expressing deep concern for the massacre of innocent people. It demanded that Armenian troops withdraw from all occupied Azerbaijani territory. This may have appeared to support Azerbaijan's diplomatic position in the conflict, except that Iran never defined what it meant by occupied territory—was it only the area outside of Nagorno-Karabakh, or Nagorno-Karabakh itself?

Faced with the flood of refugees, Iran sent its own troops surging across the border into Azerbaijan. This drew a fierce response from Moscow who did not want to see the conflict internationalized. "Whatever their motivation," said a Russian Foreign Ministry spokesman, "We cannot show any understanding or support for the actions of the Iranian side. The fact that Iranian armed groups have crossed the border into Azerbaijan will not only lead to a further escalation of the conflict, but also pushes it dangerously close to the verge of internationalization."[28]

[26] United Nations Security Council. Security Council Resolution 874 (1993), 3292nd Meeting. 14 October 1993, S/RES/874 (1993). Web. Accessed 1 June 2019. http://unscr.com/en/resolutions/doc/874.

[27] Mamedov, Sokbet, "Azerbaijan Does Not Consider Itself the Defeated Side," Izvestia, Moscow, 20 October 1993, p. 2 in FBIS-SOV-93-203, 22 October 1993, p. 77 as quoted in Human Rights Watch, ibid., 69.

[28] Croissant, ibid., 94.

Iran pulled back, but it had made its point: If fighting threatened Iran's borders, it was prepared to react.

The Security Council passed a fourth and final resolution on the fighting, UNSC 884, on 12 November 1993. It did not cover any new ground. It reiterated UNSC 883's notice of tension between Azerbaijan and Armenia, and condemned violations of the cease-fire.[29] All four resolutions had demanded a cease-fire and peace talks, as well as a withdrawal from occupied territory. All four requested that the parties cooperate with the CSCE and support the Minsk process. Missing from all four was a critical element: any enforcement mechanism to compel the parties to obey the resolutions.

Russia's representative on the Karabakh issue, Vladimir Kazimirov, had been dismissive of the CSCE. "The first year of the OSCE Minsk group's activities (since June 1992) showed that it can't effectively play the role of mediator, to stop or hold the spreading of the armed conflict in the new regions…(T)he Minsk group obviously underestimated the importance of stopping the bloodshed. We continued our activities in the Minsk group, trying to make it take the right path, counteracting the attempts of the Western diplomats to use this format in their geopolitical interests, directed first of all to lessening Russia's influence in the South Caucasus. In this situation we had to double our own efforts as mediator, more actively meeting with the authorities of the countries in conflict, calling them for achieving a ceasefire."

Kazimirov reported that even though the Azerbaijanis had honored their pledge not to rocket Stepanakert, the acting commander of the Karabakh Self-Defense Committee Samvel Babayan sent a note. It warned the Azerbaijanis were gathering military equipment in Aghdam and the Armenians would consider this a break in the cease-fire. The message said fighting would begin in an hour and that he would hold Azerbaijan responsible. In reviewing the message, Kazimirov commented "The very text of Babayan's letter testified to their decision to deliberately break the former arrangement that was hidden behind the epistolary tricks of the newly appointed commander from Karabakh." Despite all the problems, the Russians managed to halt the fighting for the week of 27 June 1993.

[29] United Nations Security Council. Security Council Resolution 884 (1993), 3313th Meeting. 12 November 1993. S/RES/874 (1993). Web. Access on 1 June 2019. http://unscr.com/en/resolutions/doc/884.

Kazimirov claims that in the second half of 1993, Russia succeeded in arranging two months out of six to be cease-fires. "Nobody except for Russia—neither other States, nor the OSCE Minsk group—managed to curb even temporarily military actions in Karabakh (even when they had a chance.)" US Ambassador John Maresca explained Russia's hostility toward the OSCE. "At first, Russia fully supported the Minsk Group. But in 1993 Russia reactivated its earlier independent mediation effort…The reason was clear: Russia wished to reestablish its dominance in the region and to exclude outsiders, namely the US and Turkey…Moscow would like to reestablish control of the former Soviet frontier with Turkey and Iran, and to share in Azerbaijan's oil riches. To accomplish these aims, Russia has been pressuring Azerbaijan to accept the reentry of Russian troops as a separation force and as border guards, as to give Russia a share of the oil concessions…For leverage, the Russians have used an implicit but dramatic threat: If Azerbaijan does not comply, Russia will step up its backing for Armenia…with disastrous military results for the Azeris."[30]

Russia tried again to hijack the peace process from the Minsk group in May 1994, at the meeting of the CIS Interparliamentary Assembly in Kyrgyzstan. Under Russian direction, the group issued the Bishkek Protocol. There was no mention of the CSCE, but several references to previous CIS initiatives. It repeated calls for a withdrawal of troops from Azerbaijani territory outside of Karabakh, and a limited cease-fire.[31] Russian-sponsored talks would then follow. (When Mathias Mossberg, the head of the CSCE mediating group, indicated that he would like to come to the talks, Russia refused him permission.)[32] It was a blatant attempt to remove the Western international community from the negotiating table.

[30] Maresca, John J. "Agony of Indifference in Nagorno-Karabakh," *The Christian Science Monitor*, 27 June 1994. Web. Retrieved 6 June 2019. https://advance-lexis-com.libproxy.chapman.edu/document/?pdmfid=1516831&crid=8a09ae85-de4f-4fe3-83c9-eb32ecabdd89&pddocfullpath=%2Fshared%2Fdocument%2Fnews%2Furn%3AcontentItem%3A3S3M-GXX0-005X-62JP-00000-00&pddocid=urn%3AcontentItem%3A3S3M-GXX0-005X-62JP-00000-00&pdcontentcomponentid=7945&pdteaserkey=sr0&pditab=allpods&ecomp=bfyk&earg=sr0&prid=410373d9-000d-4247-a4e5-6a1063ecbbe5.

[31] Bishkek Protocol, 5 May 1994. Web. Retrieved 3 June 2019. https://peacemaker.un.org/sites/peacemaker.un.org/files/Bishkek%20Protocol.pdf.

[32] Cornell, ibid., 122.

Kazimirov glossed over the Bishkek Protocol's lack of any mention of peacekeepers, which explains why the two sides continue to face each other on a line of contact.[33]

Kazimirov's memoirs are a unique glimpse into the Russian interpretation of the peace process. He spent a lot of time complaining about Western attempts to be involved in the peace process, without explaining why he opposed them. Similarly, he did not explain his antipathy to an Azerbaijani proposal that the peacekeepers be international rather than Russian. While Kazimirov seemed genuinely interested in achieving a peace in the region, he appeared more interested in creating and/or preserving a Russian sphere of influence. (After leaving his post, Kazimirov became an advocate for the Armenian cause. He frequently appeared on Russian television supporting Yerevan's interpretation of events.)

Russian Defense Minister General Grachev then invited the military leaders of Armenia, Azerbaijan, and Nagorno-Karabakh to Moscow. There, he ignored the fact that a cease-fire had already been in effect for four days and demanded that the participants sign another cease-fire that would include the stationing of an 1800-strong Russian peacekeeping force. Azerbaijani President Aliyev told Kazimirov that unless the Russian forces were part of a CSCE delegation they would only enter Azerbaijan "over my dead body."[34]

Azerbaijan claimed that the May cease-fire was for thirty days; Kazimirov insisted there was no time limit to the agreement. Regardless, Western powers began preparations for a "permanent" cease-fire. The draft called for a CSCE multinational peacekeeping force, but it agreed that the troops would be under Russian command. Azerbaijan rejected the proposal.[35]

The Story of Section 907

American politics is electoral politics, and the American congress is frequently swayed by the organized lobbying groups with the most members, the largest contributions, or the strength of lobbying group

[33] Kazimirov, ibid.

[34] Croissant, ibid., 111.

[35] Walker, Edward. Ibid., 21.

members' interest in a single issue. In the case of Nagorno-Karabakh, the Armenian community in the United States was fully engaged. Countering their efforts were few Azerbaijanis. As a result, after Armenia invaded Azerbaijan, seized large swaths of Azerbaijani territory by force, and continued to hold that territory in opposition to international law, the US Congress condemned Azerbaijan as the aggressor. It also failed to acknowledge that, under international law, Nagorno-Karabakh was a part of Azerbaijan.

Specifically, Congress passed the Freedom for Russia and Emerging Eurasian Democracies and Open Markets Support Act, aka the Freedom Support Act of 1992. This mammoth appropriations bill created numerous, frequently overlapping, mechanisms providing American aid to the countries of the former Soviet Union. Buried within the legislation was Section 907, prohibiting direct US government aid to Azerbaijan. "United States assistance under this or any other act…may not be provided to the Government of Azerbaijan until the President determines, and so reports to the Congress, that the Government of Azerbaijan is taking demonstrable steps to cease all blockades and other offensive uses of force against Armenia and Nagorno-Karabakh".[36]

Section 907 was so completely one sided that even as liberal a newspaper as the Washington Post took note of it. The editorial was four years after the passage of the legislation, but bears being quoted at length:

"The United States continues to intervene mischievously in the appalling conflict between Armenia and Azerbaijan. Its particular contribution is to increase the misery of a million Azeri refugees, and in that way to draw out hopes for a settlement. Why would Washington wish to conduct such a policy, which runs against its own substantial strategic, economic and political interests? It is a policy thrust upon a reluctant president by a Congress heavily influenced by Armenian-Americans. This lobby has forced tough restrictions on direct American humanitarian and other aid to Azerbaijan…

"(L)ook at the situation on the ground. First… Azerbaijan is at war with Armenia; you would not expect them to trade with each other right now. Then, it is not only that Karabakh Armenians seized and hold the long-sovereign Azeri enclave of Nagorno-Karabakh, whose turmoil sparked this war between the two formerly Soviet republics. Armenians

[36]Freedom Support Act. PL 107-155. Stat. 2532. Sec. 907. Web. Retrieved 1 June 2019. https://www.congress.gov/bill/102nd-congress/senate-bill/2532/text.

also now occupy 20 percent of Azerbaijan proper. In short, the United States is punishing the loser and comforting the conqueror, occupier and evident winner of the war…

"(W)hat is on display is ethnic political power. The irony is that its wielding may not even be to the advantage of the Armenians. They would be better served, as would the Azeris, by enlisting the United States as an impartial moderator as they traded off territory for security for Karabakh and prosperity for themselves. But instead the Armenian lobby tends to tip American policy and to invite political intervention by an imperially inclined Moscow."[37]

Secretary of State Madeline Albright protested the law to Congressman Robert Livingston. "Section 907 damages US national interests by undermining the administration's neutrality in promoting a settlement in Nagorno-Karabakh, the ability to encourage economic and broad legal reforms in Azerbaijan, and efforts to advance an East-West energy corridor."[38] Her aide, Stephen Sestanovich, also protested the law as contrary to US National Security interests. "The Azerbaijani government is strongly pro U.S. It is being helpful to us on Caspian energy questions, on proliferation, on Iranian terrorism—and on Nagorno-Karabakh. Section 907 has limited, and will continue to limit, the expansion of US-Azerbaijani relations—to no useful purpose."[39]

As Sestanovich predicted, the bill hurt US-Azerbaijani relations for many years while Armenia strengthened its ties with Moscow. In 2001 Congress passed PL 107-115 authorizing the president to waive Section 907 if it is in the national interest. While promising the government of Armenia $90 million, it also states "The President may waive section 907 of the FREEDOM Support Act if he determines and certifies to the Committees on Appropriations that to do so–

(A) is necessary to support United States efforts to counter international terrorism; or
(B) is necessary to support the operational readiness of United States Armed Forces or coalition partners to counter international terrorism; or

[37] "Armenian Lobby," *Washington Post*, 1 August 1996, A22.

[38] Cornell, ibid., 106.

[39] Cornell, ibid., 106.

(C) is important to Azerbaijan's border security; and
(D) will not undermine or hamper ongoing efforts to negotiate a peaceful settlement between Armenia and Azerbaijan or be used for offensive purposes against Armenia."

The law further reads that "The President may extend the waiver Authority…on an annual basis on or after December 31, 2002."[40] Every president from both parties has done so annually.

The Clinton administration did its best to stay out of the conflict, except for its support for the Minsk process. Armenian President Ter-Petrosyan visited the White House in August 1994. Clinton told him that he (Clinton) would follow the Nagorno-Karabakh issue personally. Ambassador Maresca then made a series of proposals that included recognizing a Republic of Nagorno-Karabakh within the Republic of Azerbaijan, and the creation of an economic free zone that would include the republics of Armenia, Azerbaijan, and Nagorno-Karabakh.[41]

The proposal went nowhere, probably because the United States was already hedging how involved it wanted to be on the ground. The US Administration seemed willing to cede the leadership of any peacekeeping efforts to Russia, something that the OSCE fought hard to prevent. At the same meeting, President Clinton told Ter-Petrosyan the United States would not object to Russian troops' presence in a peacekeeping force, "if the parties agree to it and there were clear OSCE safeguards so that we had the right sort of oversight." A month later, Secretary of State Madeleine Albright went further, echoing Russian president Boris Yeltsin's comments about the Caucasus being in Russia's sphere of influence. The United States was not against Russian peacekeeping missions in the "near abroad," she said, since "Russia has the resources, direct interests and the leadership required to help resolve the problem in this region."[42] With the United States giving signals like these, it was little wonder that Ter-Petrosyan would not agree to the US proposals without getting Russian approval first.

[40] Foreign Operations, Export Financing, and Related Programs Appropriation Act 2002, PL 107-115, Assistance for the independent state of the former Soviet Union. Sec. g (2) and g (4). Web. Retrieved 1 June 2019. https://www.govinfo.gov/content/pkg/PLAW-107publ115/html/PLAW-107publ115.htm.

[41] Laitin and Suny, ibid.

[42] Human Rights Watch, ibid., 137.

When the Republicans came to town in 2001, the new Secretary of State Colin Powell sponsored a summit meeting of Presidents Aliyev and Kocharyan in Key West, Florida. They negotiated a decentralized status for Karabakh and an exchange of territory. In the end, however, neither of the leaders believed their citizens had been prepared to accept the compromises they had made with each other. It was a lost opportunity. US co-chair Rudolf Perina said the two leaders had been "unbelievably close" to solving the conflict. In his analysis, any new peace proposal would only have minor technical changes in it, since the basic concepts for resolution had been agreed upon.[43]

Armenian-US relations took a hit in 2002 when the US government applied sanctions against the Armenian biochemical company Lizin for its sales to Iran. The president said Lizin was not a state-run company. The US Federal Register did not specify the nature of Lizin's activities, only that the sanctions were imposed under the Iran Non-Proliferation Act of 2000. Foreign Minister Vartan Oskanian effectively admitted that Lizin had sold sensitive dual-use technology to Iran despite American warnings. Oskanian seemed unrepentant and willing to continue banned sales. "Our relations [with Iran] have been on a high level since 1991, and they remain on that level today," he said. "We see no reason to introduce any changes into our policy."[44]

In 2003, Armenia allegedly assisted Iran to purchase rockets and machine guns. These were subsequently recovered in Iraq in 2007 during two Shi'a militant attacks that killed an American serviceman soldier and wounded six. The United States protested in 2008, and official Armenia did not deny the sales.[45]

Throughout the George H.W. Bush administration, the executive branch supported Azerbaijan's position in the negotiations. As an example, Secretary of State Colin Powell wrote to Azerbaijan's

[43] Danielyan, Emil. "Armenian, Azerbaijani Presidents Were 'Incredibly Close' to Karabakh Settlement," Radio Free Europe/Radio Liberty, 30 October 2003. Web. Retrieved 7 June 2019. https://reliefweb.int/report/armenia/armenian-azerbaijani-presidents-were-incredibly-close-karabakh-settement.

[44] Danielyan, Emil. "Armenia: Officials Say Sanctions Will Not Worsen Ties with U.S.," Radio Free Europe/Radio Liberty, 21 May 2002. Web. Retrieved 16 July 2019. https://www.rferl.org/a/1099761.html.

[45] "Top Armenian Officials Decline Comment on 'Arms Supplies' to Iran Allegations," Radio Free Europe/Radio Liberty, 30 November 2010. Web. Retrieved 16 July 2019. https://www.rferl.org/a/armenia_declines_comment_arms_supplies_iran/2235143.html.

Foreign Minister Elmar Mammedyarov, "The United States unequivocally supports Azerbaijani territorial integrity…and is glad to take part in a monitoring mission on the occupied territories."[46] Sometimes the support was not easy to give, as the United States wanted to remain a neutral party with good relations in both capitals. On 13 January 2005, outgoing Assistant Secretary of State Elizabeth Jones commented in a video conference call that it was in Russia's interest to have stability in areas such as Nagorno-Karabakh. She strayed into Armenian internal politics with the rest of her statement, that it was in Russia's interest "for corruption to end there—for the criminal secessionists who rule there to be removed. It is not appropriate for this kind of instability and criminality to exist right in the middle of Europe."[47] Youthful demonstrators from Baze, the Armenian Revolutionary Front-Republican, and Orinats Yekir protested in front of the US Embassy, protected by a government-provided police cordon.[48] In response to the demonstrations and to comments from the vice speaker of the Armenian National Assembly Vahan Hovannisian that Jones' comments did not represent the views of the US Government, the embassy in Yerevan issued a strong statement of support for Jones and for Azerbaijan. "US policy with respect to the Nagorno-Karabakh conflict has not changed. The United States does not recognize Nagorno-Karabakh as an independent country–and its leadership is not recognized internationally or by the United States."[49]

Since the Obama administration, the United States has returned to the practices of the Clinton administration. It has stepped away from involving itself in the Nagorno-Karabakh conflict except to continue to provide a co-chair to the Minsk process. As Chatham House noted, "Neither belligerent," meaning Armenia and Azerbaijan, "has made

[46] Mehtiyev, ibid., 11.

[47] "Assistant US Secretary of State's Statesmen's (sic) Hinder Peace Process Says Karabakh ARF," Asbarez, 20 January 2005. Web. Accessed 1 June 2019. http://asbarez.com/51209/assistant-us-secretary-of-states-statemens-hinder-peace-process-says-Karabakh-arf/.

[48] "Youth Demonstration Vocalizes Concern about US Remarks on Karabakh," Asbarez, 19 January 2005. Web. Retrieved 1 June 2019. http://asbarez.com/51204/youth-demonstration-vocalizes-concern-about-us-remarks-on-Karabakh/.

[49] "ARF Bureau Member Hovannisian Slams Jones' MKR Statement," Asbarez, 19 January 2005. Web. Retrieved 1 June 2019. http://asbarez.com/51207/arf-bureau-member-hovannisian-slams-joness-mkr-statement/.

an unambiguous commitment to a Euro-Atlantic orientation."[50] The conflict therefore does not appear to be part of the US-Russian great power rivalry, despite Russia's heavy involvement in the issue. It seems that Washington has ceded the Caucasus to Russia's sphere of interest.

The Peace Process

Armenian President Levon Ter-Petrosyan traveled to Washington, DC in August 1994 to meet with President Bill Clinton and encourage investment in Armenia. He told Clinton that he would welcome several thousand Russian soldiers deployed between the Armenian and Azerbaijani forces. He said it was the best way to keep the peace and to protect the security of Armenians in Nagorno-Karabakh. Petrosyan naively denied that the Kremlin would have an ulterior motive for placing its forces in the southern Caucasus. "There are forces in Russia which dream of re-establishing the Soviet Union or re-establishing the Russian empire," he said. "But I'm confident that the officials who are in power in Russia do not have a goal of re-establishing Russia's empire." Clinton replied that he would have no problem with a Russian peacekeeping force, provided it was acceptable to the OSCE.

The Azerbaijanis, however, did not approve. Having worked hard to get the Russians out of their territory, they were in no mood to invite them back in. Their Ambassador to the United States, Hafiz Pashayev, outlined the conditions that would be needed to accept foreign troops in their soil. Pashayev said it would be better to have monitors instead of peacekeepers, that they could only come if there was a timetable for their withdrawal, and it would be preferable if the international force came from many countries instead of Russia alone.[51]

In September 1994, the OSCE's Committee of Senior Officials complained of Russian unilateralism. Committee members from NATO and neutral countries complained that Russia had recently initiated an

[50] Broers, Laurence. "The Nagorny Karabakh Conflict: Defaulting to War," Chatham House, Russia and Eurasia Programme, July 2016, 2. Web. Retrieved 1 June 2019. https://www.chathamhouse.org/sites/default/files/publications/research/NK%20paper%2024082016%20WEB.pdf.

[51] Greenhouse, Steven. "Armenia Says It Would Welcome Russian Peacekeeping Offer," *The New York Times*, 12 August 1994. Web. Retrieved May 2019. *AcademicOneFile*, http://link.galegroup.com/apps/doc/A174456657/AONE?u=chap_main&sid=AONE&xid=ae0b330b.

Armenian-Azerbaijani summit in Moscow without informing the CSCE, that it had snubbed a meeting organized by the CSCE's Minsk group (to which Russia itself belonged) and had pressed for a Russian/CIS peacekeeping force to be deployed in Karabakh rather than a CSCE-sponsored multinational force—including Russia—that the Minsk group sought. Delegates pointed to the apparent contradiction in Russia's policy of seeking to make the CSCE superior in status to regional security organizations while simultaneously undercutting it by unilateral action in the East.[52]

In December 1994, at the same meeting where they changed their name from the CSCE to the Organization on Security and Cooperation in Europe (OSCE), that organization pledged to enhance the CSCE's role in warning, conflict prevention, and crisis management through the use of peacekeeping operations and missions. It obliquely criticized Russia's attempt at unilateralism, diplomatically requesting individual member's actions to be harmonized into a single, coordinated effort. The CSCE/OSCE also agreed to send a multinational peacekeeping force of 3000 to the region after all sides agreed to a cessation of the conflict. It was the first time the CSCE/OSCE offered to take on a peacekeeping role in an armed conflict. At the same meeting, a decision was made that Russia should be a permanent chair of the group.[53] This was later changed, in 1997, establishing three co-chairs: Russia, France, and the United States.

In March 1995, the co-chairs received their mandate from the OSCE. The language was quite strong on ruling out attempts at unilateral peacekeeping. "The Co-Chairmen will realize full co-ordination in all mediating and negotiating activities, harmonizing them into a single coordinated effort within the framework of the OSCE…The Co-Chairmen will, jointly and in full parity…make joint efforts in order to strengthen the cease fire; develop a common basis for negotiations with the parties to the conflict…assist the Chairman-in-Office in developing a plan

[52]"Daily Report," Radio Free Europe/Radio Liberty, 20 September 1994. Web. Retrieved 6 June 2019. http://www.friends-partners.org/friends/news/omri/1994/09/940920.html(opt,mozilla,unix,english,,new).

[53]Conference for Security and Cooperation in Europe, *Budapest Declarations*. Regional Issues, Intensification of CSCE action in relation to the Nagorno-Karabakh conflict. 5–6. Web. Retrieved 5 June 2019. https://www.osce.org/mc/39554?download=true; Human Rights Watch, ibid., 141.

for the establishment, composition and operation of a multi-national OSCE peace-keeping force…jointly chair the regular consultations of the Minsk group, dispatch jointly to the Minsk group members…jointly and continuously inform and consult…jointly inform…visit jointly, or when appropriate separately, on an agreed basis…"[54]

The OSCE subsequently summarized the function of the Minsk group as follows:

- Provide an appropriate framework for conflict resolution in the way of assuring the negotiation process supported by the Minsk Group;
- Obtain an agreement of the parties to cease armed conflict in order to permit the convening of the Minsk Conference;
- Promote the peace process by deploying OSCE multinational peace-keeping forces.[55]

The group held its next summit meeting in Lisbon, Portugal in 1996. At the instigation of Azerbaijan, the Chairman in Office inserted an annex to the summit's final declaration. It said no progress had been made to resolve the Nagorno-Karabakh conflict and the issue of the territorial integrity of Azerbaijan. It outlined three principles that were supported by all members of the Minsk group, but that one of the participating states (Armenia) was not willing to accept. These included the territorial integrity of the Republic of Armenia and the Republic of Azerbaijan; self-rule for Nagorno-Karabakh within the Republic of Azerbaijan; and, security for the whole population of Nagorno-Karabakh.[56]

[54] Organization for Security and Cooperation in Europe, *Mandate of the Co-Chairmen of the Conference on Nagorno-Karabakh Under the Auspices of the OSCE ("Minsk Conference")*. Vienna: 23 March 1995. Web. Retrieved 5 June 2019. https://www.osce.org/mg/70125?download=true.

[55] Organization for Security and Cooperation in Europe, Updated Survey of OSCE Long-Term Missions and Other OSCE Field Activities. Vienna: 26 August 2005. Web. Retrieved 5 June 2019. https://www.osce.org/secretariat/16311?download=true.

[56] Organization for Security and Cooperation in Europe, Lisbon Document 1996, Annex One. Web. Retrieved 5 June 2019. https://www.osce.org/mc/39539?download=true.

In response, Armenia had its own annex inserted into the documents. It stated the first Annex presupposed the future status of Nagorno-Karabakh, which was supposed to be the subject of negotiations.[57] The dueling annexes reflected the central point of contention between Armenia and Azerbaijan. Armenia believed the principle of international law that should determine Karabakh's status was the self-determination of the inhabitants. Since the area had been cleansed of Azerbaijanis shortly before the war, that would result in either an independent Karabakh or one annexed to Armenia. Azerbaijan, by contrast, believed that the overriding principles were state sovereignty and the inviolability of international borders. The two annexes had another, long-term consequence: Armenia refused to sign the larger document and walked out of the summit. Karabakh Armenians walked out as well—never to return to the negotiating table.[58]

In May 1997, the Minsk co-chairs introduced a peace package. It called for the Armenia army to withdraw into the Republic of Armenia, for the Karabakh forces to withdraw into the 1988 borders of Nagorno-Karabakh, and the Azerbaijani forces withdraw far enough to create a buffer zone. Once the withdrawals were completed OSCE peacekeeping forces would patrol the no-man's land dividing the various sides. The peacekeeping forces would then oversee the return of the permanent inhabitants into the demilitarized zone, Shusha, and the Shaumian district. The blockade of Karabakh would be lifted. Azerbaijan would lease the Lachin corridor to the OSCE. Finally, diplomatic relations between Armenia and Azerbaijan would be restored. In a second document, the co-chairs recognized the international borders of Armenia and Azerbaijan, and that Nagorno-Karabakh was within the boundaries of Azerbaijan. It also promised the former oblast a form of self-determination.[59] This was the so-called "package" deal in which most steps occurred simultaneously. President Arkady Ghukasian of Karabakh rejected the document brusquely, likening the co-chairs of the Minsk Group to the "troikas" of

[57] Organization for Security and Cooperation in Europe, Lisbon Document 1996, Annex Two. Web. Retrieved 5 June 2019. https://www.osce.org/mc/39539?download=true.

[58] Croissant, ibid., 120.

[59] Organization for Security and Cooperation in Europe, *Comprehensive Agreement on the Resolution of the Nagorno-Karabakh Conflict*, July 1997. Web. Retrieved 5 June 2019. https://www.legal-tools.org/doc/4b2ddb/pdf/.

judges that had condemned innocent people to death in Stalin's purges. Baku cautiously encouraged further work on the proposal but remained dubious about the plan.[60]

In September, the Minsk group tried again, offering a "step by step" or "phased" proposal in which each element acted as a confidence-building measure to be completed before the next element.

The buffer zone between troops would remain unoccupied until there were further negotiations. Similarly, the status of Nagorno-Karabakh, Lachin Corridor, Shusha, and the Shaumian district would be the subject of negotiation after the military withdrawal was completed.[61] The Armenian Foreign Ministry announced his country accepted the proposal and was awaiting word on the sequencing of events.[62] Azerbaijan also accepted the proposal as a basis for negotiations, but Karabakh Armenians said no. Since troops had to be withdrawn before negotiations began, Stepanakert believed it would have surrendered its greatest advantage (Azerbaijani territory that it occupied) before the negotiations began. In rejecting the plan, Karabakh's representative said that they wanted a package proposal, and they suggested that either Armenia or Iran could act as a guarantor of Karabakh's security.[63]

A surprise to all was the reaction of Armenian President Ter-Petrosyan who endorsed the proposal. Baku reacted warily, but Azerbaijani presidential foreign policy adviser Vafa Gulu-Zade told Interfax on 30 September that he was "personally satisfied" with Ter-Petrosyan's statements.[64] Ter-Petrosyan was approaching the problem as a pragmatist, placing Armenia's national interest over that of Karabakh.[65] The Armenian political opposition condemned the president for a defeatist attitude and

[60] Laitin and Suny, ibid.

[61] Organization for Security and Cooperation in Europe, Agreement on the End of the Nagorny Karabakh Conflict, December 1997. Web. Retrieved 5 June 2019. https://www.c-r.org/downloads/Accord17_22Keytextsandagreements_2005_ENG.pdf.

[62] "OSCE/Minsk Plan for Karabakh Accepted," Radio Free Europe/Radio Liberty, 9 October 1997. Web. Retrieved 5 June 1997. https://reliefweb.int/report/armenia/osceminsk-plan-karabakh-accepted.

[63] "Newsline-October 13, 1997," Radio Free Europe/Radio Liberty, 13 October 1997. Web. Accessed 5 June 2019. https://www.rferl.org/a/1141514.html.

[64] "Newsline—October 1, 1997," Radio Free Europe/Radio Liberty, 1 October 1997. Ibid.

[65] Cornell, ibid., 127.

proposed that the peace proposal be put to a referendum within Armenia and Karabakh,[66] something to which the president did not agree. Ter-Petrosyan's realism and willingness to compromise eventually drove him out of office, to be replaced by the former head of Nagorno-Karabakh, Robert Kocharyan.

Kocharyan's new foreign minister was a US citizen from Syria named Vartan Oskanian. In June 1998, Oskanian made the announcement that Armenia was willing to accept less than full independence for Karabakh, but they would not accept mere autonomy within Azerbaijan. This might have been a signal of Yerevan's willingness to compromise, but Oskanian went on reflecting the new administration's harder line on Karabakh. Oskanian threatened that if the deadlock in negotiations were not broken, Armenia might take unilateral action to include the possible unification of Karabakh with Armenia. The international community expressed its alarm, and the Foreign Ministry had to walk back Oskanian's words a few days later. The statements were not to be taken out of context and "characterized in ways that are unfounded."[67]

Oskanian's words found an echo in Karabakh. "Azerbaijan has oil," said Arkady Ghukasian, the Karabakhi "president." "But only we can contribute the necessary stability to give it value. Everyone here is armed. I cannot exclude a partisan war if we are surrendered to Azerbaijan. We are going to decide our own fate."[68]

Having been stymied with both the package proposal and the step-by-step proposal, the Minsk group came up with a third alternative in November, the common state proposal. This was the brain-child of the former head of the Russian KGB, Prime Minister Yevgeniy Primakov. The proposal said that Nagorno-Karabakh and the Republic of Azerbaijan were common states. The two entities would sign an agreement on the divisions of responsibilities and mutual delegation of powers. In other words, the Minsk negotiations would result in an agreement for more negotiations. The proposal then included several items that would be totally unacceptable to any sovereign country: Nagorno-Karabakh, under international law a part of Azerbaijan, would have the authority

[66] "Newsline—November 13, 1997," Radio Free Europe/Radio Liberty, 13 November 1997. Web. Retrieved 5 June 2019. https://www.rferl.org/a/1141536.html.

[67] Laitin and Suny, ibid.

[68] Williams, Daniel. Ibid.

to enter into agreements with foreign countries; the enclave would be given veto power over Azerbaijan's ability to enter into agreements if it affected Karabakh's interests; it could appoint its own diplomatic representatives within Azerbaijani diplomatic facilities abroad; it would have its own constitution, and Azerbaijani law would only be valid within Nagorno-Karabakh if it did not contradict the new Karabakh constitution; they would have their own flag and national anthem, and only Nagorno-Karabakh could issue passports to its inhabitants; Nagorno-Karabakh could have representatives in the Azerbaijani parliament and participate in Azerbaijani presidential elections, but only Karabakh representatives could participate in Karabakh elections; Azerbaijani security forces were forbidden to enter Nagorno-Karabakh except with permission from Stepanakert; the official language of Karabakh would be Armenian, not Azerbaijani Turkish. In short, except for the name, it established Azerbaijan as a subordinate entity to Nagorno-Karabakh, with Stepanakert having veto power over many of Azerbaijan's sovereign rights.

The common state proposal left the status of Lachin for future negotiations; it said residents of Shusha and Shaumanian district could return to their homes to be protected by Nagorno-Karabakh security forces. There would be a phased withdrawal of forces along the lines outlined in previous proposals, with the demilitarized zone to be patrolled by UN peacekeepers.[69] In seeking to address Armenian demands for self-determination, the Minsk group had shorted Azerbaijani demands for sovereignty and inviolability of international borders.

Presidents Kocharyan and Aliyev met twice in April 1999, on the sidelines of other diplomatic events. The face-to-face meetings restarted talks that had stalled, but the exact nature of the discussions is unknown. At one of the meetings, the 1992 "Goble Plan" was proposed whereby the Lachin corridor would be surrendered to Armenia in return for a corridor across Armenia linking Azerbaijan to its exclave of Nakhichevan. The plan was opposed in Azerbaijan because it could be interpreted as surrendering Karabakh to Armenia. In Yerevan, the plan was opposed because it would mean the loss of its southern border with its ally Iran.[70] The peace

[69] Conference for Security and Cooperation in Europe, "On the Principles for a Comprehensive Settlement of the Conflict over Nagorno Karabakh," November 1998. Web. Retrieved 7 June 2019. https://www.c-r.org/downloads/Accord17_22Keytextsandagreements_2005_ENG.pdf.

[70] de Waal, ibid., 274–175.

process soon stalled again, however, as Armenia faced the aftereffects of the October 1999 shootings in parliament.

President Putin opened 2001 with a trip to Baku to get the peace talks started again. Together with French President Jacques Chirac, he sponsored summit meetings in Paris in February and March. The two Caucasus presidents appear to have agreed to a land swap similar to the Goble plan as a condition of peace: Armenia would retain control of the Lachin corridor, and Azerbaijan would gain a Mehri corridor linking Azerbaijan proper to the exclave of Nakhichevan. Opposition figures in both capitals opposed the plan when it became known.[71]

Not to be outdone, Secretary of State Colin Powell sponsored his own summit meeting in Key West. It was the high-water mark of summit diplomacy, but the two Caucasus leaders walked away. The American Minsk co-chair and the Armenians were convinced that the principles had been agreed upon; Azerbaijan claimed only a number of alternative suggestions had been discussed with no agreement.[72] Aliyev and Kocharyan met 21 times over the course of their presidencies, but peace eluded them.

The Minsk co-chairs established the Prague Process in 2004, a bilateral channel by which the deputy foreign ministers of Armenia and Azerbaijan could communicate. Nothing of significance emerged from the arrangement, but it kept contact alive between the two countries.

The European Union tried to circumvent the Minsk process with new proposals of their own: Armenia would withdraw from five of the occupied regions surrounding Nagorno-Karabakh; Baku would reopen cooperation with Yerevan including the rail line that had been closed since the beginning of the conflict. The proposal came from Swedish Parliamentarian Per Gharton, who was the EU's rapporteur on the Caucasus. The proposal did not get far; when Gharton made his report to the European Parliament, the parliamentarians stripped his report of the recommendations.[73] It would not have survived in any case, as Armenian Foreign Minister Oskanian dismissed the proposal on procedural grounds.

[71] "Caucasus Report: July 1, 2002." Radio Free Europe/Radio Liberty, 1 July 2002. Web. Retrieved 1 July 2019. https://www.rferl.org/a/1341865.html.

[72] Mehtiyev, ibid., 3.

[73] "European Parliament Calls for Stronger EU Engagement in South Caucasus," Radio Free Europe/Radio Liberty, 27 February 2004. Web. Retrieved 8 June 2019. https://reliefweb.int/report/armenia/european-parliament-calls-stronger-eu-engagement-south-caucasus.

"Armenia does not support separate initiatives that are different from the OSCE Karabakh settlement package," he said.[74] Azerbaijan, of course, welcomed the proposal to get large swaths of its territory back in return for minimal concessions.

Azerbaijan got a boost from an unexpected quarter in August 2004, when Armenian-ally Iran sent its president Mohammad Khatami to Baku to improve bilateral relations. Khatami reiterated Iran's commitment to Azerbaijan's territorial integrity,[75] signaling its disagreement with Armenia over its occupation of Karabakh.

Turkey tried to get into the act, holding a tripartite meeting on the edge of the 2004 Istanbul NATO summit. Turkey discussed getting more involved in the peace process, possibly even playing a role as mediator. Moscow was not amused, since if anyone was going to be a mediator outside of the Minsk process it was going to be the Kremlin.[76]

The Parliamentary Assembly of the Council of Europe (PACE) also had an opinion on the conflict that seemed to place the majority of the blame for the continued stalemate on Armenia. It reaffirmed that "Independence and secession of a regional territory from a state may only be achieved through a lawful and peaceful process…and not in the wake of an armed conflict leading to ethnic expulsion and the de facto annexation of such territory to another state." Having declared that Karabakh's method of seeking independence violated international law, it continued: "The Assembly reiterates that the occupation of foreign territory by a member state constitutes a grave violation of that state's obligations as a member of the Council of Europe." It also suggested that if the Minsk process failed to reach a settlement, Armenia and Azerbaijan should take the case to the International Court of Justice in The Hague. As a tip of the hat to the Armenian negotiating position, the resolution also called on Azerbaijan to resume direct contact with representatives from Nagorno-Karabakh.[77]

[74] Mehtiyev, ibid., 5.

[75] Abbasov, Shahin. "Iran-Azerbaijan Relations: On a Better Footing After Khatami's Baku Visit." Eurasianet, 10 August 2004. Web. Retrieved 15 July 2019. https://eurasianet.org/iran-azerbaijan-relations-on-a-better-footing-after-khatamis-baku-visit.

[76] Mehtiyev, ibid., 5.

[77] "The Conflict over the Nagorno Karabakh Region Dealt with by the OSCE Minsk Conference," Resolution 1416 (2005), Parliamentary Assembly of the Council of Europe. Web. Retrieved 8 June 2019. https://assembly.coe.int/nw/xml/XRef/Xref-XML2HTML-en.asp?fileid=17289&lang=en.

Baku tried to send a goodwill signal to Armenia when in the summer of 2004 members of the Karabakh Liberation Organization were arrested. This group of hardliners funded by the Azerbaijani government disrupted a NATO Partnership for Peace conference being held in the "Europe" hotel in Baku. They even attempted to assault its participants for inviting Armenian officers to Baku. "These officers represent the occupational army, exclaimed Akif Nagi, the chairman of the KLO". "Their hands are soaked in blood. They have raped our women and killed our children. There is no place for them in Baku."[78] The initial response of the government was proper. The activists were put on trial and given lengthy sentences for sabotaging a NATO-sponsored event. After a public outcry, The government backtracked and publicly admonished the court for the "tough verdict." The KLO activists were released.[79] The incident showed again that the public was not prepared to support government actions that hinted at compromise.

Armenian and Azerbaijani presidents Kocharyan and Ilham Aliyev met in Warsaw on 15 May 2005 on the sidelines of the Council of Europe summit. In line with a "gentlemen's agreement" of confidentiality on the contents of negotiations, neither side divulged details of what the two presidents discussed. Armenian MFA spokesman Hamlet Gasparian stated, however, that the Warsaw meeting opened the way for a continuation of the "Prague talks" between foreign ministers Mammadyarov and Oskanian.

The two ministers met, and Azerbaijan's foreign minister Elmar Mammadyarov dropped a bombshell. He announced that Armenia was prepared to agree to withdraw from all seven occupied provinces surrounding Nagorno-Karabakh. Talks were underway to create a timetable. Whether Mammadyarov was leaking results of the talks, or spreading propaganda to put Armenia on the defensive, there were howls

[78] Ismailzadeh, Fariz. "The Karabakh Liberation Organization Protests the Visit of Armenian Officers." The Central Asia-Caucasus Analyst, 30 June 2004. Web. Retrieved 5 May 2019. https://www.cacianalyst.org/publications/field-reports/item/9131-field-reports-caci-analyst-2004-6-30-art-9131.html.

[79] "The Rise and Fall of Samvel Babayan." Ibid.

of protest from the Armenian side. Gasparian categorically denied the truth of Mammadyarov's remarks.[80]

For his part, former Azerbaijani negotiator Vafa Guluzadeh did not believe any talks would come to a successful conclusion, because Russia did not want them to succeed. "Because Russia is not yet ready for that. Russia spares no effort in trying to stay in the region, so the signing of a peace agreement by Yerevan and Baku would mean the pull-out of the Russian military bases from Armenia in the near future," he said.[81]

In November, Haik Kojandian, an advisor to Defense Minister Serzh Sargsyan, suggested a step-by-step proposal that included all the elements of the OSCE proposal, only in reverse order: a referendum, to be followed by peacekeepers, to be followed by rehabilitation of the conflict zone.[82] The first stumbling block in the negotiations was always trying to reconcile Armenian claims of self-determination with Azerbaijan's claims of sovereignty. Kojandian had now introduced a new stumbling block that the Russians use to impede progress in peace talks, the question of sequencing steps that needed to be taken.

Foreign Ministers Oskanian and Mammadyarov met informally on 4 December 2005 with the Minsk group co-chairs, on the sidelines of the annual OSCE foreign ministers' meeting in Ljubljana, Belarus. They laid the groundwork for a summit meeting of the principals to be held in February. The summit meeting between Presidents Kocharyan and Aliyev took place in Rambouillet, outside of Paris, on 10 February 2006. As the meeting date approached, the OSCE expressed readiness to help deploy an international peacekeeping force if the two presidents agreed on it. Belgian Foreign Minister Karel de Gucht said this would allow the two sides to solve any issues that might remain after the summit.[83] Armenian Foreign Minister Oskanian said there was a paper which outlined

[80] Fuller, Liz. "Azerbaijan: Armenia Denies Agreeing to Leave Seven Occupied Districts," Radio Free Europe/Radio Liberty, 19 May 2005. Web. Retrieved 8 June 2019. https://www.rferl.org/a/1058945.html.

[81] Mehtiyev, ibid., 14.

[82] Fuller, Liz. "Armenia/Azerbaijan: Will Presidents' Meeting Yield Progress Toward Karabakh Peace Deal?" Radio Free Europe/Radio Liberty, 27 January 2006. Web. Retrieved 8 June 2019. https://www.rferl.org/a/1065154.html.

[83] "OSCE Offers Peacekeeping Help in Nagorno Karabakh," Radio Free Europe/Radio Liberty, 25 January 2006. Web. Retrieved 8 June 2019. https://www.rferl.org/a/1065082.html.

the basic principles of an agreement and which both sides accepted.[84] The Karabakh Armenians, however, struck a sour note. On February 22, "president" Arkady Ghukasian called on Kocharyan's administration to stop acting as a go-between, and instead promote direct talks between Azerbaijani officials and Karabakh representatives. "When Baku starts to negotiate with Nagorno-Karabakh, for me it will mean that Azerbaijan tries to solve the problem," he said.[85]

President Aliyev told his cabinet that Azerbaijan would never compromise on the question of its territorial integrity,[86] raising a high bar for the summit. The Minsk Russian Co-Chair kept the hope of a compromise alive, by disregarding Aliyev's comments. "We remain optimistic…These words are not addressed to us. We haven't heard anything of the kind and, therefore, cannot comment on this."[87] The talks, like so many others, ended in failure. The OSCE co-chairs said the discussions had been "intensive," but had failed to make progress.

The two presidents reacted badly to the failure at Rambouillet. President Aliyev gave a speech on 1 March in which he said negotiations with Armenia were a dead-end, that Karabakh would always be Azerbaijani territory, and that he was prepared to take whatever steps were necessary to secure Karabakh. President Kocharyan reacted the following day, warning that if "whatever steps were necessary" meant the use of military force, that he would give legal recognition to Nagorno-Karabakh's independence. "But if the moment arrives, when Azerbaijan indeed unequivocally says that the time is right for them, that they have to strengthen their army and in the future will solve the Karabakh issue by force, then our steps should be as followed: firstly, de jure recognition

[84] "Nagorno-Karabakh: Minsk Group Co-Chair Hopes for 2006 Progress," Radio Free Europe/Radio Liberty, 1 February 2006. Web. Retrieved 8 June 2019. https://www.rferl.org/a/1065304.html.

[85] Khachatrian, Haroun. "Armenia Cautiously Optimistic about US Diplomacy Concerning Nagorno Karabakh," Eurasianet, 21 March 2006. Web. Retrieved 8 June 2019. https://reliefweb.int/report/armenia/armenia-cautiously-optimistic-about-us-diplomacy-concerning-nagorno-karabakh.

[86] "Aliyev Vows Nagorno Karabakh Will Remain Part of Azerbaijan," Radio Free Europe/Radio Liberty, 1 February 2006. Web. Retrieved 8 June 2019. https://www.rferl.org/a/1065337.html.

[87] "Garabagh Mediators Praise Outcome of Talks in Armenia," 3 February 2006. ReliefWeb. Web. Retrieved 8 June 2019. https://reliefweb.int/report/azerbaijan/garabagh-mediators-praise-outcome-talks-armenia.

of Nagorno-Karabakh by the Republic of Armenia."[88] In response, President Aliyev said if he did not see any progress in the peace talks, he would leave the negotiations.[89]

The presidential road show next went to Bucharest, in June 2006. When this summit resulted in failure, the co-chairs decided to go public with a joint declaration. The co-chairs had submitted a series of proposals they considered to be a combination package/step-by-step approach. Everything, including the status of Nagorno-Karabakh would be decided at one time (the package), but implementation could take place in stages over a long period (the step by step). The co-chairs announced they were withdrawing from the peace process but would be willing to reengage when the presidents showed political will and initiative to reach a peace process.[90] The new American co-chair, Matthew Bryza, characterized the proposals that had been rejected: "These are the best proposals made so far. I would say that we are closer to peace than ever before. But I can't guarantee that the presidents would use their sovereign right to accept these proposals or make changes that would suit both sides."[91]

The co-chairs resumed their activities in September 2006. They held a variety of meetings with the foreign ministers in Moscow, Paris, and Brussels. This led to the third presidential summit of the year, at the CIS November summit meeting in Minsk. Both sides emerged giving optimistic statements.

The co-chairs met again in November 2007, in Madrid. They negotiated the "Madrid Principles," which became the basis for all subsequent

[88] "Armenia/Azerbaijan: Tensions Rise Over Nagorno Karabakh," Radio Free Europe/Radio Liberty, 3 March 2006. Web. Retrieved 8 June 2019. https://www.rferl.org/a/1066339.html.

[89] "Azerbaijan Warns Armenia on Karabakh Negotiations," Radio Free Europe/Radio Liberty, 16 March 2006. Web. Retrieved 8 June 2019. https://www.rferl.org/a/1066775.html.

[90] Dehdashti-Rasmussen, Rexane. "The Conflict over Nagorno-Karabakh: Causes, the Status of Negotiations, and Prospects," in *OSCE Yearbook 2006*. Institute for Peace Research and Security Policy at the University of Hamburg/FISH (2006), 199–200. Web. Retrieved 8 June 2019. https://ifsh.de/file-CORE/documents/yearbook/english/06/Rasmussen-en.pdf.

[91] "Matthew Bryza: Peace Talks Not Deadlocked Despite Exhausted Mediating Effort," Today.az, 10 July 2006. Web. Retrieved 8 June 2019. http://today.az/view.php?id=28010.

negotiations. The document said the presidents of Armenia and Azerbaijan were instructing their foreign ministers to negotiate a peace agreement taking into account the following principles (among others):

1. The final legal status of Nagorno-Karabakh would be determined through a plebiscite allowing the free and genuine expression of the will of the population of Karabakh.
2. All the Azerbaijani territories around Nagorno-Karabakh under Armenian control would be returned to Azerbaijan's control in stages, and international peacekeepers would be deployed.
3. Kelbajar district would be placed under transitional international monitoring by an OSCE commission that would include Armenian and Azerbaijani representatives.
4. A corridor would link Nagorno-Karabakh to Armenia.
5. Azerbaijan would commit not to send military personnel or equipment beyond the current line of contact, with the exception of police units (in equivalent proportion with civilian population as pertains to police units deployed in other Azerbaijani provinces) and with the exception of border detachments and associated equipment along the Azerbaijan-Iran border (at a level equivalent to those maintained per kilometer along the eastern Azerbaijan-Iran border).
6. The sides would pledge non-use of force against each other, including in Nagorno-Karabakh and around Nagorno-Karabakh.
7. The rights and privileges of the inhabitants of Karabakh during the interim period would be finalized by the parties with the participation (in a form to be agreed) of Nagorno-Karabakh representatives.[92]

Like previous proposals, implementation details were left for future negotiations. Madrid had become the basis for the Minsk process, but those details were never resolved. Would the plebiscite take place before or after the withdrawals? Who could participate in the plebiscite: current residents or all residents (meaning those who fled the violence and were living elsewhere)? What questions would be included that would allow the world to know the free and genuine expression of the will of the people? When

[92] "Madrid Principles—Full Text," ANI Armenian Research Center, 11 April 2016. Web. Retrieved 12 June 2019. https://www.aniarc.am/2016/04/11/madrid-principles-full-text/.

would the peace monitors arrive? Where would they be stationed? What would be their role? The questions were endless.

The United Nations continued to take note of the Frozen Conflict in Karabakh. In March 2008, the General Assembly passed a resolution reaffirming continued respect and support for the sovereignty and territorial integrity of the Republic of Azerbaijan within its internationally recognized borders. It also demanded the immediate, complete, and unconditional withdrawal of all Armenian forces from all the occupied territories of the Republic of Azerbaijan. While General Assembly resolutions are not binding on the members, they do reflect their opinion. In that respect, it was also important that the resolution said, "no State shall recognize as lawful the situation resulting from the occupation of the territories of the Republic of Azerbaijan, nor render aid or assistance in maintaining this situation." Such language is a condemnation of any country actively supporting a movement that does not respect the sovereignty and territorial integrity of the country.[93]

Presidents Aliyev and Sargsyan met in June 2008 in St. Petersburg on the sidelines of the annual meeting of the CIS. It was the first meeting between presidents since Sargsyan replaced Kocharyan in April. They had a chance to meet a few days earlier at the NATO summit in Bucharest, but Aliyev refused. At the Russian meeting, the two leaders gave their foreign ministers authorization to continue talks.[94] To build on the momentum, Russian president Medvedev engaged in shuttle diplomacy. He visited Baku in July and Yerevan in October. These efforts were capped on 2 November, when Medvedev hosted both Aliyev and Sargsyan in Moscow. Little is known about the discussions that took place, but there was considerable optimism going into the meeting. Russian foreign minister Sergei Lavrov thought the two sides were on the verge of a breakthrough, describing the possibility of a breakthrough as "very real."[95]

[93] United Nations General Assembly Resolution 62/243 "The Situation in the Occupied Territories of Azerbaijan," Adopted by the General Assembly on 14 March 2008. Web. Retrieved 8 June 2019. https://www.un.org/en/ga/search/view_doc.asp?symbol=A/RES/62/243.

[94] "Analysis: Presidents Give Green Light for Continuation of Karabakh Talks," Radio Free Europe/Radio Liberty, 12 June 2008. Web. Retrieved 18 June 2019. https://www.rferl.org/a/1144604.html.

[95] "Aliyev, Sarkisian to Meet in Moscow," Asbarez, 29 October 2008. Web. Retrieved 18 June 2019. http://asbarez.com/59432/aliyev-sarkisian-to-meet-in-moscow/.

Nothing came of the talks, however, as President Sargsyan had no room to maneuver. Days before the summit, the Dashnak party threatened to leave Sargsyan's coalition government if the president "betrayed national interests" by agreeing to cede any of the occupied territories.[96] In other words, the Dashnaks refused to allow Sargsyan to fulfill the terms of the Madrid principles. Despite the obstacles, the two leaders would agree to speak again in January 2009 on the sidelines of the World Economic Forum in Davos, Switzerland. Armenia sent Foreign Minister Edward Nalbandian[97] instead of President Sargsyan, however, and so this opportunity for further summitry was missed.

Armenia held the position that officials in Nagorno-Karabakh should be a separate party to the talks. This position was undermined by one of its own. Jirayr Sefilyan, a Lebanese-born Armenian military commander and political figure who was involved in the capture of Shusha in early May 1992, and later continued to serve in the armed forces of both the "NKR" and Armenia. Sefilyan said in a newspaper interview, "Who are we kidding? The whole world knows that the army of the NKR is a part of the Armenian armed forces, that the budget of the NKR is financed from the budget of Armenia, and that the political leaders of the NKR are appointed from Yerevan. It is time to consider Karabakh as a part of Armenia, one of its regions. In the negotiation process the territory of Karabakh should be considered as a territory of Armenia and no territorial cession must be made."[98]

The European Partnership Summit in Prague gave the two leaders another opportunity to speak in May 2009. Minsk co-chairs were upbeat. "Presidents Aliyev and Sarkisian were able…to reduce their differences on our Basic Principles and generally agree on the basic ideas that they came here to discuss," American co-chair Matthew Bryza said. Days later,

[96] Fuller, Liz. "'Moscow Declaration' a Victory for Armenia," Radio Free Europe/Radio Liberty, 3 November 2008. Web. Retrieved 18 June 2019. https://www.rferl.org/a/Moscow_Declaration_A_Victory_For_Armenia/1337592.html.

[97] Synovitz, Ron. "Turkish PM Shows New Foreign Policy Assertiveness at Davos." Radio Free Europe/Radio Liberty, 30 January 2009. Web. Retrieved 19 June 2019. https://www.rferl.org/a/Turkish_PM_Shows_New_ForeignPolicy_Assertiveness_At_Davos/1376933.html.

[98] Interview with Jirayr Sefilyan, Armenia Today, 29 October 2008, as quoted in Chiragov and Others v. Armenia, European Court of Human Rights, 16 June 2015, 18. Web. Retrieved 29 July 2019. https://www.echr.am/en/events/chiragov-and-others-v-armenia-gc.html.

however, the head of the international relations department of Azerbaijan's presidential administration, Novruz Mammedov, disagreed. He said that the co-chairs were deceiving world public opinion by claiming progress when there was none. He even suggested that Bryza had an ulterior motive for the false statements. Mammadov implied that Bryza was intentionally lying to US Secretary of State Madeline Albright and US President Bill Clinton in a bid to get a promotion. "Armenia's position was very unconstructive," Mammadov said. "They did not want to take a single step toward resolution of the conflict and once again made their claims on Azerbaijan's territory."[99]

The presidents met again the following month, at a meeting in St. Petersburg with the co-chairs. Both reported progress, without stating what that progress might be. Mammadov said the meeting was more productive than the Prague summit.[100]

On a Russian television channel, President Aliyev brought new hope to the stalemate. Since one of the major sticking points in the Minsk process was the future status of Karabakh, Aliyev said he was willing to defer making a decision on this point for up to a hundred years. The president was willing to settle for the return of five of the seven occupied districts surrounding Nagorno-Karabakh, with Kelbajar and Lachin reverting back to Azerbaijan after five years.[101]

A different political game played out in October 2009, when Turkey and Armenia signed two sets of agreements to normalize relations. Had these agreements gone into effect, the people of both Armenia and Azerbaijan would have been outraged: Armenia because Turkey had not agreed to recognize the events of 1915 as a genocide, and Azerbaijan because Turkey would reopen the border with Armenia without any progress having been made on Karabakh. In Armenia itself, opposition parties led a firestorm of criticism against agreements with the ancient

[99] Fuller, Liz. "Is the Karabakh Peace Process in Jeopardy?" Radio Free Europe/Radio Liberty, 15 May 2009. Web. Retrieved 19 June 2019. https://www.rferl.org/a/Is_The_Karabakh_Peace_Process_In_Jeopardy/1732576.html.

[100] Babayan, Aza. "Armenia, Azerbaijan 'Satisfied' with Fresh Summit," Radio Free Europe/Radio Liberty, 4 June 2019. Web. Retrieved 19 June 2019. https://www.rferl.org/a/Armenia_Azerbaijan_Satisfied_With_Fresh_Summit/1747084.html.

[101] Fuller, Liz and Emil Danielyan. "Is a Formal Karabakh Peace Agreement Within Reach?" Radio Free Europe/Radio Liberty, 8 July 2009. Web. Retrieved 19 June 2019. https://www.rferl.org/a/Is_A_Formal_Karabakh_Peace_Agreement_Within_Reach/1772434.html.

enemy. In Azerbaijan, the Foreign Ministry issued a statement saying that normalization of relations between Turkey and Armenia prior to the desired withdrawal of Armenian forces from occupied Azerbaijani territory "directly contradicts Azerbaijan's national interests and casts a shadow on the brotherly relations between Turkey and Azerbaijan."

Not wanting to oppose Azerbaijan's supporters in Turkey, Prime Minister Erdogan announced that he would submit the accords he had signed to parliament for ratification, but only after Armenia withdrew from Karabakh. Erdogan cited opposition to the agreement among the Turkish electorate, and potential opposition from the General Assembly if he tried to have the agreements approved without there being peace between Armenia and Azerbaijan.[102] The willingness of Turkey and Armenia to normalize relations was considered an early foreign policy victory for the American Obama administration; Erdogan's refusal to submit the agreements to parliament was an American defeat.

The June 2010 summit in St. Petersburg ended in controversy. The Armenian side claimed that Russia had presented new proposals; the Azerbaijani side said that the Russian proposals were old news, having been distributed over a year ago. Regardless of the age of the Russian proposals, Azerbaijan president Aliyev was not happy and left the summit a day early. The following day was the worst cease-fire violations in two years, in which one Armenian and four Azerbaijani soldiers were killed.[103] Two weeks later, at the CIS Summit in Ukraine, the two leaders refused to talk to each other.

Iran heard that one of the proposals being considered in the Minsk process was an international peacekeeping force, in which the United States might contribute troops. They opposed the American presence unequivocally. Speaking in Yerevan, the Iranian ambassador to Armenia

[102] Fuller, Liz. "Will Serzh Sarkisian's Biggest Gamble Pay Off?" Radio Free Europe/Radio Liberty, 15 October 2009. Web. Retrieved 19 June 2019. https://www.rferl.org/a/Will_Serzh_Sarkisians_Biggest_Gamble_Pay_Off/1852787.html.

[103] "Azerbaijan Says No New Peace Proposals," Radio Free Europe/Radio Liberty, 6 July 2010. Web. Retrieved 19 June 2019. https://www.rferl.org/a/Azerbaijan_Says_No_New_Karabakh_Peace_Proposals/2092584.html.

Seyed Ali Saghaeyan said Iran "would not allow" the deployment of American forces, as such forces would pose a serious threat to Iran.[104]

A new controversy now arose, over the status of the Stepanakert airport. Authorities in the secessionist enclave announced they were repairing the facility and launching Artsakh Air with flights between Yerevan and Stepanakert. Azerbaijani authorities were outraged and pointed out that they had closed the airspace over this part of their sovereign territory. "We notified that the airspace over Karabakh is closed," said the head of the Civil Aviation Organization Arif Mammadov. "The law on aviation envisages the physical destruction of airplanes landing in that territory."[105] Sargsyan decided to play chicken and upped the ante by stating he would be on the first flight. Azerbaijan backed down and said they would not threaten civilian aircraft.[106] The entire episode may have been a charade on both sides, as the airline never started services.

June 2011 found the two leaders together again, this time in the Russian city of Kazan. As the Kazan meeting approached, mediators said substantive differences were small, but it was not clear whether the leaders had the political will to present a deal to their citizens. As usual, a joint statement was issued that the leaders agreed on a number of issues, but those issues were never enumerated. Both sides then blamed the other for the talks' failure. Armenia charged Azerbaijan with adding additional demands to the Basic Principles; Azerbaijan charged Armenia with making maximalist demands and an unwillingness to compromise.[107] An unnamed diplomat involved in the talks said that the talks were "not a make-or-break meeting" and that work on an agreement would continue.

[104] "Iran Opposes Any U.S. Peacekeeping Role for Karabakh," Radio Free Europe/Radio Liberty, 24 June 2010. Web. Retrieved 19 June 2019. https://www.rferl.org/a/Iran_Against_Any_US_Peacekeeping_Role_For_Karabakh/2081078.html.

[105] "Azerbaijan Threatens to Shoot Down Karabakh Planes," Asbarez. 16 March 2011. Web. Retrieved 19 June 2011. http://asbarez.com/94194/azerbaijan-threatens-to-shoot-down-karabakh-planes/.

[106] Grigorian, Marianna. "Nagorno-Karabakh: Waiting for Air Artsakh," Eurasianet, 6 May 2011. Web. Retrieved 19 June 2019. https://eurasianet.org/nagorno-karabakh-waiting-for-air-artsakh.

[107] Grigorian, Marianna and Shahin Abbasov, "Nagorno-Karabakh: Are Baku and Yerevan Getting to Yes, or Going Nowhere?" Eurasianet, 27 June 2011. Web. Retrieved 19 June 2019. https://eurasianet.org/nagorno-karabakh-are-baku-and-yerevan-getting-to-yes-or-going-nowhere.

The diplomat admitted that the two sides had made less progress than mediators had hoped. "It was clear in the talks that there is still a great deal of mistrust between the sides," he said. "We all felt it would be possible to achieve more."[108]

By the end of this meeting, peace talks were deadlocked. Azerbaijan had reached its limits on compromises. Bolstered by oil sales and weapons purchases, it believed time was on its side. Armenia stopped considering the occupied territories surrounding Nagorno-Karabakh as bargaining chips. Instead, hardliners began to mine history for proof these lands were part of Armenia's patrimony.[109]

Things began to heat up on Azerbaijan and Armenia's southern border. Azerbaijan believed Iran was actively trying to destabilize its government. An Israeli think tank reported in 2007 that the Azerbaijan Ministry of National Security arrested 16 members of the Northern Fighters of Imam Mahdi, a group monitoring Western and Israeli diplomatic missions who had ties to the Revolutionary Guard. In 2009, the Islamic Party of Azerbaijan organized in Baku anti-Israel demonstrations. This was an Iranian-funded formerly legal political party whose leadership had ties to Iran, Hizballah, and Jaish Allah terrorist organizations. Authorities had canceled its party registration in 1995 when its senior members were indicted on charges of treason and posing a threat to state security.[110]

In January 2012, Baku arrested two people accused of plotting to kill two teachers at a Jewish school in the capital. In February, the government announced the arrest of another suspected terrorist group allegedly working for Iran. In March, the national security ministry announced the arrest of 22 Azerbaijani citizens who had been trained in Iran by the Revolutionary Guard. Authorities seized automatic assault rifles, grenades, ammunition, and explosives. The group allegedly planned to attack diplomatic missions, the offices of a Jewish organization, the local

[108] Barry, Ellen. "Azerbaijan and Armenia Fail to End Enclave Dispute," *The New York Times*, 25 June 2011. Web. Retrieved 23 May 2019. *Academic OneFile*, http://link.galegroup.com/apps/doc/A259721565/AONE?u=chap_main&sid=AONE&xid=e42ae803.

[109] "Armenia and Azerbaijan: A Season of Risks," Briefing 71. International Crisis Group Europe (26 September 2013), 3–4.

[110] Murinson, Alexander. "Iran Targets Azerbaijan," The Begin-Sadat Center for Strategic Studies, BESA Center Perspectives Paper 110, 23 June 2010. Web. Retrieved 15 July 2019. https://besacenter.org/perspectives-papers/iran-targets-azerbaijan/.

headquarters of BP, and an American-themed fast food restaurant.[111] In retaliation, Iran arrested two Azerbaijani poets on espionage charges. They were released in September.[112]

Following a series of cease-fire violations in July 2014 that left a score of dead, Russian unilateralism returned to the forefront. President Vladimir Putin invited Aliyev and Sargsyan to meet with him in Sochi. Neither of the other Minsk co-chairs were invited to the event. The two Caucasus presidents met each other there in August 2014, and then had individual meetings with Putin. They issued a statement committing themselves to a peaceful resolution of the conflict, but released no details about either the summit discussions or the discussions with Putin. Aliyev put a positive spin on the lack of Western participants, thanking Russia for its efforts. "Russia, as our close friend, partner and neighbor, certainly plays a special role in the settlement process," he said as the meetings began.[113] Not to be outdone in the field of unilateralism, US Secretary of State John Kerry held his own summit meeting with the principals the following month on the sidelines of a NATO summit meeting in Cardiff, Wales. Like the Sochi event, there were no results. The presidents met again in September on the sidelines of a NATO conference,[114] and in October 2014 when French President Francois Hollande invited the Minsk co-chairs to join the presidents in a summit he sponsored. Since there was a sharp disagreement at this latter meeting about the meaning of "final status," no joint statement was issued at the end. Another summit was held in December 2015 in Zurich, sponsored by Switzerland.

Aliyev's Sochi praise of the Russians represented more than a tactical move but reflected a change in the geopolitics in the Caucasus. Russian

[111] "Azerbaijan Arrests '22 Iranian Spies,'" *The Telegraph*, 14 March 2012. Web. Retrieved 15 July 2019. https://www.telegraph.co.uk/news/worldnews/Middleeast/azerbaijan/9144424/Azerbaijan-arrests-22-Iranian-spies.html.

[112] "Iran Releases Azerbaijani Poets Accused of Spying," Radio Free Europe/Radio Liberty, 5 September 2012. Web. Retrieved 15 July 2019. https://www.rferl.org/a/iran-azerbaijani-poets-spying/24698533.html.

[113] "Putin Urges Karabakh Peace as Aliyev, Sarkisian Meet in Russia," Azatutyun, 10 August 2014. Web. Retrieved 20 June 2019. https://www.azatutyun.am/a/26523369.html.

[114] Aghayeva, Seba. "Meeting of Azerbaijan, Armenian Presidents Emphasizes Need to Sign Big Peace Agreement," Azvision, 8 September 2014. Web. Retrieved 29 July 2019. https://en.azvision.az/news/2688/meeting-of-azerbaijani-armenian-presidents-emphasizes-need-to-sign-big-peace-agreement.html.

troops had invaded Abkhazia and South Ossetia in Georgia in 2008, and the West failed to respond. In 2014, Russia seized the Crimea and instigated a war of secession in eastern Ukraine. The West again failed to respond. It became obvious in the Caucasus that the West was limiting its involvement. In addition, in spite of massive human rights violations in many countries within the former Soviet Union, the West seemed to ignore the abuses within Russia but to focus on allegations in Azerbaijan.

Perhaps signaling the authorities' unhappiness with this Western cavalier attitude of criticizing friends but not competitors, Azerbaijan raided the Baku offices of Radio Free Europe/Radio Liberty in December 2014. Authorities seized computers and ordered the office closed. The attack followed months of extreme anti-Western rhetoric by top Azerbaijani government officials—including accusations that the United States ambassador to Baku had engaged in "gross interference." The president's chief of staff, Ramiz Mehdiyev, published a 13,000-word article claiming that the C.I.A. was contriving regime changes in the post-Soviet space (the so-called color revolutions). It also called Azerbaijan's human rights activists a "fifth column" of the United States.[115]

While the United States incurred the wrath of Azerbaijan, trouble rocked the Armenian-Russian alliance. In January 2015 Russian private Valery Permyakov killed a family of seven, including two babies, outside of the Russian military base in Gyumri. Contrary to Armenian law and Russo-Armenian treaties, he was not handed over to local law enforcement agencies for prosecution. Before the murder trial began, Permyakov's commanding officer and other crucial witnesses were decommissioned and sent home to Russia. Permyakov himself was found guilty of the charges and extradited back to Russia.[116]

There were additional killings of Russian-on-Russian,[117] but in 2017 an Armenian killed a Russian serviceman assigned to the base. Authorities

[115] Kucera, Joshua. "Azerbaijan Snubs the West," *The New York Times*, 9 January 2015. Web. Retrieved 23 June 2019. *AcademicOneFile*, http://link.galegroup.com/apps/doc/A396595743/AONE?u=chap_main&sid=AONE&xid=d69346d7.

[116] Grigoryan, Armen. "New Controversies Swirl Around Russian Military Base in Armenia," Eurasia Daily Monitor 14/66, The Jamestown Foundation, 16 May 2017. Web. Retrieved 16 July 2019. https://jamestown.org/program/new-controversies-swirl-around-russian-military-base-armenia/.

[117] "Russian Soldier Found Stabbed to Death in Armenia," *Moscow Times*, 15 June 2015. Web. Retrieved 22 July 2019. https://www.themoscowtimes.com/2015/06/15/russian-soldier-found-stabbed-to-death-in-armenia-a47377.

charged the twenty-year-old subject with having mental health problems.[118] In December 2018, another murder occurred, when a Russian soldier was charged with beating an Armenian woman to death.[119]

The European Court of Human Rights added a twist to the peace discussions with an important legal ruling that negated Armenia's claims that Karabakh was either an unrecognized independent state or an internal Azerbaijani problem. In the landmark decision "Chiragov and others v. Armenia" the court ruled that Nagorno-Karabakh was under the control the Republic of Armenia, and that Yerevan was responsible for what occurred under its occupation. "Armenia, from the early days of the Nagorno-Karabakh conflict, has had a significant and decisive influence over the 'NKR,' that the two entities are highly integrated in virtually all important matters and that this situation persists to this day. In other words, the 'NKR' and its administration survive by virtue of the military, political, financial and other support given to it by Armenia which, consequently, exercises effective control over Nagorno-Karabakh and the surrounding territories, including the district of Lachin."[120]

In September 2015, following some artillery exchanges, the Minsk co-chairs met separately with the Foreign Minister of Armenia Edward Nalbandian, and with the Foreign Minister of Azerbaijan Elmar Mammadyarov, to discuss the need to reduce tensions along the Line of Contact. The Ministers agreed to continue preparations with the Co-Chairs for the next presidential summit at a future unnamed date. They also encouraged the two sides to accept an OSCE mechanism to investigate cease-fire violations, a proposal that Armenia accepted.[121]

The rapporteur for the Parliamentary Assembly of the Council of Europe (PACE), Robert Walter, tried to investigate the situation. Azerbaijan agreed to a meeting immediately, but Armenia offered several postponements. Finally, the Armenian representative to PACE wrote that

[118] "Russian Soldier Stabbed to Death in Armenia," Radio Free Europe/Radio Liberty, 22 April 2017. Web. Retrieved 22 July 2019. https://www.rferl.org/a/russian-soldier-stabbed-to-death-armenia-gyumri/28446224.html.

[119] "Russian Soldier Charged in Death of Armenian Woman, Lawyers Say, Radio Free Europe/Radio Liberty, 18 December 2018. Web. Retrieved 22 December 2019. https://www.rferl.org/a/russian-soldier-charged-in-death-of-armenian-woman-lawyers-say/29662520.html.

[120] Chiragov and Others, ibid., 68.

[121] Organization for Security and Cooperation in Europe, *Press Statement by the Co-Chairs of the OSCE Minsk Group*, 26 September 2015. Web. Retrieved 1 June 2019. https://www.osce.org/mg/185746.

she could meet with Walter in Yerevan, but that Armenia could not arrange a visit to Karabakh. That required the approval of the Karabakh authorities. In a report that he later wrote about these events, Walter expressed surprise since Armenia had arranged a visit to Karabakh by a high-level French delegation during the same period. As for the Karabakh authorities, they would not grant permission for Walter to visit, since he was working on the resolution discussing "occupied territories of Azerbaijan"—terminology they could not accept.

Although denied access to Armenia and Karabakh, Walter visited Baku. There he met with members of the Azerbaijan parliament. He reported that for most MP's, Russia was at the origin of the conflict and part of the problem. It was impossible for it to be part of the solution. They argued that, without Russia's interference, Armenians and Azerbaijanis could reach a solution. Walter also noted that the Armenian side no longer hid the presence of their troops in Nagorno-Karabakh. There was a regular exchange of senior personnel between the Armenian Armed Forces and the so-called "Nagorno-Karabakh Republic Army." As an example, in June of 2015, Lt. Gen. Levon Mnatsakanyan, the Deputy Chief of Staff of the Armenian Armed Forces, was appointed Minister of Defense of "NKR" and Commander of the "NKR Army." His predecessor, Lt. Gen. Movses Hakobyan, was then appointed as Deputy Chief of Staff in Yerevan. In fact, the Armenian Minister of Defense, Seyran Ohanyan, served as Commander of the "NKR Army" between 2000 and 2007. This should not have been a surprise, given that Presidents Kocharyan and Sargsyan had both emerged from Nagorno-Karabakh.

PACE approved a resolution from their Committee on Political Affairs and Democracy. The resolution could not pass, however, as passage requires a unanimous vote. It reiterated some of the points from their 2005 Resolution on the conflict. "The Assembly reaffirms that independence and secession of a regional territory from a State may only be achieved through a lawful and peaceful process based on democratic support by the inhabitants of such territory and not in the wake of an armed conflict leading to ethnic expulsion and the de facto annexation of such territory to another State. It reiterates that the occupation of foreign territory by a member state constitutes a grave violation of that State's obligations as a member of the Council of Europe and reaffirms the right of displaced persons from the area of conflict to return to their homes safely and with dignity."

This was a clear repudiation of the positions of Armenia and the de facto authorities in Karabakh. In fact, the resolution endorsed Azerbaijan's positions in the negotiations:

"The Assembly calls for:

14.1 the immediate cessation of violence across the line of contact and the border between Armenia and Azerbaijan, including the withdrawal of all military equipment and the cessation of military activity in the vicinity of the region;

14.2 the demilitarization of the line of contact on both sides;

14.3 the implementation of the first steps toward a peaceful settlement, namely: the withdrawal of Armenian armed forces and other irregular armed forces from Nagorno-Karabakh and the other occupied territories of Azerbaijan; the establishment of full sovereignty of Azerbaijan in these territories and the convening of the plenary meeting of the Minsk Group to establish an interim status for Nagorno-Karabakh guaranteeing security and internal self-governance, with an agreed corridor linking Armenia to Nagorno-Karabakh; and other confidence-building measures, including an access corridor to Nakhichevan." It called on Russia to stop providing weapons to both sides and labeled the Republic of Armenia an "occupying power."[122]

Not surprisingly, since the resolution undercut the Armenian negotiating position, the Armenian representatives at PACE dissented. The main issue they raised was that the very title of the report being prepared was one sided in favor of Azerbaijan and prejudged the conclusions. They urged PACE not to adopt the resolution.[123] Armenia could not accept the PACE resolution for the same reason it could not accept any peace plan: namely, the inability of large sections of the Armenian population to surrender land captured during the 1992–1994 war, even though the surrounding territories had been seized originally to act as bargaining chips.

[122] Walter, Robert. "Escalation of Violence in Nagorno-Karabakh and other occupied territories in Azerbaijan," Committee on Political Affairs and Democracy, Parliamentary Assembly of the Council of Europe. PACE Document 13930, 11 December 2015. Web. Retrieved 17 November 2020. http://assembly.coe.int/nw/xml/XRef/Xref-XML2HTML-en.asp?fileid=22255&lang=en.

[123] Walter, Robert (rapporteur). "Escalation of Violence in Nagorno Karabakh and other Occupied Territories of Azerbaijan." Parliamentary Assembly of the Council of Europe Report 13930, 11 December 2015. Web. Retrieved 20 June 2019. http://assembly.coe.int/nw/xml/XRef/Xref-XML2HTML-en.asp?fileid=22255&lang=en.

There was a flare-up in the fighting on 2 April 2016, the worst cease-fire violation in twenty years. A new cease-fire was established through Russia's efforts. President Putin called for a halt to the fighting on 5 April, and the cease-fire went into effect the following day.

Russia was not the only regional power concerned with the fighting. Alarmed by a howitzer attack that landed on Iranian villages near its northern border, Iranian Foreign Minister Mohammad Javad Zarif telephoned Armenian Foreign Minister Nalbandian on 5 April 2016 and offered to play a role in peacemaking if both sides consented. He repeated the offer of Iran's good offices at a trilateral meeting with Azerbaijani and Turkish foreign ministers. To emphasize the seriousness of Zarif's proposal, Iranian President Hassan Rouhani telephoned the Azerbaijani and Armenian presidents the next day with the same offer.[124] Russia and Iran then joined together for some shuttle diplomacy. Iran's efforts did little to further the peace process, but it sparked new contacts between Tehran and Baku (there were already good contacts between Tehran and Yerevan).

President Putin visited Baku in August 2016. The Russian leader announced his intention to forge a strategic partnership with Azerbaijan, expand trade links, and to strengthen military cooperation in the Caspian Sea. Days later, however, Russian Defense Minister Sergei Shoygu announced Russia would provide more military training for Armenian soldiers, and he described Russia's military base in Armenia as a "guarantor of stability" in the Caucasus.[125]

Aliyev and Sargsyan would meet twice during 2016, in May in Vienna and in June in St. Petersburg. There were no breakthroughs. Putin defended his sponsorship of the St. Petersburg summit against the charges of unilateralism. "We often hear that Russia is trying to monopolize the work related to the settlement of the Nagorno-Karabakh conflict and push other mediators aside," he explained. "That is a misconception. The trilateral summits on the Karabakh issue with the participation of the Russian President—there have been more than twenty such summits—perfectly

[124] Azizi, Hamid Reza. "Will Iran and Russia Join Forces on Azerbaijani-Armenian Conflict?" Kafkassam, 16 April 2016. Web. Retrieved 20 June 2019. https://kafkassam.com/will-iran-and-russia-join-forces-on-azerbaijani-armenian-conflict.html.

[125] Ramani, Samuel. "Why the Russia-Azerbaijan Alliance Is Weaker Than It Looks," *The World Post*, 22 August 2016. Web. Retrieved 29 July 2019. https://www.huffpost.com/entry/why-the-russiaazerbaijan_b_11608854.

complement the efforts by the OSCE Minsk Group co-chaired by Russia, the United States, and France to settle this conflict. It should be noted that US and French representatives attended the concluding part of the abovementioned trilateral summit in St. Petersburg."[126]

The two tried again in October 2017, the first time in over a year that the two had formal discussions (although they met informally at a CIS gathering a month earlier). It appeared that these meetings were taking place solely for the purpose of holding meetings, form over substance. In the meantime, relations cooled between Baku and Moscow as evidenced by the Azerbaijani government refusing Moscow's nominee for Ambassador. A Duma spokesman stated "the Committee of the State Duma of the Russian Federation on CIS Affairs, Eurasian Integration and Relations with Compatriots supported (Georgy) Zuev (deputy director of personnel in the Russian MFA)'s candidacy for the post of Russian ambassador to Azerbaijan." Despite this support, President Putin had to cancel the assignment because of Azerbaijan's non-concurrence due to Zuev's pro-Armenian views.[127]

The serious diplomatic act of issuing a non-concurrence was probably because the Kremlin took a variety of steps deemed offensive by the Azerbaijani government, to include Russia and Armenia engaging in large-scale joint exercises. In May 2017, Moscow dissolved the All-Russian Azerbaijani Congress (ARAC) whose key leader was President Aliyev's daughter.[128] Azerbaijani Foreign Ministry spokesman Hikmet Hajiyev said the decision caused deep regret. "In general, we regard the decision to eliminate ARAC, which played an important role in the development of humanitarian relations between Azerbaijan and Russia, as an unfriendly step from the political point of view, which severely impacts the

[126] "An Overview of the Azerbaijan-Iran-Russia Trilateral Summit in Baku," Special Dispatch No. 6569, Middle East Research Institute (MEMRI), 11 August 2016. Web. Retrieved 20 June 2019. https://www.memri.org/reports/overview-azerbaijan-iran-russia-trilateral-summit-baku#_edn12.

[127] Tarasov, Stanislav. "Moscow and Baku Balance on the Brink of a Diplomatic Scandal," Regnum, 28 November 2017. Web. Retrieved 28 July 2019. https://regnum.ru/news/2350888.html.

[128] Goble, Paul. "Russian Overreach Calls into Question Baku's Balanced Foreign Policy," Eurasia Daily Monitor 14/157, Jamestown Foundation, 5 December 2017. https://jamestown.org/program/russian-overreach-calls-question-bakus-balanced-foreign-policy/.

development of the strategic partnership of the two countries at a high level," he told Azerbaijan's state news agency.[129]

Viewed in Cold War terms, the cooling of relations with Russia should have meant a strategic opening for the United States. Instead, US Congressmen belonging to the "Armenian Caucus" in the House of Representatives poisoned the well. They blundered into accepting an Armenian invitation to illegally cross the international border of Azerbaijan and visit Karabakh. Frank Pallone, David Valadao, and Tulsi Gabbard crossed into the occupied territories on 20 September 2017. They met with members of the Karabakh "legislature". Afterward, Pallone issued a statement that "We believe the people of Artsakh should have the right to self-determination and have security mechanisms." Baku reacted angrily. Foreign Ministry spokesman Hikmet Hajiyev called the visit a "provocation aimed at undermining efforts of the co-chairs of the OSCE Minsk Group, including the United States, in settling the Nagorno-Karabakh conflict." Hajiyev announced the three American congressmen were blacklisted from visits to Azerbaijan. "Pallone, Valadao and Gabbard paid an illegal visit to the occupied Azerbaijani territories, thus breaching Azerbaijani law," he said.[130]

In September 2018, President Aliyev met in Dushanbe, Tajikistan with the newly elected Armenian Prime Minister Nikol Pashinyan. The talks took place on the sidelines of a meeting of the CIS. The two agreed that their defense ministers would reduce cross-border incidents, open a hotline between commanders on either side of the line of contact, and to continue negotiations.[131] The two met again in St. Petersburg at a dinner hosted by Russian President Vladimir Putin. They discussed the possibility of prisoner exchange but failed to reach agreement.[132] A third meeting

[129] Jardine, Bradley. "Russia Closes Azerbaijani Diaspora Organization," Eurasianet, 22 September 2017. Web. Retrieved 28 July 2019. https://eurasianet.org/russia-closes-azerbaijani-diaspora-organization.

[130] "Azerbaijan Blacklists Three US Lawmakers for Visiting Nagorno-Karabakh," Radio Free Europe/Radio Liberty, 23 September 2017. Web. Retrieved 29 July 2019. https://www.rferl.org/a/azerbaijan-blacklists-three-us-lawmakers-visiting-nagorno-karabakh/28752231.html.

[131] Kucera, Joshua. "Aliyev and Pashinyan Hold First Talks, Agree on Tension-Reducing Measures," Eurasianet, 1 October 2018. Web. Retrieved 19 June 2019. https://eurasianet.org/aliyev-and-pashinyan-hold-first-talks-agree-on-tension-reducing-measures.

[132] "Another Pashinian-Aliyev Conversation Reported," Azatutyan, 7 December 2018. Web. Retrieved 19 June 2019. https://www.azatutyun.am/a/29643463.html.

took place in Davos at the World Economic Forum. They discussed the history of the conflict, and the current situation, but did not engage in substantive talks.

The Americans thought that the Pashinyan government represented new hope for the peace process but outgoing Ambassador to Armenia Richard Mills acknowledged there were still difficulties. Mills said he hoped the political transition would generate more discussion on Armenia's options but was struck by how little discussion there was about acceptable solutions. "What I did hear was a little disturbing because it appeared to be a step back from where we were," he said. "I was surprised when I first got here and found out that most Armenians I met were adamantly opposed to the return of the occupied territories as part of a negotiation settlement." He noted that return of land was one of the core principles of the Madrid Principles. "It has long been my government's understanding of why the occupied territories were originally seized; they would be a land for a peace option," he said. "So I was very surprised that there was no support for that anymore." He said "the harsh reality is that any settlement is going to require the return of some portion of the occupied territories." He added that the status quo is no longer in Armenia's favor - from closed borders to the strain on the country's material and human resources to corruption.[133] This was not a message the new Armenian political elite wanted to hear.

One week later, US National Security Advisor John Bolton arrived for an official visit. He encouraged Pashinyan to take advantage of his electoral popularity to engage on Nagorno-Karabakh. During press interviews in Yerevan, he said "If … the resolution of the Nagorno-Karabakh is the primary issue on the Armenian political agenda, there is no better time to try and take decisive action than right after that (Parliamentary) election."[134]

Prime Minister Pashinyan interpreted Bolton's words as unwelcome pressure. "John Bolton, or anyone for that matter, cannot speak on my behalf," he said. "They are moving forward with the logic that they

[133] Titizian, Maria. "U.S. Ambassador Mills: I leave Inspired and Hopeful," EVN, 15 October 2018. Web. Retrieved 16 July 2019. https://www.evnreport.com/politics/u-s-ambassador-mills-i-leave-inspired-and-hopeful.

[134] Tamrazian, Harry. "U.S. Expects 'Decisive Action' on Karabakh from Armenia," Radio Free Europe/Radio Liberty, 25 October 2018. Web. Retrieved 16 July 2019. https://www.azatutyun.am/a/29563885.html.

have some kind of ownership of the Karabakh issue, and now they are attempting to sell it to me, without asking my opinion."[135]

In December 2018, Iran's minister of intelligence and the minister of communication visited Baku. In return, Azerbaijani speaker of the National Assembly Ogtay Asadov visited Tehran and met with Iranian President Hassan Rouhani. The diplomacy was capped in January 2019 when Mohammad Bagheri, Iran's Chief of General Staff of the armed forces, visited Baku for two days. He met with President Aliyev and other senior officials. The two countries agreed to expand bilateral relations, further strengthen their military and security cooperation, increase trade, and work mutually on the completion of the North-South Transportation Corridor. As for Nagorno-Karabakh, Bagheri reaffirmed on behalf of the Iranian government the territorial integrity of Azerbaijan. While this had always been Iran's official position, the restatement in Baku seemed to indicate some space between Iran and its Armenian ally.[136] By contrast, however, Iranian President Ruhani himself visited Yerevan in December, indicating the basic thrust of Iranian-Armenian cooperation would continue.

Iran again offered their services as mediator. Tehran's former Ambassador to Azerbaijan Mohsen Pak Ayeen told a news service that, "If both parties are interested, Iran is ready to intervene with goodwill and respect for the territorial integrity of the two neighboring countries and help settle the issue in a way that would serve their national interests."[137] The offer was met with silence, perhaps because it was made via the media instead of through diplomatic channels.

Aliyev and Pashinyan held formal talks under the auspices of the Minsk group in Vienna on 29 March 2019. It followed a number of meetings between their respective foreign ministers. While it was the two leaders' fourth meeting, it was the first time that the meeting was the agenda,

[135] Kucera, Joshua. "After Bolton Takes Aim at Russia and Iran, Is Armenia the Collateral Damage?" Eurasianet, 30 October 2018. Web. Retrieved 19 July 2019. https://eurasianet.org/after-bolton-takes-aim-at-russia-and-iran-is-armenia-the-collateral-damage.

[136] Hodaei, Alireza. "Iran and Azerbaijan Strengthen Ties for First Time in More Than 40 Years," TRT World, 22 January 2019. Web. Retrieved 15 July 2019. https://www.trtworld.com/opinion/iran-and-azerbaijan-strengthen-ties-for-first-time-in-more-than-40-years-23530.

[137] "Ex-Envoy: Iran Ready to Mediate in Nagorno-Karabakh Dispute," *Financial Tribune*, 16 March 2019. Web. Retrieved 28 July 2019. https://financialtribune.com/articles/national/97221/ex-envoy-iran-ready-to-mediate-in-nagorno-karabakh-dispute.

instead of the two talking on the sideline of another event. They agreed to an unprecedented commitment to prepare their populations for peace. "I cannot say that there has been a breakthrough, revolution, or landmark event in the negotiating process," Pashinyan told members of the Armenian community of Austria. "But it is very important that a new process, which allows us to talk about our agendas, ideas and issues, has begun."[138]

On the same day in Vienna, Armenian Defense Minister David Tonoyan took a more defiant note. He rejected the idea of returning the territories surrounding Karabakh. "I declare that the formula 'territories for peace' will no longer exist," he said. "We will reformulate it as 'new war-new territories."[139] Despite Pashinyan's electoral mandate, he faced as difficult a struggle as his predecessor in bringing his government to the peace table.

The foreign ministers met in Moscow on 15 April at talks sponsored by Russia, but all the Minsk co-chairs attended. No breakthrough ensued, but the two sides committed to take measures to give relatives of people held in custody access to their loved ones. The ministers "expressed their willingness to start concrete work on establishing contacts between people."[140]

Prime Minister Pashinyan joined former president Sargsyan in Shusha, Karabakh for an Armenian victory celebration on 9 May 2019. It marked the 27th anniversary of Armenian forces capturing the Azerbaijani-inhabited town. The presence of the Armenian republic's current and past leaders reinforced the role of Armenia in the occupation of the territories.[141]

[138] "Armenia-Azerbaijan Summit Described as 'Positive' 'Constructive,'" Radio Free Europe/Radio Liberty, 30 March 2019. Web. Retrieved 19 June 2019. https://www.rferl.org/a/armenia-azerbaijan-summit-vienna-positive-nagorno-karabakh/29850997.html.

[139] Elliott, Raffi. "Pashinyan, Aliyev Meeting: Positive, but Inconclusive," *Armenian Weekly*, 1 April 2019. Web. Retrieved 19 June 2019. https://armenianweekly.com/2019/04/01/pashinyan-aliyev-meeting-positive-but-inconclusive/.

[140] "No Breakthrough Evident at Nagorno-Karabakh Talks in Moscow," Radio Free Europe/Radio Liberty, 14 April 2019. Web. Retrieved 29 July 2019. https://www.rferl.org/a/armenian-azeri-foreign-ministers-to-discuss-nagorno-karabakh-settlement-in-moscow/29880374.html.

[141] "27 Years since the Armenian-Azerbaijani Battle for Shusha/Shushi," *JAM News*, 9 May 2019. Web. Retrieved 31 July 2019. https://jam-news.net/27-years-since-the-armenian-azerbaijani-battle-for-shushashushi/.

The Minsk group co-chairs engaged in another whirl of shuttle diplomacy on 27–30 May. They met with Pashinyan in Yerevan and with Aliyev in Baku. In both capitals, they also held consultations with the respective foreign ministers and defense ministers. Finally, they met with the de facto authorities in Nagorno-Karabakh, and with the Chairman of the Azerbaijani Community of Nagorno-Karabakh (living in Baku.) They presented concrete proposals to further the Minsk process (no further information), and the foreign ministers of Armenia and Azerbaijan agreed to a further meeting which was then held in Washington, DC.[142]

The US Congress decided to intervene again. In 2015, under heavy pressure from the Armenian National Committee of America (ANCA) Congressmen Royce and Engle had introduced a bipartisan proposal calling for the placement of gunfire locators, and observers on the line of contact. They also called for the withdrawal of snipers, heavy arms, and new weaponry from the line. The proposal went nowhere but, in 2019, it was included by California Representative Judy Chu in a basket of amendments to the National Defense Authorization Act. Amendment number 97 passed the House on a voice vote. The amendment did little to advance the peace process, especially after Rep. Chu told ANCA "The campaign of terror against the people of Artsakh must end."[143] The use of the term Artsakh, and the description of the lawful government of Azerbaijan's efforts to reassert its sovereignty over its own territory as terrorism, demonstrated that the amendment was not meant to be a neutral measure but an attempt to consolidate the status quo.

Yerevan had long demanded that Karabakh Armenians be allowed to rejoin the peace talks. Their absence meant they could disagree with any settlement Armenia and Azerbaijan made. This came to the fore in preparations for a meeting of the Minsk co-chairs in Moscow in July 2009. French co-chair Bernard Fassier told reporters before the meeting that the two sides were in agreement on all the basic principles except two, the future status of Nagorno-Karabakh and the nature of security guarantees for the Armenian population there. In response, Nagorno-Karabakh

[142] "Co-Chairs Say They Have 'Concrete Steps' for Karabakh Peace," Asbarez, 31 May 2019. Web. Retrieved 1 June 2019. http://asbarez.com/181078/co-chairs-say-they-have-concrete-steps-for-karabakh-peace/.

[143] "US House Passes Chu Amendment to Strengthen Artsakh Cease-Fire," *Armenian Weekly*, 12 July 2019. Web. Retrieved 31 July 2019. https://armenianweekly.com/2019/07/12/us-house-passes-chu-amendment-to-strengthen-artsakh-cease-fire/.

"defense minister" Movses Hakopian said no one had asked Karabakh to withdraw from the Azerbaijani districts it occupied and the enclave's leadership had no intention of giving them up.[144]

Diplomacy was turned on its head in November 2020 when Armenia accepted a Russian ceasefire proposal to halt the six week war. In return for allowing Armenian forces to withdraw from Karabakh, Armenia granted Azerbaijan control over all the lands they recaptured, and a corridor between the main part of Azerbaijan and Nakhchivan. To keep the two sides separated, Russian peace keepers will patrol the Lachin corridor for five years. There will also be a role for Turkey which, as of this writing, is under discussion.

Conclusion

Israel's former foreign minister Abba Eban once made the comment, "The Palestinians have never missed an opportunity to miss an opportunity."[145] In many ways, the same can be said about the Armenian-Azerbaijani peace talks. The basic points for an agreement over Nagorno-Karabakh have been known to both sides for two decades, and yet political leaders on both sides have been unable to accept the agreement. Nationalist sentiments that were stirred up (intentionally by the Armenian side) to help in the nation building process are notoriously difficult to oppose at a later date. This has made it extremely difficult to sell any compromise to the peoples of the Caucasus. Both sides have to make serious efforts to convince their populations of the benefits of ending the conflict, or all the diplomatic meetings in the world will have no effect. The Russian ceasefire has the support of the Azerbaijani population, but Armenians have rioted in the streets of Yerevan. At least one of the two protagonists will seek to continue the conflict.

[144] Fuller, Liz. "Minsk Group Co-Chairs Hopeful of a Karabakh 'Breakthrough,'" Radio Free Europe/Radio Liberty, 10 July 2009. Web. Retrieved 18 June 2009. https://www.rferl.org/a/Minsk_Group_CoChairs_Hopeful_Of_Karabakh_Breakthrough_/1774141.html.

[145] "Israel's Diplomatic Giant Eban Dies," BBC News, 18 November 2002. Web. Retrieved 5 August 2019. http://news.bbc.co.uk/2/hi/middle_east/2486473.stm.

CHAPTER 6

Final Thoughts

This volume has attempted to describe the military, political, economic, and diplomatic steps that have been taken to define Nagorno-Karabakh—and also to demonstrate the costs to all sides from this "Frozen Conflict." The Soviet Union/Russia is not the progenitor of ethnic conflict, nor did it have the ability in the 1980s and 1990s to stop it. Russia has, however, become an expert at using those conflicts to further its own political ends. In Karabakh, villagers that argued with neighbors and threatened violence with axes and old hunting guns suddenly found themselves aligned with groups armed with tanks, artillery, and aircraft. Playing both sides against the middle, Russia has emerged as the indispensable party in any peacemaking/peacekeeping operation. It is in this respect that the war between Armenia and Azerbaijan is a created conflict: Russia supplied the weaponry to create a hot war in 1992, and it has supplied the diplomacy that has kept the conflict "frozen" but not resolved ever since. As a result, Russia has troops stationed in Armenia, it owns the commanding heights of the Armenian economy, and it is Azerbaijan's major weapons supplier. It now will have peacekeepers on Azerbaijani territory until 2025. The winner of this frozen conflict is not Armenia, Azerbaijan, or the inhabitants of Nagorno-Karabakh (living there or as internally displaced persons). The winner is Russia.

What remains to be examined is the legal status of the participants. The conflict between Armenia and Azerbaijan, as already described, is

J. J. Coyle, *Russia's Interventions in Ethnic Conflicts*,
https://doi.org/10.1007/978-3-030-59573-9_6

based on the reliance of each side on competing principles of international law. For Armenia, the overriding issue is the right of a people to self-determination. This principle, taken in its abstract, would give any minority people the right to secede from a larger political body and form its own state. Nagorno-Karabakh would have the ability to secede from Azerbaijan and obtain its independence. Kurds living in Armenia would have the right to secede. Within this new Kurdish state, Armenians would have the right to secede and rejoin Armenia. The principle continues ad absurdum until one could discuss individual blocks of individual streets seceding from whatever country in which the inhabitants reside if those inhabitants share a common ethnicity. Most of the English Midlands would now be divided into Pakistani, Indian, Bangladeshi, and Chinese statelets.

For Azerbaijan, the two principles of international law are state sovereignty and the legitimacy of international borders. Faced with Russian efforts to expand their influence by supporting minority groups throughout the former Soviet Union (except inside the borders of the Russian Federation), countries such as Moldova, Georgia, and Ukraine are equally firm on these principles. The inviolability of state borders has been a long-established principle of international law—World War II was fought to halt German and Japanese violations of this principle by their invasions of neighboring countries. Armenia tries to claim that it supports the inviolability of borders by denying its role in the Nagorno-Karabakh conflict. The European Court of Human Rights, however, ruled in "Chiragov and others v. Armenia" that Yerevan has violated this basic principle of international order.

State sovereignty has been challenged two times since the collapse of the Soviet Union: by the West in the case of Kosovo and by the Russians in the case of Crimea. In both cases, the result has not been universally accepted and has been challenged by states in the international order. In Nagorno-Karabakh, however, all countries—including Armenia—claim they respect Azerbaijan's sovereignty over the former oblast. Armenia's official, legal position is that the fighting is a matter internal to the Azerbaijani state. Where Armenia parts company with the rest of the world, however, is their goal for the future of the enclave: they claim that the principle of self-determination supports an independent existence for Karabakh.

It is an argument worthy of consideration. There is a general principle in international law, however, that a people can only secede if both the secessionists and the recognized state agree. Based on this, Nigeria fought and kept Biafra, the Philippines fought the Huks, Oman held onto Dhofar, the American North fought the American South. In Texas v. White (1868), the United States Supreme Court ruled that the states of the Confederacy never separated from the United States. They said it was impossible, since the constitution only provided for how states could join the union, and not leave it. It said that once the state had joined the American body politic it had become a member of an indestructible union.[1]

In the case of Nagorno-Karabakh, the Soviet Constitution of 1977 provided a mechanism by which a republic could leave the union but—like the American constitution—had no provision that authorized an oblast to secede. Since Nagorno-Karabakh declared its independence while the Soviet Union still existed, it tried to perform an act that was literally impossible. The fact that self-determination requires the approval of both sides of the conflict still remains. While there have been plebiscites and demands from the Nagorno-Karabakh "legislature" for secession, this has never been approved by the authorities in Baku because of the absence of the Azerbaijani population from the region (and thus unable to participate in a plebiscite) and the lack of consent by the central government.

Even if Baku agreed to give the enclave its independence, it still leaves unanswered the status of the provinces surrounding Nagorno Karabakh whose population was ethnically Azerbaijani before the war. Multiple UN resolutions have reaffirmed the inadmissibility of acquiring territory by force. The international community does not recognize ethnic cleansing, and the 4th Geneva Convention prohibits an occupying power from changing the ethnic composition of the occupied territory. Article 49 prohibits mass forcible transfer from an occupied territory, except for security reasons and—in the event of a security evacuation—the population is to be returned to their homes as soon as hostilities cease.[2]

Article 49 also prohibits the occupier transferring part of its own population into the occupied territory, yet Armenia did exactly that with Syrian

[1] Texas v. White, 74 U.S. 700 (1868). Web. Retrieved 5 August 2019. https://supreme.justia.com/cases/federal/us/74/700/.

[2] International Committee of the Red Cross (ICRC), "The Geneva Conventions of 12 August 1949," 151. Web. Retrieved 5 August 2019. https://www.icrc.org/en/doc/assets/files/publications/icrc-002-0173.pdf.

refugees. Most Syrian Armenians are descendants of Armenians fleeing the Ottoman Empire during World War I. Pushed out of Syria since 2011 by the Syrian Civil War, approximately 20,000 have made their way to Armenia where they are greeted as citizens. Housing programs run by Armenian NGOs and the Armenian government settled these new arrivals in Nagorno-Karabakh, and in the area surrounding the enclave such as the Lachin corridor.[3] Karabakh authorities want to provide incentives to attract more refugees, labeling them "enhanced security."[4] This violates another principle of international law.

The international community has done nothing to enforce international law concerning this conflict. They have not stopped the intentional targeting of civilians, indiscriminate use of force, ethnic cleansing, seizure of territory by force, violation of a UN member state's sovereignty; they have done nothing to enforce four UNSC resolutions or to halt the movement of settlers into occupied territories. If it is the responsibility of the Armenian and Azerbaijani governments to prepare their populations for peace, it is the responsibility of the international community to insist on that peace—and respect for the law of nations.

[3] Allen, Jeremy. "The (Re)Settlers of Karabakh: How Regional Nationalism Has Weaponized Syrian Refugees," *The McGill International Review*, 23 October 2018. Web. Retrieved 5 August 2019. https://www.mironline.ca/the-resettlers-of-karabakh-how-regional-nationalism-has-weaponized-syrian-refugees/.

[4] Avetisyan, Armine. "'Enhanced Security': Armenian Settlers in Nagorno Karabakh," OC Media, 3 October 2018. Web. Retrieved 5 August 2019. https://oc-media.org/enhanced-security-armenian-settlers-in-nagorno-karabakh/.

Index

J. J. Coyle, *Russia's Interventions in Ethnic Conflicts*,
https://doi.org/10.1007/978-3-030-59573-9

Y

Z

The manufacturer's authorised representative in the EU is Springer Nature Customer Service Centre GmbH, Europaplatz 3, 69115 Heidelberg, Germany. If you have any concerns regarding our products, please contact ProductSafety@springernature.com

Printed and bound by CPI Group (UK) Ltd, Croydon, CR0 4YY
30/09/2026
02225466-0018